My Time, My Truth

C. Ayla Joyce Matheson

Burlington, Vermont

Onion River Press
89 Church Street
Burlington, VT 05401
info@onionriverpress.com
www.onionriverpress.com

ISBN: 978-1-966607-22-9

Library of Congress Control Number: 2025912527

Momma, I did it! I'm a published writer, and this book is dedicated to you!

Thank you for your courage. From the ashes of my devastated childhood, a new life emerged—one I had only dreamt of. You bravely reached out and took my hand when I offered it, giving us precious time to recreate our relationship. I am eternally grateful for your willingness to own your truth, as painful as it was. It is because of this that we've enjoyed some truly wonderful adventures as mother and daughter and ultimately becoming friends!

Contents

Dear Reader,

I feel it's important to share a few things before you dive into this book.

If you're thirteen or older and you've lived a life where your innocence is intact, where you know you are worthy, loveable, and enough, and you feel safe, this book might not be the best fit for you right now. Seriously. I'd rather protect that precious innocence of yours. It's rare and valuable, and I want to respect that.

This book delves into some pretty heavy topics. You'll encounter themes of a darker, more challenging world. If you're not ready to explore those, that's totally okay. It's perfectly fine to acknowledge that such things exist without needing to immerse yourself in them.

If you've experienced trauma like rape, feeling disvalued, or physical, emotional, and spiritual abuse, please know with all my heart that it was not your fault. Your DNA contains in its blueprint the potential for abuse. For some of us (like me) my Soul's evolution required a trigger to get set off. My love, that is why I am here. To assist in our evolution, which is taking place right now. The choice to transmute abuse and dehumanization into a beautiful life experience of transformation and living a life meant to be lived as love is my intention. To know love, the dark is a necessary part.

If you are still reading, I know this book is meant to speak to you. Here's a mantra to remember if you get triggered. Take a deep breath, place your hand on your heart, and say it with me as I have done every day for years. These words come from my coach, Jody Marquis:
"I am grateful to know, feel, and embody myself as...
Lovable. Worthy. Enough.
Even on my most challenging days.
Even when doubt creeps in...

Even when I feel lost, stuck, or unseen...
I choose to love myself more!
Because at the core of who I am—
beneath all layers of experience, belief, or story—
I am whole and always will be...whole!

Write it down and use it as your bookmark!

This book explores challenging experiences like fear, mistrust, dehumanization, and lack of consent. Through these explorations, I hope to shed light on what love truly is. I encourage you to look for the silver linings in your own story and to understand and embrace your true self as love. When difficult emotions arise, I've found Jody Marquis's L.O.V.E. Now Method to be helpful: Listen and observe with curiosity; Open your heart to love; Veer your thoughts away from fear; and Embody your next aligned action.

If you read my book and need support, please don't hesitate to reach out. You can email me at ayla@gracewaychrysalis.com or connect with the Graceway Chrysalis Facebook page. My website www.gracewaychrysalis.com will be a place to connect with the Grace Way Chrysalis community.

With care,

C. Ayla Joyce Matheson
www.gracewaychrysalis.com

Preface

When I was twelve I was told (by God) I someday was to write my autobiography. I remember at the time feeling excited but also puzzled as to what about my life could ever warrant a life story important enough for others to read. I knew that at my young age I already had the experience of having a bizarre childhood, up to that point! I figured that at age twelve I was pretty grown up after having experienced such diverse cultures as my South Bronx, New York experience and before that my life in Costa Rica, which was pretty awesome.

So at that early age I was always seeking unusual life experiences to fit what I had already experienced. I was just expanding on it. I saw myself as the heroine in my life, but I also was dealing with self-loathing and low self-esteem. Somehow these two—the heroine and self-loathing—didn't fit seamlessly together. I remember being painfully shy and frightened of my own shadow, but I loved the kids who were on the "outside" of popularity! The strange and weird kids were the kids I identified with.

I am a spiritual seeker and have always been attracted to the mystics, and at one time I seriously thought I was going to enter a convent when I was of age to choose my future. I was desperately searching to understand the power of the Christ. Was this a real power? Was it a power I had in me all the time? How did I access and activate this very magical super power? I was so curious and made finding out about Christ's love and power to heal, my mission in life. I was hungry to know the truth!

This truth-seeking journey is the story you are about to read! Thank you for going with me on this trip! And oh what a trip it has been. I'd love to hear your feedback. You can reach out to me at www.gracewaychrysalis.com.

Introduction

In 1966...

My dad, a gregarious, handsome, easy-to-give-a-smile kind of guy, was an Episcopalian minister and missionary who spoke beautiful Spanish. He identified more with the Latino people than his own Anglo-Saxon roots. He was an easy-going man with simple tastes who loved to tell stories. Repeatedly, oblivious to the fact that you may have heard them once, twice, or even more! Dad loved Latin music, especially the magical sound of the steel drums, the culture, and he talked with his hands, like any Romance-language speaker.

My mother, Gwynneth, was shy and introverted. She struggled with the social expectations set forth for a minister's wife, like having to wear a hat and gloves to church every Sunday service. Pants were not worn out in public. She was expected to run church groups, volunteer or lead church events, and host dinners on occasion. While in fact, Mom was a writer, a poet, sculptor, and painterly kind of woman who enjoyed the outdoors, her horses, and dogs. The most challenging expectation for her to live up to was the unimportance of her voice as the wife of a minister.

My dad's first Spanish-speaking mission took our family of four to Costa Rica where we lived in beautiful, sweet harmony with the natural environment for the last two of the three years that we were there. In the small village of Escazu, we had sugarcane fields on one side of our *casita* and coffee bean fields bordered on the other side. In the distance, standing watch over us, was the majestic, active volcano Irazú.

We were happy. Mom had horses and immensely enjoyed giving riding lessons to the local kids. I had my own large pony that I rode in the fields flanking our home and around the house and underneath a huge mimosa tree, which stood as a sentinel in our front yard. My older brother seemed content, my baby sister was a happy baby, and life was good. My uncle Clay, Dad's kid brother by twelve years, had come to live with us. He was having trouble in his high school, so he was invited to finish high school in Costa Rica. I grew to love my uncle. He didn't seem that much older than me because he was still in high school. And he was warm and friendly towards me. He welcomed my presence, asked me questions, and I loved his enthusiastic laugh. He joked with his big brother, my dad, loved being outdoors, and gave my family a lot of loving attention, appreciative of the opportunity he was given to be in Costa Rica.

Life seemed to be rolling along smoothly until Mom was pregnant again with her fourth child, and then it wasn't! We were moving. The diocese encouraged large families. Mom, being shy and a don't-make-waves kind of personality, gained strength from admiring another minister's wife who had four children. She made the job of raising a large family look saintly and easy. Mom aspired to be seen this way, living a Godly life in selfless service. But my mother did not have the temperament, the mental stamina, or a caregiver's compassion towards those in need of whom she was to serve—the other major expectation of the minister's wife. A fourth pregnancy put my family into a pressure cooker, with the timer set. Dad, struggling with the added responsibilities of providing for his larger family and a wife who had begun railing against her duties as a minister's wife, had a nervous breakdown. This truth was shrouded in an ashamed secrecy well into my adult life, until the truth came out.

The Episcopal Diocese began looking for a post for my dad. It was decided to move my family back to the United States where the pressures from living in a foreign country would be eradicated. While the church sought to find an appropriate parish, my family of five, with a very pregnant mother, moved twenty-two times that year. Yes, twenty-two times! Finally, the bishop of the New York Diocese found a new mission for my family.

From left to right: Katherine, Greg, Kevin, and me, 1961

I'll never forget what it felt like to drive through the tall, steel, spiked gates, a gateway to the forgotten ones in the inner city of New York, and into the bowels of the Bronx, a gateway to hell. The neighborhood we found ourselves in was infested with drugs, prostitution, and gang violence. Broken families and sexual abuse were rampant among the young girls, raped by fathers, brothers, uncles, cousins, or just strangers, with no consequences—no legal consequences, that is. Many girls were pregnant by the age of thirteen or fourteen, because their periods started. The patterns laid before them by their mothers, their grandmothers, and their mothers' mothers were too strong to be denied in this environment of destitution. The reality, grim and sad, prompted this impression of my mother's in 1961:

THE SLUMS

The smell of death lingers here
life is too much to cope with
buildings crumble, windows break
paint peels, people quake.
Everything is wrong from beginning to end.
People are born to starve to death
with bones exposed to the wind and the cold

Death lingers and grabs as it can
the weak, the helpless, the unknowing man.
Does anyone survive this hell on earth
this crumbling peeling quaking dearth?
Did God arrange for this way of life
or is it because of human strife?
Why do we wrap up in comfortable fleece
and refuse to see the naked beast?

Readers, Change is upon us! It is 2025 as I finish this story. It is my greatest desire, and I set this intention as I send this book out into the world: May we have the courage as individuals, a society, a nation, and in the world at large to choose unconditional love when fear and love collide. When love wins, and one's truth is spoken, moral courage is grown. I pray we have many who are growing their moral courage because we need more, much more love in the world since unconditional LOVE and living an authentic and Soulful life, is all there is!

I had a dream one night back in the early 90s... *On a neon sign which was floating in the sky above me, flashing on and off—on and off, Paradigm Shift-Paradigm Shift—Paradigm Shift....*

C. Ayla Joyce Matheson

Chapter 1

1963

Bride Doll Betty was hideous. She was three feet tall, dressed in a cheap, white-satin wedding gown, and she had blond hair, bright, red painted toenails, and high heeled shoes. The Bride Doll had a white veil which could be taken on and off, or pulled down over her face, for a more modest and demure look. How could this ugly doll be my mommy's going away gift to me? I just wanted a baby doll to snuggle with. Not this thing—I hated this doll.

I was seven years old, turning eight soon. Not a teenager yet. I just wanted Thumbelina, a soft, squishy, cuddly baby.

Mommy and I went shopping the week before she went into the hospital, walking hand in hand through the littered, stinky streets of our neighborhood, 149th Street and St. Ann's Ave. in the South Bronx. I was a tiny little thing, with long, strawberry blond hair and bright, sparkly eyes, brilliantly blue in color. I was always ready to break into a big smile, which I am told lit up my whole face. I was such a contrast in this new neighborhood, like a marshmallow in a cup of hot cocoa.

I didn't understand where Mom was going or why she was going away. I knew that I was terribly homesick for our beautiful life left behind in the mountains of Costa Rica. So, now Dad's mission work was with the Spanish-speaking communities in the Episcopal Diocese of New York. My dad loved it here in the

South Bronx, loved its people and the language. He dressed wearing bright, colorful shirts when he wasn't in his black shirt, pants, and white collar. He was a strikingly handsome man, with a large dimple in his cheek when he laughed, which was often. During his services, Dad's voice, strong and resonant, filled the nave of the church as he preached. Listening to him sing the canticles was magical for me as he had a beautiful, rich tenor voice. He prided himself on his flair for the vestments he wore; the one place where he could allow his eclectic and gregarious personality shine was when he stood before the altar. In Costa Rica, Dad loved the local, open-air markets we had left behind. He loved the scents, the bargaining, talking to all the vendors, many of whom were members of his congregation, and they loved him. He bought the native woven belts, woven on the backstrap loom, to wear as a stole over his white or black cassock. Sometimes a favorite lady vendor, flirtatious with the *Padre*, gifted him a new stole, giggling as she let him pick one out.

When he was in his white cassock, with his arms opened wide, sleeves flapping, he seemed like an angel of God, preaching the word of our Lord in beautiful Spanish with a native accent.

Dad, a brilliant man, was also filled with fear. He believed all were created equal, but with exceptions! The "queer" ones were sick, misguided, and needed God's healing and forgiveness. Adamant was he in his belief that "they" were not born "that" way. Their souls needed saving. First Nation peoples' spiritual beliefs and ways of life, their ceremonies, and rituals he believed were heresy. Evil, as Christianity taught its ministers. This was one of the many anomalies in my dad's glass house. People either really liked my dad or really despised him for his lack of empathy. Dad was a proud man with a healthy ego. He was also a traditional male who believed women should be pregnant and in the home as a homemaker. Men ruled the house, and Dad had the last word, always. Another anomaly was that he was a bully and seemed to enjoy needling my mom until she flew into one of her hysterical rages. When this happened, the veins in her neck popped out, her eyes changed, and her face contorted. This mom was wicked scary. Dad laughed and called her the "mad woman." He said continuously that she was crazy.

Mom, the total opposite of Dad, was easily able to have her emotions set off into a rage by my dad. She was extremely sensitive and an empath who was left-handed. When she was a girl in the 1930s, her left hand was tied behind her back, forcing her to use the right. Left-handed girls were thought to be witches, and it was believed that dark Spirits could inhabit their bodies and lead them astray, into evil ways, once a girl entered womanhood. My mother's mom, Monica, a devout Christian, came from old-school thinking around the male being the dominant figure in the family. She served her husband and the boys; the future men in the family as she saw it. Their wish was her command.

When I visited my grandmother, she ordered me around, making it sound like a great honor to serve the "men" their drinks. But they were not "men"—it was my brother, for Christ's sake. Tea, hot or cold. Never liquor, beer, or wine. Sherry on special occasions. I would knock on the library door with a tray in my arms, ready to wait on my brother, my dad, and my grandfather, Bumpy, who retreated to the library and played chess. I loved my maternal grandfather, Bumpy—*Bon Pere* my grandmother wanted us to call him, to acknowledge her own French roots. *Bon Pere* sounded like "Bumpy" to us kids, so he became "Bumpy." He was a kind and gentle man with red hair and very shy. His hazel eyes changed color with his moods. He suffered from bouts of depression, during which time my maternal grandmother, Nana, hovered over him, impossibly protective. "Shhhh," she continuously scolded me. "Your grandfather needs quiet. Shhh. Shhh." Just my presence must have been noisy because I was quiet as a mouse.

Mom's roots were conventional all the way. She was trapped in the old paradigm and raised to be "seen but not heard," as I was being raised. She had a lonely childhood, with two older siblings who were the shining beacons and garnered all their mother's attention. Her relationship with her father was a sensitive one, as he understood who she was, she being like him in personality. They would cuddle in her bed as she was being soothed for the night's sleep, him reading stories to her in his lilting Welsh accent. She loved her dad, and she was the apple of his eye.

Mom shared with me how everything changed abruptly one night when she was a young teenager. They were enjoying their nightly snuggle, wrapped in his big arm curled into the crook of it, when her mother came flying into the room, accusing him of molesting his daughter. He wasn't. It was nothing of the sort, but her rage frightened my gentle grandfather. Sadly, he didn't ever feel comfortable snuggling with my mother again. The ritual they enjoyed of him reading aloud stopped. Her father withdrew and became more reserved around her, intimidated by his wife's false accusations and afraid to be demonstrative in his love for his daughter.

Her mother, Monica, was jealous of her. She watched her daughter grow into a beautiful, young woman—if still a bit skinny and too tall—making derogatory remarks to my mom. My mom was hurt and puzzled by this new, cold-shoulder treatment from her dad, and thought she had done or said something wrong. She was extremely lacking in self-confidence in her tall, gangly body, which was beginning to bud out into a woman's body. But around animals, especially horses, my mom was comfortable. She loved horses and dogs, and they loved her back. They loved her in a way her parents couldn't. She bonded with horses, much the same as her grandfather Solon had, whom she had never met. She preferred to be around animals, with their unconditional love, more than people.

Thriving in college, finally feeling her oats and freedom, she excelled in hockey, much to her surprise. Mom also had filled out in her body and grew into herself, becoming a head turner! She became pinned to my father, John Kelley, before she went away to Agnes Scott College in Decatur, Georgia. In her second year of college, Dad proposed to her. He had recently graduated from seminary and was ready to begin his life as a missionary. She was torn, feeling empowered in her newly discovered life. But when his offer came again, it was, "marry me now, or never." Mom withdrew from school and married him. She resented her decision and him, for making it be a "now or never" option, and stuffed her true feelings.

Why wasn't he able to wait for me to finish school? she wondered when she was in one of her dark moods, filled with resentment.

My little body, petite and fragile—birdlike fragile—was engulfed by the couch and the seriousness of the adults around me. The atmosphere felt suffocating as I was told by my parents that Mom was going away for quite a while. I wasn't going to see her at all during this time. She was going into a special hospital where she could be cared for, because she was not happy. I knew this. I heard her crying, wailing, and sometimes screaming behind her closed bedroom doors. She scared me with her unhappiness. I wanted to make her feel better.

She was taking me out to buy me the baby doll I had been begging for, for weeks. A Thumbelina doll. Thumbelina had a soft, peach-pink, fabric body, her legs and arms were rubber, her head moved, and her bright blue eyes opened and closed when you moved her back and forth. I wanted her badly. I had spotted her several weeks before in the store and had been pestering my mom for her.

When we got to the store, I made a beeline for the shelf upon which I had seen Thumbelina sitting in her box, waiting to be bought. I picked the box up lovingly and was so happy to finally have this baby to hug and play with. But as we were walking by the other dolls, with Thumbelina secure in my arms, Mommy took a big box with the Bride Doll inside off the shelf. At three feet tall she was as big as I was. And hideous.

What? I screamed in my head. She was taking the Bride Doll box up to the register.

"But Mommy, I don't want her. I want Thumbelina. **You said I could buy what I wanted.**" My voice got stronger but it was quivering. Then I croaked out, in a broken voice, "I don't like her." And even more softly, I said, "She's scary," but to no avail.

Mom seemed to be in a daze, and my protest was not fazing her in the least. She took Thumbelina in her box roughly from my arms and shoved her at the cashier. In a flat, unemotional voice, she asked her to return Thumbelina to the shelf.

"We'll take this doll," she said firmly and got her wallet out to pay. I was in tears, struggling to not scream at her in the store: *I hate you. I don't want this hideous thing. What is wrong with you, Mommy?* What I said so softly was, "You told me I could buy the doll baby that I wanted. I don't like this one. She's creepy." I burst into tears as we are leaving Thumbelina behind with the bewildered clerk, her sad, knowing eyes looking at me.

• • •

I was groomed to be Betty, the little Bride Doll, and to step into Mommy's shoes, as Daddy's little hostess. My daddy, his boss, and the vestry men often met in our home. During these occasions, while Mommy was in the hospital, I was dressed up. I was dressed up in a frilly yellow dress which came above my knee. I wore fancy black patent leather shoes to carry the tray out to the men. Oh, and I had to wear a little frilly apron. I remembered someone giving it to me! I had another apron I preferred from Costa Rica. It was handmade of muslin, with a brilliant, deep, sky-blue ribbon (the color of Mother Mary's mantle) bordering the apron. Embroidered on it was a Costa Rican scene of an ox cart going to the market, which reminded me of its colorful wheels rolling along the dusty, dirt roads outside my home. The apron I loved had flowers and birds embroidered randomly around it, making it look like the ox cart was going on its *paseo* to the market through a field of wildflowers. No words were spoken as I was handed instead the yellow frilly one to put on. This was more appealing to them. What I liked didn't matter.

I felt weird. The big smile plastered on my face felt frozen, and my eyes were sad. I felt like there were two Mes. I knew Daddy didn't like it when I got sad and cried because I missed my mommy and my brothers and sister. I had a new baby brother I didn't even know and didn't see often. Slowly over time, my young brain blamed my baby brother for having been born, making Mom go away.

About a year and a half after he was born, as Mom prepared to go away, my younger siblings were moved to my grandparents' country home in Wilton, Connecticut. My older brother was sent to live at St. John's of the Divine Cathedral in Manhattan, becoming a choir boy at age ten and a half. I got to see him every so often when he came home for a long weekend. But he didn't pay me much attention, as he was too busy running wild with his friends through the barrio. I did not have that freedom. I stayed within the steel gates.

I was always being told that I had great hips. Good for birthing babies. My smile, cemented on my face, was commented on regularly, and how sweet I was, too. So bright my eyes were, was the comment, that they sparkled with light. It seemed that my destiny, as far as my dad was concerned, while Mom stayed silent in her absence, was to marry and have children. Lots of them. I would be a pretty wife. The church's community of clergy and the bishops who led them were encouraged to have large families. The church frowned upon a minister and his wife if they didn't want children at all. That was a mortal sin.

The Bride Doll, Betty, stood by herself in my bedroom corner, staring at me with vacant, glass eyes. I hated her and finally moved her into my closet, so I didn't have to look at her, ever. The church had an open-door policy which meant the front door was never locked. Anyone could walk in off the street and enter our home if they wanted to see my dad for some problem. My mom hated this policy and fought with Dad about it before she went into the hospital. It frightened her to not be able to lock her home at night. Or during the day, for privacy.

"Nope. That is not the way it is here," Dad argued. "Get used to it. It's our new life as a minister's wife, in service to our Lord God." His reply was harsh and impatient with Mom. She struggled to keep her shit together. Until she finally couldn't and admitted herself to a private hospital.

My bedroom was the closest to the front door of the parish house, now our home. I was scared that my room was the first room in the house. I had nightmares of someone coming in and taking me, and my voice, screaming, would not be heard, as the bedroom next to mine was empty. As was the one around the corner, next to the kitchen; this was my older brother's room. Dad's room was at the end, behind the living room, and he could never hear my crying at night. Because on the other side of Dad's bedroom was the church's gymnasium, reaching two stories high. Basketballs were heard slapping against the wall of Mom and Dad's bedroom 'til late in the evening when the gym finally closed.

Looking out of my bedroom windows, there was a big vacant lot. It was bare dirt with grassy patches. Two scraggly trees were trying to grow. In between this vacant lot, there was an alleyway. This was directly below my windows and was about seven feet wide and six feet tall. It was narrow. Young neighborhood boys, around nine or ten years old, hung out in this alleyway. They gathered in groups of three or four, each with a small brown paper bag scrunched up at the top and held tightly in their fists. Inside the brown bag was a tube of airplane glue, which they sniffed. They got high as kites flying on a string and became nasty. If they happened to catch a glimpse of me playing in my room, they quickly pulled down their zippers, whipped out their dicks, put their hands around them, and jerked them up and down while hurling obscenities at me. The first time it happened I watched their dicks engorge, fascinated. Startled and frightened, the next time I saw them I dropped to the floor and curled up against the wall with my arms wrapped tightly around my knees. I squeezed my eyes shut, trying to block the sound of their voices.

This became a daily ritual for the boys, and I, with my fantasy world below the windows, crawled around on the floor so I couldn't be seen.

March 6, 1963 – ADMISSION NOTE – THE NEW YORK HOSPITAL, WESTCHESTER DIVISION, NEW YORK. excerpt from Gwynn Kelley's journal.

The patient was brought to the hospital today by her husband who was a rather "tackily" dressed Episcopal minister with a small mustache. Mrs. Kelley was neatly dressed, co-operative, and polite. She seemed somewhat ill at ease when she related her symptoms. It appears that she has a long history of moodiness, irritability, and depression. She feels at the present time that she is about to "lose control of herself"... She admitted to being terribly depressed at times and would cry a great deal and might have feelings of wanting to end her life. There have been no overt suicidal gestures, however. The patient quite willingly signed the voluntary application and accompanied the supervisor to Hall IV.

"So here I am locked up. Oh, my God, what have I done? The doors are locked! I hang on to the thin thread of my truth and my courage. I signed myself into this hospital on the advice of my doctor. I have the key. If I signed in, I could sign myself out. I hold on for dear life."

My mother was gone for fourteen months. After she left, I remember a nightmare that began haunting me. *I am standing on a precipice. On one side is a roaring river with huge, jagged rocks, and wild, swirling eddies. On the other I see serene fields and gentle valleys, which go on as far as my eyes can see. I want to fly. My feet are anchored to the stone precipice. All I hear, deep in my bones, above the roaring of the river below is: Am I crazy like my mother? Am I crazy? Am I crazy like my mother? Yes. Yes. Yes, came the haunting chant in response. In the distance there is always a light, carried by my dad, which I am trying to reach but I can't. I precariously run and run along this edge but can't reach the light carried by my father.*

During my waking hours and in the depth of the night, I asked myself that repeatedly, because my father always referred to me as being "just like your mother," whenever I cried or tried to share my feelings. *So, are you?* I asked looking into my eyes, in the mirror. *Are you crazy? Are you a mad woman?*

I remembered wondering as a child, *When I finally leave my parents' home, will this scary stuff stop?* The vibration of love, my birthright, as my father's God/Creator intended, was rewired. Fear became the rising voice deep in my belly, squeezing my heart's voice shut so I wouldn't speak the truth. My natural, loving heart felt replaced with a terrified, fearful, and not to be trusted heart voice. My natural fear response, wired in my belly, was re-wired deep to my heart to mean mistrust, fear, and ultimately self-loathing, and the place of right-decision-making, during my mother's stay in the private mental hospital, became judged and wrong. So this meant, as I matured and needed to make more difficult choices, if my belly and lower root feelings were triggered—wired to fright, fight, or flight—I took this to mean "go for it" as my authentic personality had changed.

At times while Mom was gone, the experiences I had were terrifying. I realized knowing terror was not the same thing as being afraid. Terror was the deeper, darker root of fear. It was the underbelly of fear where dehumanizing treatment was accepted and used to silence those who threatened the agenda of the dark, shadowed world, where fear reigns supreme. Terror was palatable in the air to my hyper-sensitized awareness of the world around me.

In this small, vulnerable childhood world of mine, the adults around me were mean-spirited but appeared to be masking as caring people. I saw through this. I somehow was a threat, a danger to "them, the men dressed in black." As a little girl in this world, I knew there was nothing I could do but beam my love to those who hurt me and tried to shut me up. Do what I was taught Christ did: turn the other cheek!

This ability of mine, to see others as they truly were, was shamed. I was impregnated with enormous shame, confusion, and guilt, which was reinforced weekly during my dad's church services. The confusion I felt came at me from the strange world of adulting. I watched and listened to all that surrounded me and informed me. I felt as though another me began to grow inside. Like a split in my brain happened. The voices I heard did not agree. They fought. I heard in church that whatever was happening in our lives was part of "God's plan." Was it? Painful, bad things were part of a plan? That didn't feel right in my gut. I began to get stomach aches. I couldn't wear anything tight around my belly. It ached all the time.

Because I was so different from the children around me, I watched people. Not being included at certain times allowed me to create an intrigue with the space between myself and others my age. My girlfriends in the South Bronx knew I was going to leave them. I didn't understand this because I had nowhere to go. My family had left me, so I didn't understand the ocean of difference between us. When I looked into my own eyes, I noticed the light beaming love was eventually replaced. My eyes looked dull. I remembered because I was turning nine soon, on September 25th. It was 1964. I saw evil. My name, Cynthia, even had the word "sin" in it. It must be that I was one of the bad ones. "I need cleansing, I am a sinner," I repeated every Sunday in church.

The eyes that looked back at me were lifeless and flat. I was sad the spark was hidden. The dull eyes felt hate, and they were the eyes I loathed when I looked in the mirror. They looked back at me, forlorn. I felt this power, dark and forbidding, pulsing through my veins, deep in my bones, growing. I felt it most when I danced to a pounding Latino rhythm, feeling my body move, gyrating my hips and pelvis to the music.

I wondered about this power. I related to Mary Magdalene, the whore in the Bible I heard stories about. Jesus accepted her, though, and didn't shun her like everyone else did. I related deeply to her and believed that Jesus would not forsake me. I saw all around me the whores and hookers were an accepted part of the culture in our community. Not many opportunities were available for girls to change patterns that may have come from their mothers and grandmothers. Especially the young teen pregnancies! Whether the girls got involved with sex because they needed money, got raped and pregnant, became hooked on drugs, or a boy who they liked was connected to the underbelly of the community getting them involved, whores and prostitutes were here to stay.

I dreamed when I was sitting in our church, looking up at the larger-than-life painting of Jesus, surrounded by animals and children, that I was up there on his lap, surrounded by his love and the love from the animals. There was an angel that sat to his right, above and behind him. Angel Gabriel. It was a peaceful and loving scene. I was comforted when bad things happened, or I was just feeling scared and alone to be on Jesus' lap, surrounded by his love and the animals that were with him. Merging into this painting was often my refuge of safety.

In my body, I knew men were afraid of this woman, Mary Magdalene. She belonged to no one. No man owned her, but rather she gave her body in exchange for her freedom. She represented so many of the women and girls who I knew and played with—seen as whores, who were raped and abused, and became free with their bodies. Detached.

The men dressed as black crows paid homage to this ancient evil which ran rampant in our barrio. Afraid of the light, which embodied kindness, generosity, forgiveness, compassion, empathy, and God's love, they were threatened by its existence in the neighborhood and intended for it to be snuffed out. Their intention was for terror to reign supreme so they had control. An eye for an eye, a tooth for a tooth...

Deep in my tiny, fragile bones I wondered how they knew that I embodied and had been supercharged by the vibrant and living light of Source, which they perceived as being the powerful Light of Christ? I had never told anyone about my strange experiences in Costa Rica, other than my dad and mom, after it happened. Dad laughed and said I had a very active imagination! Mom was curious but laughed with Dad.

The "black crows" believed there were those born who carried the authentic power of the Creator, the Holy, Living Spirit of Christ, which when activated performed what the church called "miracles." This threatened the power held within the priest's hands. It threatened evil's existence.

Cynthia at the ocean in Costa Rica, 1958

Having just moved from St. Louis, MO, where I was born, I was living in Costa Rica then. We first lived in the capitol for a short while. There was a beautiful, huge poinsettia tree on the corner of the house, which reached to the second floor, greeting my mother every day with its cheerful presence. The blossoms were huge and dark red with a bright yellow-gold center, like a button. Dad had welcomed a beautiful huge, green parrot into our lives named Beanie. Beanie sat outside on the verandah near and under the branches of the poinsettia tree. He knew how to whistle—the Wolf call, which was supposed to announce an attractive woman's arrival! Often Dad, while sitting on the verandah, would be mistaken as the one whistling at the gorgeous women approaching down the sidewalk. Dad sheepishly shrugged his shoulders and lifted his hands, gesturing, "it wasn't me."

We had a maid, Tina, who cared for my family, cooking, cleaning, and watching us kids—my brother and me. I liked Tina. She had a warm smile, with soft, brown eyes, and thick black hair, and she wore a tight bun at the nape of her neck. Her dresses were bright and colorful, and she sang as she worked. Her black beans and rice were a constant smell in our kitchen. We had them for breakfast, lunch, and dinner, with a side of some kind of stewed beef, chicken, or pork, or fried eggs. Plantains were also a part of our meals, three times a day. Cooked, mashed, fried— they were green, or dark black and wicked ripe, or just yellow, like a regular banana. I loved these foods and gobbled down Tina's cooking.

I was told I had quite the temper when I didn't get my way. This was attributed to being a redhead, although my hair was strawberry blond. I think Tina was there to care for us, as Mommy and Daddy were very busy with our new life. Mommy struggled with the language and had a hard time communicating with Tina. Dad, on the other hand, was fluent, thriving and easily making friends with everyone he met. Greg, my older brother, went to first grade at a private Catholic school run by nuns, and I went to a nursery school at the same place, for the morning. I wore a navy-blue skirt, starched white shirt, knee socks, a tie of some kind, and black shoes. I was uncomfortable because it was so hot, but off we went to school, being walked there by Tina on the dusty road.

Our house was a big, two-story, square house with beige stucco on the outside and dark wood trim. It was kind of on a hill, with a big, fenced-in backyard. It was lush and green, with tropical trees and flowers everywhere. The air was warm and breezy, but the walls of our home felt confining. I couldn't see over the edge to the other side, as they were too high and could not be seen through. The yard sloped down and had lots of play areas. I don't remember much interaction with others outside my family and the bishop's family. We were isolated behind our walls.

Having a hot temper if I didn't get my way or felt ignored, I had outbursts of rage. I was a very sensitive child with only Tina paying attention to me, and I demanded to be heard and seen! On one of these occasions, I cried, screamed, and threw myself on the floor, kicking and holding my breath until I turned blue and fainted. Still, I got nothing from my parents, other than their annoyance. Annoyed but not sensitive or caring enough to ask me what my trouble was. These bouts of rage grew in their fury until finally Mom consulted with my pediatrician for advice. She was told first to ignore me, making sure I was safe and away from the stairs, so if I was to faint, I wouldn't tumble down the stairs from the second floor. Eventually I would stop my fit, he told her. If this didn't work, his second suggestion was to put me in a cold shower. She did and it worked. It stopped the tantrums.

After our time in San Jose, with city living, we moved out into the country. *El campo!* The air was luscious, sweet, and filled with wonderful, tantalizing scents from the sugarcane and coffee bean fields flanking our home. We had a beautiful, huge, soft, fluffy pink mimosa tree, which danced in the wind, in front of our home. Our house was primitive compared to the big city house we had just left. The rooms were small, bunched up next to each other, with a living room, kitchen, etc. all in one room. But it was the Earth and her beauty which captivated my attention. Even to the point of coming inside one night, when a scorpion lay in my bed. As the covers were drawn back, preparing me for my cozy night's sleep, there it was! Hiding under my covers. Mom shrieked. Dad ran into the kitchen and brought back a huge *machete* and chopped the thing in half, in my bed. Then they proceeded to try and tuck me in for the night as he explained that scorpions liked to live in our shoes, too. Of this fact, we were reminded by our new maid, Chiquita, again in the morning after Dad recounted the episode. So, every night we all went through a shoe examination, dumping them upside down, making sure the nasty rascals were not in our rooms.

Sleep? Not a chance in hell was I able to fall asleep after that just happened! So, I lay awake at night wondering about the land our home had been built on...the scorpion's home. My dad reminded me that these are black ones, not the red ones, which were poisonous and whose bite was much nastier. Oh great. That made me feel a whole lot better!

A wild, sensuous nature abounded in this new home of mine. Mom found a barn close to our home and bought a horse. Coronation was his name. He was a Paso Fino walker, and my mom was in heaven, thriving. She had gotten a few students to teach, including me, and acquired a small, gray pony for me to ride. The mimosa tree became a great friend. I loved riding my pony under it, my tiny legs stuck straight out as I pulled him to a stop. Standing on his back, I stretched my arms up and hung onto a branch. Dangling, I hung tightly as my pony went around the tree again, allowing me to drop onto his back. We spent endless hours doing this. The horse, tree, and I became a threesome. And the tree, I discovered, was magical. She spoke to me, but not like humans did. Her voice came as a whisper through my skin, flowing into my body, imprinting me with her wisdom. The wisdom of Earth people connected me forever to Mother Earth—*Pacha Mama*, in Quechua, the language of the ancient Incas. I spoke with the tadpoles that swam in a half-moon culvert waterway which ran beside our home. I heard the voice of the coffee bean flowers before the beans grew and ripened. Most deeply of all, I heard Irazú, the magnetic and grand volcano which stood high up above our home. On Sundays, my family gathered for *paseos*. Packing a huge picnic lunch, we saddled up and rode our horses up to the volcano. We stopped at a large, flat, grassy area, where we picnicked. We unsaddled the horses, tethered them to one another, and allowed the horses to graze and roam. At this time, my family consisted of my older brother, Greg, me, my mom, dad, and my dad's kid brother, who was twelve years younger, Clay, who was quickly becoming my favorite person in my whole, small world. Clay had sandy blond, brown hair, twinkling, brilliant green eyes, and a sweet, warm smile that lit up his whole face. I related to him because he didn't seem to be old, like my parents. He played with me, talked to me, answered my many questions, and didn't treat me as though I were invisible and a bother like a fly buzzing around the food laid out on the ground, to be swatted away.

During these fun family rides, I always tried to ride next to Uncle Clay, so I could show off! While the others were resting, I, being curious, wanted to investigate the center of the volcano, but walking to the edge and peering over gave me vertigo, spinning my world too fast. I tried to do this holding Uncle Clay's hand. While no one was paying attention to me, I dropped onto my knees, and then my belly, and crawled, slithering like a snake to her edge. He kept my secret, loving the curiosity and bravery I had. As I looked deep down into the vortex of the mouth, it was like a big, gaping vulva, bubbling blood red lava. Intense. During one of these moments, I left my body and flew around the perimeter, down, down, down I went. I felt the hot wind in my hair and felt the heat and its intensity on my skin. And then I catapulted back into my body, like an arrow shot and hitting its mark. Ka-BAM! I was in my body, lying flat on Mother Earth, pondering. Whew...that was wild flying free as a bird, not confined to this small body. Mother Earth had burned her mark into me, claiming me as one of her own, on that day, in 1960.

So, when we finally arrived at our new home in the South Bronx, in 1962, I grieved the loss of Mother Nature's lush and vibrant presence in my surroundings, flowing through my veins. I missed my uncle and his playful, easy love, after he returned to his home in Missouri. I missed the other neighbors' children playing in the culvert beside me, surmounting any language barrier there could have been in our way.

Now, I saw vacant buildings, some burned out. I saw trash cans, either full or dumped over, and men sitting on the edges of filthy sidewalks. I saw children of all ages, running around unsupervised, laughing, and playing in the streets. I wanted badly to join them in their ruckus play and laughter. Kicking a can and running after it, until a car came, looked like great fun. I heard mothers yelling from their windows to their kids. I saw scrawny little trees trying to grow, surrounded by concrete and soil that looked like concrete, hard and cracked. The sounds of horns beeping, the smell of exhaust, garbage sitting in the summer sun, urine-baked bricks, and stale alcohol permeated the neighborhood. And then I saw the gates...the gates into our new home. Gates into a holy hell. Tall, black, forbidding, and spiked at the top. There was a hump of a hill to our right, and an alley to our left, behind a low wall where the cars parked. Next to the hump of land, which I realized was a graveyard, stood a beautiful, old, majestic church with tall, bright red doors, held with wrought iron hinges and wrought iron scrolling. It was beautiful, standing majestically on the rise above the neighborhood. Straight ahead was a large, barren, dirt yard. Kids were playing kickball, jacks, and several girls were jumping rope as the dusty, parched soil kicked up with each jump forming a cloud around the girls. Up a short distance away and off to the right and sitting atop a hill, I saw another big house. Maybe that's our home, I prayed.

There were people gathered around our car as we drove in through the gates of the church. It was like we were celebrities as our car crept along. Kids dropped their games and came running, yelling, and screaming, waving their hands excitedly to greet us while the adults hung back, many holding babies in their arms. Many of the women holding babies, I noticed, looked like young girls themselves... I didn't see many men. Boys and teens I saw, but not many grown men, other than the men of the church in their more formal clothing. And the priest, dressed in black with his stiff, white collar, was among the throng of people.

We were greeted warmly and taken to our new home, up a cement sidewalk, in between the church and the graveyard, to the parish house. There were four stone arches creating an "L" shape with the church, St. Ann's, and its parish house. As we looked up at the parish house, we were told by the lead priest that to the far right was the gymnasium, then the offices, while our apartment was above all the offices on the second floor. Up the long stairs and next to our apartment to the left, through a dark hallway, was a huge vacant area which served as a clothing drop off and pick-up for people in our community.

As we entered our apartment and made our way past the cubicle, which was the kitchen, and into the living room, my eyes widened in horror as the three beautiful Palladian windows, with sun pouring through them, overlooked the graveyard. It looked like an old graveyard, as many of the stones were crooked or cracked and broken, while some of the bigger, wealthier headstones stood tall, stately, and lonely in what seemed to be a forgotten graveyard right outside my front door.

I felt very visible to the people I was meeting. I was gawked at, my body and skin were touched, and on some occasions, my head was patted and cheeks painfully pinched.

Something strange happened to me when I was being noticed in such a dramatic and bizarre way. When I made eye contact, I could feel my essence, my energy, being drawn away, as if sucked out of me. As the sucking happened, I noticed I was filled with a sweet, calm, effervescent presence. Love from my heart. As this energy flowed through my veins, a tingling sensation happened, along with a buzzing sensation which vibrated through my entire body. It swelled as it flowed into my chest, down through my arms, and into my hands so they felt like I had baseball mitts on. It then shot out my fingertips. I couldn't stop it. I felt relaxed with my heart wide open. My eyes filled with *light* and through my eyes a bright beam of laser-focused *light* shot forth. I couldn't control any of this. It happened when my empathy was touched, like a facet being turned on. As I felt and watched *light* flowing and surrounding many who seemed lost and with broken hearts, I "saw" their haunted, hungry eyes soften when touched by the flow of *light*. I watched a slow, lazy smile creep across their faces as they were warmed by the *light*—God's Light. This light was the energy turned on by Gaia, in Costa Rica. This made me a powerful channel as I channeled the light from SourceLove!

Where had the sweet, intoxicating power I received from Mother Earth's unseen energies gone? I wondered when alone, sitting on the floor in my bedroom in the South Bronx. Was this the same energy that I had grown accustomed to in my old life in Costa Rica? Or was this what I heard preached about in church, the Light of the Christ, as Dad and the lead priest claimed? Were they one and the same? Did this—what I was filled with—flow through all living things? When I filled and expanded with the buzzing energy, were they one and the same? I pondered this in church, drunk and mesmerized by the music, incense, and the flickering candles, but I found no answers. The prayers all taught that it was the Light of Christ, the Holy Spirit in us if we were baptized, which was filling me with this power. Hmm…. The prayers and the Bible readings didn't mention the beauty and power within Nature. I never heard anything about power existing within all living things. Was this church power inherent within our Mother Earth and all living things? My belief in this truth and the memory of my mimosa tree experience was fading. Dad made fun of it, anyway, and said it wasn't possible for a tree to talk to me!

The church's elders, the lead priest, Dad, and his vestrymen, who were responsible for the priest's salary, the upkeep of the church, dad's pay, and its grounds, and to ministering to the poor and needy in the community, got wind of this power I possessed. It was Nature's raw power turned on, inherent in me that they perceived. I was seen by them all the time, as I served them at Dad's special vestry men's gatherings in our apartment. They knew I was alone and vulnerable, without a caregiver watching over me. I was sweetmeat and ripe for picking.

These men wanted dominion over the neighborhood. They wanted no bright lights—rebels. Any perceived light was to be snuffed out. In the hearts of these men, and in the streets of this neighborhood, there was no place for the light with its wild, chaotic, expansive, and all-encompassing nature, spreading love and generosity to those in need. No. These men were single-minded in their desire and pursuit to rule the neighborhood with a cold, hard, iron fist, treating those under them as their subordinates. The lead priest believed that the gang members and the young kids who were hankering to follow in their brothers' (or cousins', or fathers') footsteps needed his kind of "tough love." The church's leader, a rough, tough, angry boy himself, was in a big man's body, wielding tremendous power over his parishioners. He, with help, terrorized the neighborhood with a dark and sinister belief system, eons old, and used fear as his weapon. They were men with strange and unorthodox ideas.

I remember Dad and his cronies discussing the thefts that were happening in the church. The candlesticks were stolen, the offertory plate, and a few other significant items, items the kids must have thought had value. In truth, the candlesticks were brass, as were the other things that were stolen. The men figured the kids must have thought these things were gold. After the vestry men left and Dad was sitting with his boss, he excitedly shared a plan he thought was brilliant, with Dad. He enrolled my father in doing it. Dad was to climb up into the cupola of the church and take a BB gun with him and shoot anyone who tried to break into the church. Dad, I remember, was hesitant. He didn't seem very comfortable with this tactic. He was used to gentle Costa Rican souls to save, not an all-out war zone. Even though the gun shot BBs and not bullets, it still was a glaringly violent act against these kids.

"An eye for an eye, a tooth for a tooth," Dad's boss reminded my father with a wicked gleam in his eyes that didn't get past me. I was frightened. I saw my daddy struggling to go along with this plan.

Said, with a sneer, "You don't have a weak stomach now do you, John? We deal with problems differently here. You need to thicken your skin up and get with the program. And quick."

Silence ensued. I was frozen in place and pretended to melt into the walls.

Finally, after a deathly silence that seemed to go on forever, Dad said, "Yeah, sure. I get it, Father. I get how you handle things. You're the boss. I'll be up there. Where's the BB gun?"

Chapter 2

1961-1966

Our church was the oldest one in the Bronx, built in 1841 as a memorial to the family of Gouverneur Morris II. The address was 295 St. Ann's Avenue, between E. 139th and E. 141st streets. The building was a charming roughhewn building made of randomly coursed fieldstone, shaped in the style of a Latin cross. It was "a forgotten 'country churchyard' in the heart of the sprawling city" by the Landmarks Preservation Commission. The church had a primordial feel to it, because underneath the church altar, in a vault, was buried the wife of Gouverneur Morris II, along with other famous family members, who he re-interred in the vaults, below the church, in the catacombs. The estate of Gouverneur Morris II was originally 1,900 acres, the largest estate that stretched from the Harlem River to the Bronx River and as far north as Crotona Park.

"But ironically the building of Saint Ann's marked the end of Morrisania and the green world of lower Westchester. 1841 might be called the year the modern Bronx was born, and Gouverneur Morris II was one of its creators. In the year he built the chapel, Morris sold 200 acres of his estate to Jordan Mott for the foundry town of Mott Haven, the first important industrial development in lower

Westchester. In the same year, the New York and Harlem Railroad (of which Morris was Vice President), having bridged the river from Manhattan, pushed its tracks northward—on Morrisania land—to Fordham. Along this earliest train route from New York City, which reached White Plains by 1844, sprang up the new villages (one named "Morrisania") that were to populate the 23rd Ward on land purchased from the Morris estate.

Gouverneur Morris II became a millionaire, and created a new city, by opening his cherished private realm to the manufacturers and immigrant workers of the modern world. He also opened his family memorial to the growing neighborhood, donating it as a parish church, and stipulating that there always be free pews—unusual at the time— for "all persons coming to the said church to worship." Morris seems to have anticipated—with what mixed feelings? —that St. Ann's would someday be an anachronistic country church hemmed-in by busy streets." David Baty

I was sure Gouverneur Morris did not foresee the downfall of his beautiful vision into becoming one of the toughest neighborhoods in America. Mott Haven became a rat and drug-infested project, broken down and forgotten by city officials.

Around the left side of the building, facing the church and to the south, there were steps that went down below the church, shut off to regular foot traffic by steel gates that were locked with a heavy, old, black padlock. This part of the church was mysterious. The Puerto Ricans believed it was haunted, because of the bodies that lay silent in their concrete resting places. No one was allowed down there. It was seriously off limits except for the one big day of the year when the catacombs were opened.

Halloween was a big celebration! For the neighborhood kids, it was the biggest one of the year, because no one had money to celebrate Christmas. Christmas was a sad letdown in our community. But Halloween was a different animal entirely, and the kids were pumped. They loved this holiday most of all because of their rich history of honoring their saints, spirits, ancestors, and demons. They also honored and named Evil because they had first-hand experience of its existence in the world. They knew the shadow of darkness well as it was part of their everyday lives, in that community.

My favorite person in my new home was Maria. In her native land, on the beautiful, gentle island of Puerto Rico, an ocean breeze can be felt 365 days a year, as lovingly recounted to me by Maria Carmona. As she hugged herself and pulled me in close, too, she told me that it had the best weather of any place on this sweet Earth. Maria's skin was dark as night, with just the whites of her eyes and her brilliant, white teeth flashing in a huge smile as she spoke longingly of her home. It was her Heaven on Earth. Maria was a petite woman, with smooth dark skin, and always smelled sweet, like jasmine. She had large breasts, a small waist, and was a five-foot powerhouse. Her eyes were dark, big, and inquisitive. She was twenty-three years old and had four children by three different fathers. Her first child, Peachy, was born when she was fourteen. Cookie came next, then Gigi, who became my best friend. And Carlito was Chan and Maria's son. They loved each other passionately and playfully. Their home was a warm and welcoming place for me. They were married in the church before we had moved into town. It was sweet to see that they were in love. It was obvious from the sexual innuendos, intimate touches, and their shared laughter. Chan loved his black-skinned Mama—more like worshiped her—and she loved her little, skinny Chan. They were an odd couple, as Chan was a lot older than her, like he could be her father's age. He was diminutive in size, next to the robust and vivacious Maria. To me, he felt a bit shifty and gave me the creeps. But I loved Maria so I never spoke of my discomfort. I was happy she felt cherished and content living within the church's protective gates, on the back side of the property. Maria was the maid for Father Mercy. She cleaned the church, parish house, and Father Mercy's home, up on the hill, which sat majestically in front of Maria and Chan's home. Chan was the church janitor. His arms were sinewy and strong. He had long, boney fingers with big knuckles. Everyone cracked their knuckles, which made them dark. Their house was a two-story, wood frame, beat-up old clapboard house, which looked about ready to collapse from neglect.

But it was a house, not an apartment. It had three bedrooms, a small galley kitchen, a small dining area where their talking parrot lived, and a rectangular living room, which ran the length of the house. All the furniture appeared new, as it was covered in plastic. I guess it was new because it was still covered in plastic, which I thought odd. The couch was cold and stiff to sit on. But Maria was proud of her shiny, plastic-covered furniture.

"It will always look new," she said one time when I asked, after a while, why she didn't take off the plastic.

"*Mi hija*, [my daughter] I pay extra for dis," she retorted proudly.

I loved Maria. I loved the warmth of her home, the smoky, rich, scent of the air when I entered without knocking, from cigarette smoke and incense. I loved the colorful, wild chaos that was embodied in this house, as it reminded me of Costa Rica. Kids flying in and out all the time, laughter, and the screams of their spider monkey sitting in its cage, calling out for attention, added to the cacophony of sounds. And let's not forget the talking African Grey parrot, which lived in the dining room, adding his vocals to the sounds of family life. Diana Ross and the Supremes always played in the background, blaring, when Maria was cleaning. I'd walk into her home on her cleaning days, and she'd be dancing around the living room with her broom, pretending she was a star! She was a star in my little world. She was my guardian angel who watched over me, as best she could, while my mama was gone and my siblings were all living away from home. I preferred this home to my silent and sad house, which overlooked the graveyard with its spiked fencing around it, and the dirty, baked-urine-smelling alleyway behind our house.

The best memories of living in the South Bronx were of being in Maria's home with all my friends. The birthdays were the best. Maria went all out with colorful and garish decorations, lights flashing, a spinner ball with mirrors on it which sparkled on the walls as it turned. Loud R&B music was pounding its slow, sexy, smoky music, and Latin music blared also. And *piñatas* were always a big hit! As the sun began its slow descent, we played spin the bottle, which was a big thriller for us kids. We all giggled as we kissed and had to be kissed. Some of the boys tried to slip their tongues into my mouth, which was disgusting. I'd squeal in disgust and mask it with laughter anyway. I'll never forget the feeling I had, watching all the kids laughing and dancing except me. I was painfully shy and withdrawn in these social situations. I was standing in a corner watching, silently, and uncomfortable in this peach-skinned body. Maria danced over to me, slow and sexy-like, with her hot pink lips. She laughed gently and pulled me out on the dance floor. She got in front of me, put her hands with hot pink, long nails, on my hips, and said, "Come on, lil white girl, shake your hips." She proceeded to shake my hips, got me all revved up, laughing and giggling, and finally something burst free, and I cut loose.

Dancing became my passion! Maria had unlocked a taste of joy in my closed, sad, and heavy heart. Too heavy was my heart for a little child of seven. Dancing became my happy place.

I'll never forget the first time Mom saw me dance, after she had come home from the hospital. I was in the living room; Dad was playing his favorite Herb Alpert album and I was rocking it. Gyrating my hips, rocking them back and forth, laughing, and shaking my booty. Dad was enjoying the scene, relaxed and dancing, too, near the record player. I had my top half shaking one way and my bottom another, off in another world. When I finally opened my eyes, with the stopping of the music, I glanced at my mother, suddenly feeling super uncomfortable. Naked. She was glaring at me, with her hand covering her mouth, in horror. "Who taught you how to dance that way?" she yelled at me. "You stop that right now and go to your room. That's disgusting." Her eyes were wild and flashing daggers at me. I felt them like invisible darts hitting my heart. "You look like a whore dancing that way. Go. Out," she spit out.

With my head bowed and my eyes tearing up and hidden, I whispered, "Maria. We dance at the parties she has for us kids." I sulked to my room, feeling ashamed.

Dad sat, silent.

Day of the Dead was just around the corner. It was a big deal in this Puerto Rican neighborhood. Father Mercy asked my father to assist him in the preparation for the Day of the Dead service and the haunted house, which was set up every year. It was a tradition and was the church's biggest ritual that the kids talked about and always looked forward to.

The plan Dad was to follow was all laid out for him. He first had to contact the butcher to acquire the blood, eyes, and brains of cows. These would be put in bowls on an altar, which Father Mercy was to set up. Father Mercy was a tall, big-boned man, and he looked very strong. His hands were huge. The thing I remember about him was a purple blood blister on the bottom left side of his lip. I knew this because he invited me to sit on his lap occasionally, during my dad's gatherings for the vestry men and his boss. I hated sitting on their laps when they invited me into them. I wanted to yell at them, "No, I don't want to sit in your lap. Go screw yourself." If I said that, I'd get into big trouble for being rude and having a fresh mouth.

Dad seemed upset about all the bizarre chores he was assigned to do. But he did it anyway. He had to. As for me, it was made clear, right from the get-go, that I was forbidden to go down into the haunted catacombs. The catacombs contained a small ante room, right under the altar, where Gouverneur's wife, Ann Morris, was buried.

The day finally arrived. The whole neighborhood was buzzing with excitement. The altar was all set up. The bowls were ready, the candles were lit all around the ante room for the effect, and candles were lit on the altar. Dad and Father Mercy had their black cassocks and black wool capes on as they welcomed the kids in. They had weird creepy music playing. They had a light shining up from the floor, illuminating the faces of my dad and Father Mercy, making them look distorted and gruesome.

The entrance was creepy enough just as it was. But Dad and Father Mercy had been busy hanging store-bought spider webs, to add to the spider webs that were already a part of the scene, naturally. The line of kids waiting at the entrance for the show to begin was mind-blowing. Hundreds of kids were present as word spread through the barrio. This was a famous event, I suppose. Determined to sneak through, I sat at the entrance, on my haunches, waiting for the perfect moment. I managed to insert myself into the crowd as it swelled through the door, squeezing myself between the crowded legs of the kids going in. I was small, so it was easy for me to be lost in the crowd. Father Mercy had boasted to Dad about how the "hoodlums" fainted like flies from fright. And it was true. Some kids didn't even make it in before they were fainting. The vestry men were there to help carry the kids out who had fainted. They, too, were dressed in those black cassocks that made them look like human crows running around.

The kids who made it up to the entrance were blindfolded. They were then led through, and their hand, being held, was placed into each bowl of goopy mess as a ghost story was told of the people whose bones were in the crypts. The kids were scared, some even shitting their pants. Even though these kids were rough and tough street fighters who carried switchblades and wouldn't hesitate to use them, they were just kids who wanted to have fun and could still be scared.

Kids who had no choice but to follow in their peers' footsteps, because this was their way of life. They are kids with few options in the neighborhood other than drugs, which made lots of money and gave them enormous power. Like being able to buy things for families in the community who were really struggling. The big daddy dealer did things like that, driving into the barrio in his fancy, decked-out car with black windows, fancy tires, and baubles hanging from the mirror. They were sights to see, with their gold chains, gold teeth, and leathers, strutting their stuff like a cock ready to fight. Some of these dealers even came to our Halloween event, and when the big daddy dealers showed up, the sea of kids parted, like the Red Sea parting for Moses. The kids were fainting like flies as Dad's maniacal laughter rang out and bounced off the concrete walls, giving way to eerie echoes that ricocheted around the room. Later that evening, when all was said and done, Dad recounted the story to me of the kids fainting and how even some shit their pants they were so scared. He was jacked up and so proud of himself for accomplishing the task at hand—to scare the shit out of the neighborhood, letting them know whose neighborhood it was. *God's or Satan's?* was the question I wanted to ask, but again I stayed silent. I knew what I believed.

While we were sitting in the living room, I caught a shadow out of the corner of my eye. I moved closer to the big Palladian windows that flanked the outer wall of our living room, which looked out onto the cemetery. I stared intently outside, watching. Had I imagined seeing something leaping over the gravestones? Maybe

I was imagining it, so heightened were my senses from having witnessed the catacombs. But Daddy didn't know this. You see, I never actually went up to the altar. Once in the room, I sat in the cold concrete corner, crouched, watching, my eyes big as saucers.

Suddenly, I yelled, "There, Daddy. There it is," and I pointed as I saw a huge, black shadow that appeared to have wings, flying over the gravestones. "Look, daddy. There it is. What is that? I'm scared."

Daddy started laughing. "I don't see anything. You're imagining something out there."

"No. I'm not." Again, I caught it out of the corner of my eye as I turned my head to argue with my daddy. "See? There it is!" I said, pointing.

"You have a vivid imagination. There is nothing out there," he said, still laughing at me. He's not laughing with me, because I wasn't laughing. I was frightened and shaking in my body because Daddy didn't believe me. I was scared. Was I imagining what I swear I just saw three times? I pondered this, and I didn't want to go to bed tonight in my bed, at the end of the hall.

I begged Daddy to let me sleep in his bed. I had done this a few times when I was really scared. If he was really upset, he'd ask me to come snuggle with him in his bed, so it seemed fine for me to ask for this tonight.

He said yes. Relieved, I ran and jumped into his bed before he changed his mind. When he finally came to bed, I snuggled right up close, on my side. I curled my tiny body against him, right in the crook of his warm, strong body. He was asleep in no time. I didn't fall asleep that easily. My mind was whirling from the days' activities, and that black shadow disturbed me. Deeply.

It felt good to be held in his arms with his warm body wrapped around mine. His light snoring was comforting. I felt safe in my crazy, upside-down world.

The next day was Sunday, and Daddy had his call from Mommy. He recounted his previous day's tales to her on the phone about the Halloween activities. He chatted on in his lively manner. Then, she must have asked how I was because he told her I was fine. He shared, laughing with Mom over the phone, about my active imagination seeing something black with wings, leaping over the gravestones, out the front window. Then he was silent for some time, listening to her. She must have asked again how I was doing.

"She scared herself silly and begged me to let her sleep in our bed. So, I let her. She looked so tiny and fragile when she asked that I let her sleep with me. She curled right up in the crook of my body and fell asleep."

Silence again as he listened.

"No," he said forcibly. "It was all very innocent. She was just scared."

Silence again followed. I could see in Daddy's face that he was upset. Mommy had said something that upset him. His eyes were sad and tired.

"Fine," he replied dejectedly. "I won't let her come into my bed. But Gwynneth," he said in a much quieter voice, "you really don't understand the circumstances. You are being unfair." He tried to protest and failed. Daddy never let me sleep in his bed again. He also was never comfortable hugging me or giving me a kiss on my cheek, like he used to do when he was happy to see me, his little companion. His little Bride Doll.

Oh God, I was sad. I lamented to Jesus in my prayers at night, alone. I was so scared and confused about what was going on.

The light from God's love was evident in the mothers' faces as they cared for their children as best they could. The women were colorful and haughty, some stunningly beautiful with their rich colors of brown skin. They were fierce in their protection and still powerless to protect. The young children's faces were innocent and sweet, with big, open eyes full of hope with their mothers' and grandmothers' love. This, of course, was before they were touched with fate. The drugs, rape, pregnancy, or all of it was an almost certain future for these children. Very few escaped. My brother Greg's best friend was one of the young people who did escape. Peachy got a full scholarship to attend St. John's of the Divine Cathedral school, in Manhattan, as a choir boy. He sang like a bird. So clear and sweet with power in his voice. Dad was able to get him this opportunity by talking with the bishop. A one in a million opportunity. He attended, boarded at the Cathedral, and traveled home with Greg teaching him how to be street wise!

Our St. Ann's congregation was amazingly resilient. The congregation was 90% woman and children. These women were not just any women. They were tough, streetwise proud Puerto Rican women, raised to navigate through the maze of streets which make up the South Bronx. These grandmothers were the heart of the church, and they had some stories to tell. A famous saying that I heard all the time was: *Keep moving, don't feel, and don't look back. Just keep moving forward.* The darkness of the community wasn't worth wasting time on because it would gobble up all the good and smother it. Their stories were dark, rich, hysterical, wild stories of their super-powers. The mothers were the workers and the backbone of a community dependent on the *abuelas* to help raise the children. Together they were truly the soul of the church, and it rocked with their love. The remaining family members had organized themselves to go visit their men every Sunday in prison: fathers, brothers, uncles, cousins, etc. The prison was right on the edge of the barrio. And of course, there was no transportation in or out of the barrio available, making it impossible to leave the neighborhood for better jobs. These really were God's forgotten people. The women felt it. They worked hard trying to keep their kids clean and off drugs, away from prostitution, or being raped, addicted, or one of the king pins. They worked hard at this to no avail. It was just the culture. They lived in dire situations, with faith and hope as their guiding principles.

The church services provided respite from the constant threat of danger that had taken root and spread like a malignant cancer. The singing, the colorful robes, and vestments, the smell of the incense burning, all the candles twinkling in the church, making reflections on the stained-glass windows, were beautiful distractions from what lay outside the church doors. It was a beautiful, warm interior that felt safe from harm's way. The thing I liked best of all was the huge mural of a life-sized Jesus, sitting with animals surrounding him. He had an angel to his right, and the scene was colorful and very peaceful to gaze upon. The inside of the church, with its prayers sung in the Gregorian style of chanting, and all the pomp and ritual gave these poor, destitute people a place to hope. A place to rest their tired bodies and put a religious balm on their Souls. The church propagated hope but hope that was built on dust. A hope that was built on maintaining power over its people, not empowering them. There was a big difference in these two belief systems. One heals, and the other destroys, creating victims and perpetrators.

I remember one story Dad used to love to recount. While Father Mercy was on his annual month-long vacation, the incense burner was empty after Dad's first Sunday service of the month. He asked for the burner-thing to be filled by his head acolyte. The following Sunday, when the acolyte lit up the incense, it smoked up like crazy. As the acolyte swung it up and down and around, and around, the church filled with smoke. Dad noticed that the entire church was filled with tons of neighborhood kids he had never seen. Week after week this happened, puffing Dad's chest up, as he believed that word had spread around and through the neighborhood that his preaching style was cool. He thought he was onto something, and that the kids were loving his stories. And hopefully they were. Truth be known, the acolyte had filled the incense burner with an ounce of weed. Dad's mass was a "high mass." And Dad laughed his ass off every time he recounted the story, loving the kids' ingenuity and the fact that our services were "high masses" in the Episcopal tradition, and here it was literally a mass full of high teenagers, loving what was happening to Padre Kerly, as they nicknamed him, not Father Kelley. He was bald as a billiard ball, except for the rim of gray hair around the base of his head, so this was a funny, loving joke amongst the kids.

A few years later, during my senior year in high school, I returned to visit my old neighborhood with my mom and dad. We visited St. Ann's first to find out where our friends, Maria, and her children, lived. We were given a tour of the church and saw many changes which had taken place: the biggest one being that no one lived above the church anymore, where we had lived. It had been turned into teaching rooms.

We met up with Maria Carmona and her two daughters, my two best friends, Gigi and Cookie. I remember thinking Maria hadn't changed at all. She was still a live-wire, vibrant and bubbly in her demeanor and the backbone of her family and the church. She was a bit plumper in her late thirties, wore a bright purple, skin-tight satin jumpsuit and her hair was long, jet black, and braided down her back. She had red lipstick on, and her nails were long and painted red. She wore a huge smile and was still the same warm, loving Puerto Rican mama, whose arms were always wide open to give a hug. And it felt great to be embraced by her and snuggled into her big bosom. Gigi and Cookie welcomed us while their children played on the floor. Gigi's child was three, and she was holding a newborn, several months old. She had her first baby a year and a half after we moved away, at fourteen. Cookie, at sixteen, had a two-or three-year-old and was very pregnant with her second child. I was shocked, horrified, and so grateful we had moved away when we had. I saw myself with the same plight if we had stayed even a year longer. I was devastated for my friends whose lives were as distant to mine, as lives could be. I had no words to speak as I couldn't relate to my friends who were mothers now, not young, blooming teens, like me. Well, they were still young teens, but they had grown up fast once their bodies betrayed them with their menses, and then the men and boys in their lives betrayed them.

Gigi was pretty much living with a burned-out brain from shock treatments she had received years before, when we were little. I remembered, seeing her in her current state, that Gigi disappeared for periods of time. We were never told why other than she was sick. I discovered years later she had experienced a forced silence in the form of shock treatments, which served as a warning: ***Don't tell.***

When Mommy finally came home, life was weird. I was so happy to see her and she to see me, that we fell into each other's arms, and I sobbed. I sobbed and sobbed, gasping for air, unable to breathe from my snot-filled nose.

But the seed of evil had been planted in me during the fourteen months Mommy was in the hospital. I was not the same child she had left behind. My eyes no longer sparkled. They were flat and empty and filled with fright. Extremely uncomfortable in my tightened state, free of laughter and the silliness that used to be me. Mommy asked, "Are you ok, my precious Cynthia? What's making you so sad? Mommy is home, you should be happy!"

I was afraid to speak. I had been forbidden to speak about the unspeakable. If I opened my mouth, I was afraid of what would come out. So, I stayed silent.

Mommy continued to pester me as to why I was so silent. Finally, I wrote her a letter telling her everything. What I got back was this years later:

I THREW IT AWAY

Yes, I did—it's hard to believe,
but I can't deny it.
I threw it away—trashed it—
What was written by my daughter
when she was only nine.

#

Ugly words and bleak thoughts—
I did not want to hear, so closed my ears
and veiled my eyes.
She wrote, I know not what—
but it's offensive nature
bounced off my brittle self,

#

and I in arrogant authority
tore to shreds her blackest plight,
leaving her bound and gagged for thirty years.
Caught up in man's lust this daughter so fair,
to be used in the vilest of ways.
As I stood by, her mom, not seeing,
not hearing, behind the windowpane.
Anxiety grabbed—screaming, screaming—
engulfed in anger's hell.

Written from a memory by Gwynn Kelley - February 1992

Memories too dark to live with as a small child were hidden away and forgotten until further notice. I remained silent, like a deer caught in a car's headlights. I was startled easily. I still am. I was terrified to be called on in school, so shy was I to speak. I remember one time in a brand-new school, I had a very tall Mr. Zachary as my teacher. He was a giant to me with huge, bushy black eyebrows that pointed out at the ends. He probably waxed them! He was warm and friendly and sat a lot on the end of his desk, so he wasn't so tall next to us small kids. I always sat in the back. I never spoke up. It was discovered that I didn't know any answers. My ritual became marching off to the principal's office, every morning. To Mrs. Godfrey, as my lack of any basic skills was discovered in the first week of school. I did not know how to read, write, or do any math problems. Basically, I was illiterate in the third grade. I went to Public School 30 and was the only Anglo kid in my class. The teacher was Irish and took to favoring me. I ran all her errands to the office and got to clean the erasers by hitting them on the outside of the big, brick building that was my school. I never did homework or had any assignments that I had to do while in class. I'm not sure if any of the kids learned how to read or write or do math problems either, as the disciplinary issues were a huge drain on the time my teacher had to teach. I was happy to leave the room and liked the attention I received. But I didn't learn anything.

The next school, my sister and I got transferred across the city into the Upper East Bronx. This was where Mrs. Godfrey was principal. It was an hour bus ride. Busing was happening across New York City during this time in the mid 1960s. I remember my sister and I as the only Anglo kids on the bus. I don't have the memory of my Anglo friend from our church attending the school also, yet I am told we sat next to each other on the bus, the day President Kennedy was shot and killed. My sister and I knew no one on this bus ride as none of my Puerto Rican friends attended this school with us. So, I didn't talk to anyone on the bus. I was terrified and feeling awfully vulnerable. I don't know what my little sister was feeling as she sat silently next to me. I remember reaching for her hand and holding it tightly.

I always returned to class for the afternoon with Mr. Zachery, after my morning studies with Mrs. Godfrey were completed. Mrs. Godfrey had curly red hair, wore horn-rimmed glasses, and was, as I saw her, God's saint. I noticed she was always so happy to see me. I believed she was my saint because of her name—Godfrey—and she personally tutored me the entire first year in this new school, getting me up to speed for my third-grade level.

I had lunch, Science, and history with Mr. Zachery. Sitting in the back of the room, twirling my hair, staring out the window, I imagined I heard my name being called. Next thing I knew, Mr. Zachery was bending down next to my desk asking me what the answer was. Frozen in shame because I had no clue what the question was, let alone the answer, I peed my pants. I'd had to go for a while, but I was so uncomfortable acknowledging my body's normal functions that I couldn't ask, feeling like my throat was constricted. I was ashamed to let anyone know.

The alteration of my authentic, joy-filled nature—and the snuffing of the *light* had been completed. The men had succeeded; I had become the embodiment of shame. Their intention for planting the seeds of self-loathing had taken root. I had become Betty the Bride Doll and was numb. My budding self-esteem had been rewired by the continued ridicule and derogatory comments about who I was and what I was good for. Self-hatred, shame, and guilt replaced vibrancy, trust, joy, and love. So complete was the rewiring that while in church I asked my friends to help me spell my name: sin-the-a. No adults noticed the spelling, so no one corrected the spelling of my name. I believed I was evil. A sinner of the vilest kind.

Years later, I had a dream. *I was shown a school paper. On the first-grade paper, my name was signed Sinthea.* That day I called Mom to verify this. Ironically—but not really—as this was how my healing occurred with little "stepping stones" leading the way.

That day, while cleaning out attic boxes of family memorabilia, Mom found a school paper. My name was written as "Sinthea," scrawled in a young child's handwriting. How stunning!

Chapter 3
Papier-mâché Monsters

The year was 1985.

As the embodiment of Christ's light, I was thriving in the intimate community at St. John's Episcopal Church in Walpole, NH. It was a sweet, small, stone church with a gorgeous stone fireplace at the back. My husband and two small children were excited to have found this cozy church minutes from our home. Always, a huge fire blazed on those exceptionally chilly New Hampshire winter days. The church warmed up quickly because of its stone walls and the church's small size. It took me back in my imagination to a time when life was simple. The warmth and comfort of belonging and participating was at the core of small-town communities before the days of malls, and big box company businesses. In the days when everyone knew each other and watched out for each other's children. All candles were lit, music played, sweet conversations were being whispered as shoulders met the shoulders of their friends. David, our minister at the altar, I noticed, was an elderly man in his early eighties when I first met him, with a very young wife of about forty or more years! They had two beautiful, young children and were an unusual couple, as most assumed David was the grandfather of the children and his wife, his daughter. It was the natural assumption one would jump to, given the extraordinary age difference. They were genuinely in love, and it was a sacred relationship I grew to enjoy and respect immensely. I didn't know it at the time, but David wanted to retire. He had set his heart upon me becoming the next appointed minister of this congregation. Mind you, I was not ordained. I am a priestess and seen as such by many, skilled already at calling forth and creating a sacred time for worship. It was intrinsic to my Soul's nature, only not yet known to me.

My family, David's family, and one or two other couples with children were the only young people in this congregation of mostly senior citizens. The seniors *loved* us. They loved the new, young blood, the squeals of the children, and they didn't care about any unruly behavior, so happy were they to have young blood attending church! The church had *life* again!

It wasn't long before I was invited and excited to take on the role of Sunday school teacher. But what an array of ages I had to work with! How would I ever handle this task, I pondered. I wasn't interested in following the traditional curriculum, which I was given by David. I had children aged four through ten who I had to interest, and the curriculum, as I read through it, didn't offer this.

I knew I wanted to give the children an experience of "The Living Christ," as I knew this power personally. But how can one manufacture a touching and magnificent experience of this vibrant and living energy, without an actual life experience of it? I prayed and thought deeply about this for several weeks, while in the meantime I was following the Sunday school script given to me.

Finally, it dawned on me! All children act out their anger. I believed that children really have no way of understanding the power of God's love and forgiveness unless they can have a first-hand "ah-ha" moment to awaken their understanding. Reading and talking to the kids just wasn't cutting the mustard. The stories in the Bible, though beautiful, really didn't touch kids today with anything relatable, I realized. The children had to use an experience they had, and therefore related to, as I shared my understanding of *the Living Christ, God's unconditional love.*

My brain was churning, and God's creative juices were flowing. I was filled with a vision of the kids creating "monsters," as the kids named them when I presented them with my idea. This was an aspect of their younger selves they were frightened of, or parents had named the "naughty" one, "bad," etc. We were using coat hangers and papier-mâché for the body of their alter ego. The older kids in my vision were helping the little guys shape their *monster*. I saw myself asking them to remember a time when they were "naughty or bad" and got into trouble. What had they done? How did they feel when they did the "thing" that got them into trouble? How did they feel after? What was their parents' response? I offered the kids, in this vision, different feelings to think about: angry, sad, ashamed, embarrassed, guilty, happy, uncaring, or gleeful, excited, pumped. In this vision, God gave me the entire *plan*. I saw the project in detail, and the whole thing was extremely exciting to me. I presented the idea to David with the added excitement of creating a Service of Healing in which the children presented their beloved monster and shared their story as to how they went from hating their "bad, nasty" monster to embracing their monster with love and self-forgiveness. The self-forgiveness piece felt enormously important because we are the ones who act outside of God's plan for us, which is to love all as thyself. If taught to hate yourself, then it was damn easy to hate others and act out that self-hatred on another, more vulnerable person. I wanted to teach this lesson with an experience that the children could take with them the rest of their lives.

It was amazing to me, like watching a pinball machine as the ball goes down, hitting the barriers, the lights flash on, and you hear the ping...ping. Bong, buzz, lights flashed, ping, ping. The kids got it! Easily, quickly, excitedly, and gracefully! My students understood their *monsters'* behavior. As they constructed them, they poured their hearts into their creations.

Each child was assigned a buddy, an older child helper, who would help them construct their monster. As Sundays rolled around, I relished these gatherings with these little people. As they each got out their supplies and structures, we tore newsprint up and mixed up flour and water to make the glue while the children chatted away with one another, laughing with their whole bodies. Their chatter was no ordinary chatter, though. They each recounted, one by one, their monster's behavior for the week. They talked with each other about their feelings, the punishments, and what they were learning by building their monsters.

How was this experience of making their monsters impacting them? I had stories each week that I pulled together on Christ's love and the *living energy* that is the love of Christ. I believed it was important to teach the messages of Jesus's teachings, self-love, of acceptance, forgiveness, and non-judgment, and to live in child-like wonder, remaining their authentic selves. As they were at that moment: open, receptive, curious, playful, and interested in learning. I wanted the children to feel the truth about the energy which flows through them, inspiring them and informing them. I wanted to give this to them as a foundation before the children got "indoctrinated" into our social structure of "norms." Children are present to the unseen world, in ways that most adults are not anymore. Children are wee, little Spirits, not fully landed in their human bodies until and between six and eight years of age. They are wide open channels of curiosity, generosity, kindness, acceptance, creativity, empathy, and compassion. And of course, children also have their "shadow" side, as this was what the journey of becoming human was about! We are experiencers and are here to have experiences which support our evolution and growth in love.

I believe that children, when they are born, are pure essence of:
GOD/GODDESS/SOURCE/GREAT SPIRIT
all that is, ever was, and ever will be.
Pure is the vibration of their LOVE.
And I believe where LOVE abides,
Fear cannot reside.
Children, I believe, are taught to fear those who are different...

We were not born this way. We were not born to hate. We were born of and to love. But we all come in with our DNA blueprint and our ancestral family lineages wired into our Soul's light body or electrical system.

The children worked on their living story project for about three months. We then created a Service of Healing where the children would present their "inner" monster which they had embraced and share the story of what they had learned about Christ's love, forgiveness, creativity, and healing! Truly, it was an amazing service we created, as I wrote the service with the kids' input as to how it all needed to come together and be presented to our congregation, their parents!

Finally, Sunday arrived, and the kids were over the moon with excitement. Their voices sounded like a cacophony of starlings as they flew in their amazing ballet and landed making a black cloud of a section of trees. All their beloved monsters were placed on the step up, below, and in front of the altar, while the kids took their places next to their beloved creations. One by one, each child stood and shared their experience with such pride and joy in their strong, innocent voices and with wide smiles, which spread across their faces like a crack in the clouds on a rainy day allowing the sun to shine through. At the end of the service, many came up to us and asked if we could lead the congregation on a journey such as the children had had! It was well received by all, and the children were full to the brim with love and were thrilled. They each felt so damn good about themselves and what they had learned about this shadow aspect of themselves and their superhero inner Soulful Self, to take with them through life! They grew in their understanding, discovering that love, acceptance, and that telling the truth were how to deal with the part of themselves that got them into trouble.

My time in this lovely community continued in this flow for quite some time, as I took on more and more responsibility as David's assistant. I loved my work and the time I spent in this church, with its congregation. I was amazed that I felt so comfortable in church, not being particularly religious, but more Spiritual.

Until I didn't.

My discomfort began when I became a lectern and began reading the lesson from the Bible each week, in a loud, strong, clear voice, speaking the "word of God." I was reading the lessons Jesus came to teach us and reading about the unconditional love with which God provides for our every need. Yet deep within, there was a discomfort gnawing at me. It was like the bubbling rumble of Irazú, the volcano that stood high above my family's home in Costa Rica, as the guardian and backdrop to our everyday life.

As the lectern, every Sunday, I read the Gospels of Matthew, Mark, Luke, and John. By now, I was also a chalice bearer, which meant I passed the wine, metaphorically representing the blood of Christ, following David with a plate of bread representing the Body of Christ. This tradition comes from the Last Supper, and is in the Episcopal church's Book of Common Prayers, from the service of Holy Communion. "This is my blood. Take this, and drink this in remembrance of me, and have everlasting life," I repeated over and over, while looking deeply into the eyes of friends looking back into mine.

As my internal kernel of discomfort grew, I was puzzled, as I didn't know what it was. Soon after I became aware of this discomfort, Sunday afternoons became a true "day of rest" as I took to my bed, exhausted from the morning's activities in church. I'd stay in bed for an hour or two—horizontal, as my mother called this position. She swore it was the only way the body rejuvenated itself—to be horizontal. So, I took to my bed.

With each passing Sunday, upon returning home, my bed rest grew longer. Until finally, it was for days that I felt incapacitated, baffled at the bone-deep exhaustion I was experiencing. While these exhaustion spells fell on me, I began having weird body chills that led to fevers. Months went by, and these feverish spells grew more intense and lasted longer. I talked to my general practitioner, a member of our congregation and a wonderful country doctor from England, and he was just as baffled. He asked me to come in and see him to run some tests. I did. I had no infections found in my kidney, urethra, and no urinary tract infection. The weird fevers came and went for years, with no one able to diagnose an illness. It was a mystery to the many urologists I saw in and around New England, for seven years.

Attending church services became a trigger somehow for my bouts of fever. And finally, one day the pinball machine hit the jackpot and it was payday! I no longer was able to see myself as included in the Bible teachings I read each week. I came to realize the "wrongness" in the years repeating by rote the Episcopal church's prayers, without giving a thought to *what* I was speaking.

"We do not presume to come to this thy table, oh Merciful Lord. We are not worthy enough to gather up the crumbs from under thy table."

What? What were these horrible words we spoke by rote, every week? Was there understanding for others in the words being spoken? I searched hard and couldn't find the words "she, her, mother or daughter" used in the prayers to include me, a woman. All the nouns and pronouns used were male—God was Father, breathing life into his Son, Jesus Christ. He and Him were used. Mother, Daughter, She, Her, were absent. I felt like I was missing myself.

So where was I in all of this?

Woman was whore, sinner, the deviant who talked weak-kneed Adam into eating from the tree of knowledge, the apple of wisdom. But it was I who was blamed and shamed. I was the reason "sin" began. Or so it was taught. I, woman, caused us to be thrown out of the Garden of Eden and left naked and working by the sweat of my brow, beside the beasts of burdens. It was all blamed-on woman! How could this be? I wasn't the one who made the choice to eat the fucking apple. *Adam did!* Why wasn't he blamed? Better yet, why does anyone have to be blamed, setting up the great *shame/blame/victim/complain* game in the first place? We were human. We were not meant to be perfect. We were perfect in our imperfections when we owned them. Our journey here, as I saw it, was to evolve as a Soul. We therefore needed the experiences we had causing pain. To look for the silver lining and make lemonade out of lemons!

How was this possible? The seed of rumbling discontent so deep in my Soul, churning up into my belly, had finally surfaced and exploded.

I shall never forget that day.

My family sat in the front pew where they always sat. Looking into the eyes of my dear husband, Ivan, for a second, filling myself with his love, I opened the Bible to read the week's passage. I remember, as I stood there, what I was experiencing was deep Soul sickness. I had grown weary translating the words "father, son" into an inclusive statement secretly in my mind as I spoke the words aloud. I was bone deep sick and tired of not hearing the woman, mother—the birthers of life, sisters, and daughters, she, and her—included in the scriptures I was reading each week as vibrant and essential players in all the stories. I was sick of the image of Mary Magdalene as *whore*. She was me, secretly in my heart. I no longer could translate these words to be inclusive and hold meaning for me. They didn't. The religion of my parents' ancestors simply had no place of honor for women. My blood was of the old ones: the "heretics, witches, herbalists, and midwives" from England on my paternal side and of plantation owners from the South. And on the maternal side, I was of the Vikings from Denmark, the pagans from Wales, and my great-grandmother was a finely bred Christian, Parisian woman. I could not be a part of this lie any longer. My body was dying, and no one knew why. My Soul felt like it had died. I needed a re-birth to continue living life vibrantly. Otherwise, I was living life as a walking dead person—a Zombie. Or the other I had been was a vampire, sucking the life force from others in my desperate need to fill my emptiness. Or I could be both—each half was of the other—while the beautiful pretending, giving me a false sense of the wholeness, had shattered. This was the way my mother had lived, and her mother, and her mother, and her mother before, with no voice, no say, head down, obeying. The women in my family were "mad" women. Crazy women. Too emotional. Too strong-willed and troublemakers with their constant questioning and need for creative expression. Children are to be seen and not heard; and women are to do as they are told and not complain. Do it with a smile.

Indeed, the women of my family *were* mad!!! They were, and I was damn angry at being silenced! I constantly heard myself repeat in the dark of night when I was unable to sleep from haunting and frightening night terrors: *I must be a "mad woman," too!*

The trigger for my incurable, curious, and devastating illness was that women were without respect, and therefore, in my mind, absent from the Bible. Shivers tickled my body, hardening my nipples! I felt a connection—the women's voices from my matrilineal side were silenced. Oh, we were mentioned in the Bible, but only in vulnerable, derogatory instances in which our voices were still subjugated to the men around them. I had a devastating response to this truth. I saw that the "them and they" became "me and we." This had become personal. The church of my birth, literally in which I was conceived, held nothing but half-truths and outright lies. How could I believe the stories and teachings in the Bible, when the voice representing half the population was absent? We, as empowered, simply were missing.

There were no voices of the women who surrounded Jesus' life in the Bible as wise women, or equals, disciples of his. They were sisters, mothers, and wives of the important men in the story's teachings. The two Marys and the two Marthas were the significant ones I remember. But they were second-class citizens, subjugated, and silenced. Except for the fact that when Jesus rose from the dead, the women were there. He appeared to them, and the women saw him. Not his disciples, the women. One woman. Mary Magdalene was present.

I was not satisfied with this. In fact, I found it deeply distressing and disturbing that the stories believed by my dad and so many other ministers were full of lies. And it was believed even by the population's voice which was absent: the feminine voice.

I was outraged, devastated, faithless, and without a purpose, sailing through my life, aimless, clueless. Quite frankly, I didn't care. I was dying. I knew this and felt this deep in my bones.

On this last day in church, I stood at the pulpit. I had the Bible in front of me opened to the day's passage. I remember looking at my sweet family sitting in the front of the church, all eyes on their mama, and my next action stunned me and the entire congregation. I closed the Bible. I then stated in a clear and strong voice, "I am no longer able to translate Father, Son, and Holy Spirit to mean and be inclusive of me and my kind. Women! The language simply isn't inclusive." I then went on to share, "I need to understand my own relationship with God, Jesus, the Bible, and the whole big, pile of mess I have been spoon fed since the day I was born. I love you all and am so thankful for the love and sharing we all have experienced. I am dying. And I am being called, strongly, to leave the church of my inception and my birth."

After closing the Bible and making my statement, I walked to my family, took my two children by their hands, with my dear husband following, and walked out, sobbing, and broken.

In the week following my breakdown, I received an incredible phone call from the Diocese of New Hampshire. It was my dream job being offered to me. I was offered the job of being Director of Christian Education for the Episcopal Diocese of New Hampshire. Word had traveled. They had heard about my work in St. John's in Walpole and were extremely inspired by what they had heard from congregation members. Painfully and sadly, I turned the job down. I told them that I had recently left the church because I was deeply troubled by the lies and double standards I was encountering in the Bible, the prayer book, and the whole shebang. I was angry and not in a state of mind to be able to offer to the Diocese what they wanted.

Shortly thereafter I experienced my Death—a physical near-death that transformed my life and gave me my reason to live, if I chose to do so.

Chapter 4

Sepsis Was My Killer and My Savior

It was 1988, in Walpole, New Hampshire. Poisoned blood was my killer. My own blood was toxic. It had become a cesspool of poisonous waste. With every beat of my heart, it was poisoning me, slowly, and silently killing me. Softly. Quietly, I laid for days, which turned into weeks in my bed, curled in a ball. Doctors never figured out what was going on. I'd had seven years of infections, but nothing was found in my urethra or kidneys, and no dreaded urinary tract infections. No infections anywhere, except for my scratching. My skin had lesions created with my fingernails, from little blisters rising under my skin, trying to detoxify itself. I scratched to feel something! And what was worse was that every doctor I went to see had a different take on what I needed to do. Take antibiotics only when you have sex. Take them for a period, take them for the rest of your life, take them only after sex, blah, blah, blah. It was exhausting, frustrating, and ridiculous. I went to the best hospitals and saw the best urologists I could find to solve the mystery I was living.

I was dying.

I had been bedridden for weeks, exhausted, depressed, and anxious, with night terrors growing stronger and worse every night. This time, my fever was not subsiding. It kept reading higher on the thermometer. Finally, with my temperature being seriously dangerous at 104 degrees and climbing, my husband put our children into the car and rushed me to our local hospital. I was delirious by the time we reached the hospital, with a temperature of 106 degrees. Immediately I was rushed through the receiving area and placed on a cooling blanket to bring my body's temperature down. The sounds all seemed to be far off in the distance. And I couldn't focus my eyes. All was very vague to me in those first moments at the hospital because I was floating in and around my body. I remember the blanket being cool. Very cool. My doctor, a tall, robust Englishman, with kind and gentle eyes, was speaking softly with my precious husband, Ivan. Our children were sitting wide-eyed and scared at seeing their mommy in such a state, lying so still and all wired up with tubes and machines going everywhere, clicking and purring away.

The next thing I remember I was at the top of a seemingly golden, brightly lit staircase, looking down on the body in the bed. It was still. Silent. I felt an awareness in my essence that I knew the body, but I had no emotional connection that I was aware of to the person. I could see around me in all directions, flying through the walls, above everything. My Soul floated, suspended in the comic universe as consciousness, pure and all encompassing. Vibrating to the thrum surrounding and flowing through me, I was a dancer in the cosmic ballroom.

I was brought back to the room at lightning speed. My essence was made aware of concerned murmurs coming from the people down below, gathered now, around the woman's bed. My essence was aware that the body was my human form and very badly damaged. I was shown the bruising of her Soul etched into her light body like a road map. It appeared as dark, stagnant pools of energy. I felt overwhelming love as these dark pools were made visible to my essence. Whatever the human connection I had with the young woman lying lifeless below was then lost to me. God infused (my) Soul with light. My Soul embodying Light from Source, God's Light, felt pregnant with love. And all was made of light. I cannot say for how long I experienced this *source of power*. It was as though I was plugged into the whole entire Universe, receiving. It could have been hours, when in fact it was seconds or minutes. I didn't really know.

In this brilliant moment, the task presented to me was shown as two choices. I was able to die. All was well if I made that choice. All would be understood by God.

And forgiven. Obviously, my children and husband would be devastated. If I chose to return to my body and life as I knew it, I had to discover/uncover why my body had a death wish. Only through *this* path could I discover the Truth and be free to be my authentic self. Source infused me with the awareness that I am the *Light of the world and within my cells vibrates all that was and is and ever shall be, which is love. And you shall perform miracles in my name, beloved child. Go out and spread love in the world. Be strong, be clear, be joyful, and be authentic.* I knew in my cells that I was becoming a hollow reed. I felt my identity reshaping itself as my wisdom and self-esteem grew.

Well, I'll be damned. *I am the light of the world. I am the Way.* This must be my superpower. It was this essence of love, an effervescent vitality, that was woven into and through the Universe that kept the world bound together, in unity—as One World, One People, all connected to Mother Earth. Whales traveled by this guide, the geese flew south, buds began to pop open with new life, just as the decay returned and then death. Life was always coalescing and dispersing in a cycle, and I became abundantly present to experiencing deep in my essence, Heaven on Earth.

Source continued to imbue me with this imprint: "I am the energetic make-up of atoms and molecules gathered at the precise time of (my) birth, as my mother called forth, her body in readiness. I, Soul made of God's breath, was called forth and made the choice to join with my human skin, in service to love. As an experience of life in a human body, the fullness of me on Earth wasn't lost to me, one born from Light, into this skin of blood, tissue, and bone. The sound of my cry is the first breath I take. This is the expansion of God imploding within. This first inhalation is Source being called forth to embody the new, age-defying Soul, choosing to be a human experiencer as an expression of God's Divine Love. And so it is, at the command of Divine Grace, I welcome the Soulful Self into the mind, wending its' way as it filters through my spinal cord, continuing to nourish muscles, blood, and bone as I land in my baby-body. I choose to come into consciousness to evolve as a human, living on Mother Earth, as a work of living art, in progress, as I learn to be in full creatorship with Source, my Divine Intelligence. And so it is that I make a choice and say yes! I choose to live life authentically, as unconditional love.

I am to embody vulnerability, the ability to forgive and choose love when fear and love collide, planting the seed for moral courage to grow! With this rousing rise of energy, like the winds filling a sail, I knew I had just received my superpower!

Then I heard a loud, rushing sound coursing through my body as though I was under the ocean with big waves crashing over me. Next, I saw myself hovering above the body, lying lifeless, still. The body was alone. There was murmuring outside the door, but she was alone.

I felt a pull pierce through my heart, expanding my awareness. I breathed in the One that had no name, calling upon this Great presence in a whisper: "Please. I choose life!" In the blink of an eye and a "wrinkle in time," there was a nurse by the body's side. The nurse was incandescent, radiating light. A halo surrounded her, shimmering and iridescent. As she took a breath in, she placed her hands upon (my) body, on (my) chest. I saw as she inhaled, Source flowing through her, expanding her with Light. As she exhaled, I saw strands of light flowing through her hands as she had become a hollow reed. From her lips she blew breath over my still, lifeless body. Source flowed into me; through her hands and her breath I was wrapped in a cocoon of love. In this exact instant I felt my Soul expand then smush as it separated into perfectly formed bubbles and poured like water, filling the millions of tributaries with atomic life-giving magical nutrients heading for my heart. She—I awakened and re-membered ourselves. The fever had broken. I chose to live.

When the doctor and my husband returned to the room, it appeared as though I had become a miracle. Dr. Bower had come with a heavy heart to pronounce me dead. Instead, when he returned, I was sitting up in my bed. I asked to see the nurse who was just with me.

"My Darling Cynthia, you were alone. I thought we had lost you," he replied gently, baffled by what had taken place. "You are a magnificent miracle. I really thought you had left us. Your guardian angel appeared the moment you chose to live. Brilliantly done, I'd say." His eyes sparkled with excitement and relief as he dabbed at the corner of his eyes, where tears of joy had formed. The mischievousness of the *old ones* popped through as I knew Dr. Bower was aware of his pagan roots through his British blood. He and I had enjoyed conversations during coffee hour at our church: St. John's.

Everyone let out a huge sigh of relief.

I was alone, but a nurse appeared in the blink of an eye and placed her hands upon my chest. At this moment—*Source*—merged within the body, life flowing through the veins and heart pumping. And so, it was. I had chosen life.

I wish the journey then became as simple as that. I remembered that I had a task set out before me, to find and accomplish. Kind of like the Quest for the Holy Grail! Exactly how I was going to go about accomplishing this task of discovering why my body had a "death wish" was beyond me! It was now named, which felt like a first step! But still, I had no clue. I was pretty shaken up about the whole damn thing.

My fevers were still unsolved. I still didn't have any clues given to me until the night before my visit to the Head of Urology at Mass General, in Boston. This was a short time after my near-death experience, and all was not well. I was spending most days in bed unable to rise to dress, completely exhausted. I felt like my electrical system had been frazzled and a new system was being wired up. Kind of like an old house that needs new wiring, the old system being archaic and no longer functioning safely. I was alive, but I was not well. I was weak, dysfunctional, dazed, lying, and languishing between worlds. Performing the daily tasks for the family's needs became a chore. It was coming close to the end of a year. I was dumbfounded about how to put this together. I was a mother of two young children. I was a busy lady, but I could not manage life. I asked a neighbor if she could manage my children with hers, and she opened a small day-care to accommodate my needs. Life was too fast, and I needed space. Feeling like it was all too overwhelming, too crushing for me, was the burden I still carried. I had to find out why my body had a death wish. This task put before me felt creepy, weird, and very distressing.

Soon after the NDE, I was scheduled for a nuclear medicine test, at my doctor's recommendation, down at Mass General in Boston. I'd seen scores of urologists over the past seven years, and I was tired and fed up. All had come up with different opinions about what to do, but nothing was solid, working.

During the test, it was discovered that I was allergic to iodine, the dye they filled my veins with, which lit up during the test. My throat began to shut down, and I grasped desperately at my neck. I couldn't breathe. The nurse started patting my arm. "Calm down, honey," she said. "You're fine. Just relax."

Next thing I knew, I was fighting the nurse because I was having an anaphylactic attack. And I couldn't breathe. I was clawing at my neck.

All hell broke loose as the nurse realized what was happening. She stepped it up into high gear, and finally I responded to another medicine that was used to counteract the iodine dye that I was allergic to.

I had a dream gifted to me the night before my nuclear medicine test at Mass General. Upon my arrival, after settling in, I had told my doctor about the dream, hoping I could avoid putting the nuclear poison into my body. It slipped right through his right ear and out the left without registering at all! Afterwards, we gathered again and chatted about the test. He had discovered nothing to be irregular. Kidneys were fine, the urethra was not kinked, all looked normal and healthy, I was told by the doctor. I then, quite forcibly, proceeded to recount the same dream that I had had the night before and had shared with the good doctor when I had arrived. The real parts in my dream were these: We had a farmhouse built in 1810 with an 800-gallon cistern in the basement, which was spring fed from up the hill, keeping us with a fresh, constant supply of water. In the dream, *the cistern was bone dry, and the spring was filled with silt, blocking any water flow.* My doctor, the head of urology, was an older gentleman, small boned and bird-like. He had small, squinty eyes, and his head was turned slightly away, looking at the test. His head swiveled around, and he looked at me like I was nuts.

My doctor then told me he would book me for "exploratory surgery" to see what we could find that was causing these fevers. His eyes glazed over, and he said he needed to look at his schedule to book me for exploratory surgery and turned away.

"No," I said. "I'm not going to have exploratory surgery. I just shared with you a dream I had last night." Angry and insulted because he had not even heard me, I continued, "I'm pretty sure it has something to do with my fevers."

"Come again," he replied, looking at me like I had two heads.

So, I shared my dream a third time. This time I had his attention. In the dream, the spring which fed our cistern was filled with silt, and the cistern, which was in our basement, was bone dry.

"Well," said the good doctor, scratching his chin. "Your dream is about water. Let me ask you this, how much water do you drink in a day?"

"None."

"Oh, come on. A glass a day, three glasses a day?"

"No. I've actually never had a glass of water in my life."

 I was thirty-three at the time.

Incredibly, the doctor replied, "Seriously? You've never drunk a glass of water? Ever? Well that's your problem."

He then went on to explain to me while my anger was slowly rising from deep within, "You see, the kidneys only use water to filter themselves. Everything else leaves bacteria, and I would say that your blood is toxic, and you are being poisoned by your own blood." He closed his eyes and blew out a breath. "You're suffering from sepsis. And you're a lucky girl."

"Duh," I responded. "Seeing how I just had a near-death experience, yes, I'd say that is probably the reason my body shut down. And if water was the only thing that flushes the kidneys, why was I not asked that seven years ago when my fever attacks first began? If water was so basic to healthy kidneys, why did you not ask me about water? I can't believe you guys never asked me this very basic 101 kidney health question. It has been seven years and not one urologist has asked me about water."

I was livid by this point and wanted nothing to do with the medical world. How stupid that the one most basic thing I needed, that not one urologist had asked me about during the seven years that I had been dealing with this "mysterious" illness. I was freaking dehydrated. With every pump of my heart, poison was flowing through my veins, killing my cells one by one. My own blood was poisoning me.

No water. I hated water. It had no taste, and I was to be drinking eight glasses a day, at least. I couldn't keep one glass of water down. It was a foreign taste to me, and

I didn't like it. But really, I could see that I was struggling with my "assignment," which was to discover/uncover why my body had a death wish.

The recuperation from the NDE had me continue to take to my bed. I arranged for my two small children to be taken care of by the wonderful neighbor who had created a daycare in her home. I remained flat on my back, exhausted. I spent my time combing through my mind's volume of memories, searching for the root to the self-loathing. I begged God to show it to me.

During this time, I was guided to live life one minute at a time. From one moment to the next. I figured this was what that phrase *chop wood, carry water* meant. I was leaning into this simple way of experiencing life. Leaning into appreciating every small, simple action became thrilling for me. Like hanging sheets and diapers on the clothesline. The lingering smell of the wind purifying them buzzed through my vulnerable body, filling me with a giddy joy. Cutting onions, doing dishes, cooking dinners, washing dishes all became opportunities to just simply be in the moment, my mind empty of thoughts. Other than gratitude. Gratitude was all I focused on. Grateful to be alive. Grateful for the water I was learning how to drink. And grateful for the husband I had, willing to be there for me as I dissolved into a woman needing to live one breath at a time! One act of kindness at a time.

I was remembering these events, in 1988, while I was horizontal in bed, combing through my life, trying to find the why behind this weird death wish. The experiences I was remembering were hard and eerie—traumatizing, yes. So maybe the extreme isolating and scary difference I encountered as an Anglo person in the South Bronx and then being a person on the outside when we moved to a small-town in the South was the root cause of the death wish. I knew I was different pretty much everywhere I went, and I didn't fit. I believed maybe this was my suicidal driver. Dad was forever reminding me I was *just like my mother*, and she was distraught and acted crazy. Maybe I was, too.

When I met Ivan, I was five months pregnant. I had become pregnant in Ecuador, had a failed abortion there, then found out on my nineteenth birthday on September 25, 1975, that I was still pregnant. By the time I had a second abortion, the fetus was five and a half months. And Ivan was the only friend I had who came to visit me while I was in the hospital. My parents, embarrassed and ashamed of me, wanted nothing to do with me. My father thought it would be a good idea if he announced to the faculty, where Ivan and I both were teachers, the fact that I was pregnant. Dad wanted to know, without my permission mind you, if the faculty would support me if I carried the baby to term. I was horrified when I was told by Ivan that he had made that announcement, unbeknownst to me. Why the hell did he do that? To make himself feel better because he sure as hell wasn't doing it for me!

I sifted through memories like a detailed sleuth looking for clues. Ivan and I were married June 12, 1976, in a colonial wedding in Gloucester, VA, with the reception being in Colonial Williamsburg during the 200-year-old anniversary of the founding of our nation. Our first child was born November 16th, 1979. Joselyn was a joy and a gift that scared the begeebies out of me. She was a challenge because I was terrified of her small, little infant body. Why, I wondered, because I loved babies, and she was mine! But every time I held my baby, I felt a rushing surge of energy pulsing through my veins and pushing through my body. I was frightened that this energy would harm my little one. The energy flowing through me, and into my hands made them feel like I had baseball mitts on. I felt the energy well up behind my eyes and out it streamed. My mind believed that this energy was strong enough to kill someone if the energy escaped from me, unchecked. I don't remember why I believed this. It was just what seemed to be true.

When the energy flowed, I handed my baby to Ivan or put her back in her crib. I was terrified of hurting her. Sometimes I imagined, when I couldn't soothe her screaming, throwing her against the wall to shut her up. I didn't. I never hurt my child, thank God. When these black feelings arose, I put my baby in her crib and locked her door. Yes, I could still get in, but the act of locking the door triggered something protective in me—keeping her safe from harm's way. I was protecting her from me, her mother. I was incredibly sad. I hated myself for this behavior.

Fast forward a few years, to 1988.

My body, mind, emotions, and Spirit collapsed. I was suffering from a total breakdown. Because I was in search of "why my body had a death wish," I began reading the Bible with a yellow marker in hand. I highlighted all the reading that felt like the words carried the weight of Christ's true teachings. I finished reading the Bible and realized that there were not many yellow lines running through this good book, which puzzled me. How did I know which words were the True teachings? My body buzzed, and the hair on my arms stood up from goosebumps. This spoke volumes to me. It spoke "truth" to me.

During this time, I began seeing a therapist. The same therapist was seen by both my dad, and my mom. Bill decided he would see me as well, to get the whole family history straight. This was a highly unusual practice for Bill to be seeing all of us at the same time, though not during the same appointments. However, there were a few times where the appointment with my dad overlapped my visit, and we hugged as he left and I went in. I told Bill after this happened twice, that I did not want my appointments on the same day as my dad's. It was disconcerting to pass him leaving as I was entering. I felt like I was betraying my parents by being in therapy and seeking to know "my" truth.

As I combed through life's stepping stones at the major events in my life, looking for the root, another memory bubbled up. It was Mathews, Virginia, in 1966. We had left New York and moved South as I was trying to put my finger on "why my body had a death wish rather than a desire to live." I remembered I had tried to commit suicide once by eating a whole bottle of Bayer aspirin when I was fourteen. It was shortly after my uncle Clay was killed in Vietnam, in 1968. I accidentally left my journal sitting out on the table. My mother, of course, read it and was horrified and livid with me. The aspirin did nothing but got me sick and landed me in a psych ward, after Mom read my journal.

I was relieved to be in a psych unit getting evaluated. I tried to tell my doctor that I did not get along with my parents. I was angry that my uncle was killed for no good reason. All the adults around me were saying how he was a hero, and they were so proud of him for receiving the Purple Heart. I couldn't give a shit about the medals he had won. He was dead for Christ's sake. I wanted him back.

My uncle's death was devastating to me. Clay had lived with us in Costa Rica and was the one person who treated me as though I mattered. I hated the war and didn't understand the "glory" in soldiers dying. It seemed so pointless to me and like such a huge waste. All the men who were dying were so damn young. My brother was only a few years away himself from the draft.

I was fourteen when my uncle was killed. I remember Dad walking to the elementary school to pick me up. This was extremely unusual, and I didn't like this at all. Something big was going down. Dad didn't speak to me for the whole twenty-minute walk. When we arrived, it was a somber house I walked into. Everyone was gathered on our screened in porch, and Dad read the fated letter. I sat, shocked.

I had no true friends. I was always the third or the fourth girl in a group and conveniently left out, if it suited my "friends" at that moment. I spoke differently and was made fun of because of the accent from the Bronx I had picked up. I wasn't used to the Southern habit of saying "yes ma'am, and no ma'am" when speaking to adults, so I was constantly getting sent to the principal's office for being "fresh" for my answer, "Ya, wha do ya want"? I wasn't, though. I just wasn't used to the formal Southern address my elders required of me.

We also made a very grave mistake when we first landed in Mathews, as the new family from the North. For Southerners, that was the scary word, the North. I was a Northerner in the Deep South and things were different down here, as I would soon find out. Woven into the Southern fabric, I felt the harboring of the loss of the Civil War deeply and there was great resentment.

When we first moved to Mathews, Virginia, in 1966, from the South Bronx, schools were not integrated, nor was the one movie theater. Nothing in the town that was public was integrated. I remember in Donk's movie theater there was a sign above the water fountain that read "WHITES ONLY." Pointing upstairs to the overheated, dilapidated balcony was a sign that read "COLOREDS." This was shocking to me, who had grown up as the only Anglo kid in our neighborhood. Well, except for the head priest's family. But they didn't really seem to be in the equation because they were not allowed to play with all the neighborhood kids. My sister and I were the only ones allowed to play with their two kids. We were the same age. I don't remember where Annie and her brother, Thadeus, went to school. A private school, probably, because they didn't attend school with me.

After the first month of being in this new town, we invited four of my brothers' best friends down to visit us for a week. We were on vacation, and Dad wasn't technically working yet. My paternal grandmother, who lived in Gloucester, Virginia, decided to rent a friend's cottage on the York River for us. She thought it would be a wonderful, rich time to experience the beautiful North River, a tributary off the York River and Chesapeake Bay. Our northern friends had never been crabbing before. Well, neither had I, for that matter, just having moved here. We had a great time catching those big blue claw crabs. The crabs gave us a few lessons, too, catching us with their claws pinched firmly on, which hurt like hell. I remember us shaking our hands, like a leaf shaking on its branch in the wind hanging on for dear life, trying to get a crab off our fingers. They didn't let go of those tough little, delectable beauties. We then steamed them and got to pick 'em! It was a great time and helped my family feel more comfortable in our new digs.

Peachy, Frankie, Angel, and Eugene finally had to return to New York. We were all sad to see them leave. The town was not! We now were known in the town as "n***** lovers." That was my nickname, whispered behind my back quietly and not so quietly, sometimes. We paid dearly from day one for having our brown-skinned, Puerto Rican friends visit.

Anyway, the counselor in the psych ward, when I was fourteen, told me I had really loving parents and that I needed to stop my rebellion. My parents seemed reasonable, my dad had had experience with "troubled" teens, and loved me very much. I needed to relax and accept the curfews and their rules for my own safety.

I was angry and disillusioned. I felt completely alone—devastated in my grief for the many things lost. I just didn't know what I had lost, or when or where I had lost them.

Shortly after my uncle's death, I discovered a place behind our house, in Mathews, which was on Puddin Creek. It was kind of cool, with old, snarled roots showing, making a comfortable seat for sitting on. The creek was not very much: slimy, smelly, slippery mud covered the slope down to the slow-moving water. But I liked it. The place was uncared for, like I felt, with old, rusted car parts strewn on the other bank, tires piled high, rusted rims, broken windshields, trash, and whatever else discarded from the car dealership, which abutted the creek. It felt like the perfect place to sit and nurse my beat up and bruised heart.

A memory bubbled up from deep within: I saw myself sitting on an exposed root, sobbing into my hands, grieving the loss of my uncle, when I felt a gentle tap on my shoulder. As I looked up, I saw my "uncle" shimmering. He hovered above the ground and looked like "the Christ." The shimmering Spirit was dressed in a blue jean shirt and wearing blue jeans. He had a twinkle in his eyes, and he was emanating love. Amazed, I looked at him in awe and felt as though I was embraced by his effervescence, swirling through me. I knew this was the Spirit of the Living Christ, coming in the garb of my Uncle Clay, transmitting immediate love, to give me a message. I was communicated with through the permeation of my mind or my body thought process. I felt the need arise in me, to hide and submerge myself and stay hidden, until the time came again for me to call out his name. It was communicated to me that I was pure *love*. *Love* was my *superpower*! "It will save your life when you call out my name." A buoyancy filled my cells, feeding them, plumping them up as love surged through my entire being. I felt like I had become effervescent too buzzing like a lightning bug! I will know in my bones when this time comes. And at this time, I will be gifted all I need, to complete God's plan. I was infused with knowing that my Soul had chosen an assignment that was a very special plan, requiring great courage. My parents were providing me with exactly the right "soil" to grow the needed roots for my Soul's highest evolution, from the seed of love, imbued at my birth. There are many names for the superpower which flows through my sinews, blood, and bones, from the vibrations of the Soul. *The Holy Spirit, Life Force, Qi, Chi, Prana, sparked to life when I took my first breath,* was transmitted to me. A Soulful life began when the Soul desired to embody a skin and begin the human experience, becoming a Soulful, human experiencer!

And then the Spirit essence disappeared. Poof. A lightness and effervescent quality to the air remained, as though it was tinged with electricity. My eyes saw shimmering light surrounding all things—the trees, plants, the wild grasses—and then it was gone. Evaporated as fast as it had appeared. I was left with feeling despair and filled with excitement, confusion, and ultimately, a heavy, sad heart. What did it mean to "submerge" me?

I was soon to find out.

Mom was uncomfortable talking about intimate things that had to do with my changing body. She'd get all flustered and embarrassed, impatient, and short-tempered with me, like it was something I had done that she now had to deal with, forcing her out of her small, confined comfort zone. This happened when I was about thirteen: My mom came into my bedroom and closed the door, like we were going to have a private conversation or something. I didn't know what was coming. Closing the door was never a good sign. She quickly handed me a skinny little paperback book, about *female matters* and *our time of the month*, and said, "Read it." She turned abruptly and left my room.

"Ok, Mom." I said to her back.

Mother Nature's curse was how I had heard it named and spoken about in hushed voices by other girls I hung out with. Mom never said another word to me about "female" stuff. And never talked to me about what was in the book. I was just told to read it in a gruff and embarrassed voice.

When my period finally did come, I thought I was dying. I was at swimming lessons, staying with a family whose infant I was caring for, in Newport News, VA. I happened to look down because I was feeling a weird cramping pain down there and saw blood running down my leg. I freaked, almost passing out with fright. I checked for a cut somewhere around the blood, trying to be nonchalant about it and was dumbfounded when I found no cut. I had forgotten about *the* book! My swim coach was a young, good-looking man, not a whole lot older than me...Well, he was probably eighteen or nineteen, I imagined. I thought about the skinny book Mom had given to me that I'd skimmed. This guy had noticed my discomfort. Then

I saw his eyes get big as saucers. His face turned beet red. I wanted to disappear, badly. He beckoned for me to come with him and excused me from class, taking me off to the side.

"Talk to your mom when she picks you up. You're fine. She'll know what to do," he said sensitively. "You're fine. This is normal. I promise." He winked at me, gave me a big grin, and threw his arm around me quickly, giving me a sideways hug.

I wasn't dying. What a relief to know.

When I got home, I burst into tears trying to push my way through the deep feeling of humiliation that had crowded me. Sarah greeted me with a hug. She held me at arms distance and looked into my eyes. "What's wrong?" Sarah and Carl were best friends and had an infant named Jennifer whom I adored taking care of and had started babysitting right away when she was a month old. I loved that baby to pieces. I sometimes pretended that she was mine, remembering my friends I had in the Bronx who were Moms at my age! Sarah, seeing the bond and the joy I exuded caring for little Jennifer, invited me to spend the summer with her and her husband, Carl, while they attended school at Hampton Institute, in Hampton, Virginia. I was ecstatic when I was hired for the summer to be nanny to little six-month-old Jennifer. I was pumped to live with them and be away from my family for the summer.

I mumbled words to Sarah when she asked me what in the world was going on. "Had I had a bad class?" she probed.

"No. It's not that. I'm bleeding," I mumbled out. "Down there." I pointed to my vagina. Sarah took me in her arms and hugged me. She let me go, held my hand, and marched me into the bathroom. She rummaged through the top drawer and pulled out a box of Tampons and handed it to me.

Sarah was one of my favorite people. Her husband, Carl, was a young professional-teacher-in-training and part of the Teacher Core group that was sponsored by my high school. He had a three-year contract to fill. Sarah was a big-boned woman, with big, chocolate brown, doe eyes, and long, dark brown hair. Sarah looked like Allie McGraw, the actress, to me! She always wore it loose and parted it on the side. And I thought she was gorgeous. She was muscular from spending her life on the backs of horses and was a top-notch equestrian. Sarah was my riding teacher, borrowing the horses of new friends my family had made, through the family church service. These new friends were native to the community and lived in an old beat-up, huge plantation home, which had been in the family for generations.

The Merrills had kids our ages and were a wild bunch. Their family was warm and loving; laughter rang out all the time. I loved going to their home, which was on the other side of Mathews, on the North River, which ran into Mobjack Bay. The kids were trusted and were allowed to just run through the woods, play on and in the river, without any admonishment from the parents. What a concept for me! They were trusted.

With Sarah sitting on the floor in front of me, and me sitting on the pot, I could barely look into Sarah's eyes, I was so filled with shame.

Gently, she explained to me, "A Tampon goes up your vagina to catch the blood. It has a string which dangles out that you pull the Tampon out with. You need to do this a few times a day, so it doesn't get too full and leak through. It's ok. This is normal. All is well." She sighed and took me in her arms. "Welcome darlin', to becoming a woman!" She gave me a big, warm hug. I burst into tears, mortified and so ashamed of my body. After she left the bathroom, I opened the tube, reached down to find the hole and pushed the thing up there. It didn't go in easily, that's for sure. And I was aware of it because every time I sat down, the thing hurt like crazy. Shit, was this why they called it Mother Nature's Curse? This was awful.

Five years later, I would discover the fact that I had two vaginas separated by scar tissue. Neither opening was a normal size, but I didn't know that, back then.

I switched to pads.

It was 1971, and I was fifteen-and-a-half and have just gotten my driver's license. I was a free bird—at least as free as I could be living at home with my family. To me, a license meant I could get a job. I was so tired of being broke. I had jobs; jobs I created for myself before I could drive. Like the day care that I started with three families the summer after I took care of Jennifer. I discovered I was pretty good with kids. I had six kids total. I provided the snacks while they brought their lunches. I held my day care camp in the parish house, which we lived right next to. It had a huge, big event room I turned into the summer camp room during the week, when it was not in use by Dad for church stuff. It was a great summer job, and I made $25.00 per family per week! I felt enormous pride at making my own money with an idea I came up with!

Around this same time, my aunt, who had been married to my now dead uncle, remarried. There was a sad story as Aunt Bibi and Uncle Clay had gotten divorced, which was what motivated my uncle to enlist in the Army during the Vietnam war. When Uncle Clay was home on furlough before being sent to fight, he and Aunt Bibi recommitted their love to one another, and their two little girls, and were to be remarried when he returned home from his tour in Vietnam.

Well, that didn't happen. A week before the tour was ending, he was shot in the back on his third round from rescuing two other buddies. His buddies were at my uncle's funeral. It was hard for me to be happy for these two guys who made it home. I wanted my uncle home, not these damn strangers. And I felt like shit feeling this way.

Aunt Bibi, whom I loved, eventually remarried a man named Jack. Bibi was a native of Florida. I re-met her at my uncle's funeral after having met Aunt Bibi one other time in Florida several years earlier. I immediately felt a bond with her. She had a big, fast smile for anyone, with gorgeous twinkling eyes, and starched sprayed hair that puffed up a bit on top, as the 70's styles dictated. She wore it in a kind of flip that was the in-style for the times, in Miami, Florida, in the late 60s, early 70s. She wore silky, tight clothing, and deep V-neck blouses, make-up and had gorgeous painted nails. Lots of jewelry, and was what men called a real "looker" and a real "Floridian" as my dad loved to refer to her. My aunt had two very young, beautiful, sweet little girls from her marriage to my uncle Clay, my cousins. Her new husband Jack was exciting to me because he paid me a lot of attention. No other adults gave me the time of day after my uncle Clay had died, except now my step-uncle Jack was in my orbit.

Step-uncle Jack the prick and Aunt Bibi always showed up with a big bottle of vodka and orange juice, or they would come with a bottle of rum and Coca Cola's to mix with the rum.

Aunt Bibi had just had Jack's son and was incapacitated after the birth. Jack needed help driving their Volkswagen Beetle up from Georgia, as they had just moved into Gloucester, the next town over from ours, where my favorite grandmother lived. He and Bibi had come to dinner to ask my parents if I would be able to accompany him to Georgia. He made the case that with me as a new driver, this would be a great opportunity to hone in on my driving skills.

My parents loved the idea but were hesitant. Finally, after I begged and pleaded with them, they said yes. Probably for Mom and Dad this trip was seen as a respite from me, to have a week or so of peace and quiet. You see it seemed to my father that every time I entered the house, I set my mom off into one of her rages. This was an enormous power my dad had given me... Mom didn't need me to set her off—she was just off, in a big way!

Nothing else mattered. Days later, I packed my bag, and I was heading to Georgia for a week and thrilled to be going with my step-uncle. Uncle Jack had a southern drawl and a chin that kind of stuck out like John Wayne's, reminding me of him. He was a big man, who wore jeans all the time, heavy cowboy boots, and was a huge flirt with all the women, I noticed. Making sexual innuendos with his wife, the stewardesses, and he even flirted with my mom. She didn't pay much attention to this way he had with women. She'd just blush and laugh it off, embarrassed.

I was feeling damn full of myself! When the plane was in the air and the stewardess began walking the aisles offering beverages, food, snacks, etc., my uncle ordered two rum and Cokes for himself, he told the stewardess. One of the rum and Cokes was for me, and he encouraged me by saying, "Bottoms up, young lady!" Another two drinks were ordered before we landed. I drank mine, doing what I was told. Bottoms up, and I sucked it down. I discovered I liked these! They tasted great. I was feeling way more relaxed.

Once we were off the plane and had gathered our things, we picked the car up from long-term parking. It was a cute little orange Beetle! Jack got behind the wheel, and we roared out of the parking lot. He stopped first at the liquor store to buy more rum. We then go to a mall where he proceeded to take me shopping for some "appropriate" clothing. I was uncomfortable with this. I quickly found out I wasn't allowed to buy what I wanted; Jack picked out two outfits for me. A low waisted pair of wide bell-bottomed hip huggers, which I loved, and a top that was a wraparound tie shirt, with a deep V across my chest—which I didn't love. My breasts, which had just barely budded, were accentuated. I was shy with his admiration, but I sure was proud of my titties, small as they were. Jack then bought me a bathrobe that was a tie-around-my-waist kind of robe. I had brought a perfectly good robe with me. It was dark blue velour and zipped up the front. He bought me lacy white panties, the likes of which I had never seen before—crotchless, he called them. I didn't even really know what they were as he was paying for them.

After we got home, Jack wanted me to get dressed up into my new clothes. He was taking me "out on the town" to show me a good time. I obeyed.

We drove down Peachtree Street in Atlanta, Georgia. I noticed all the flashing bar-light signs. Some advertised strippers. The first place we stopped at was a gentlemen's club. Jack lied about my age. Evidently, he knew the manager and said I was his wife's cousin, in town for a few days, to help with the final move to Virginia. It seemed to me that he frequented this joint regularly, as everyone at the bar knew him by name. We sat at the bar. He ordered two rum and Cokes. By now I was feeling good. Loose as a goose, giggling, and getting really sloppy. Jack's hand moves onto my thigh. He then encouraged me to sit on his lap, at the bar. I was shy and uncomfortable but I obliged him; I was not used to saying "no" to an adult. Meanwhile on the stage was a woman on her knees, with pasties on her nipples, wearing a thong, gyrating as though she was riding that salami. It was disgusting, if someone had cared to ask me what I thought.

Jack's hands were roaming all over my upper thighs, rubbing the insides of my thighs as he whispered in my ear, encouraging me to boogie to the music while seated in his lap. His cock hardened beneath me. I felt this through my jeans. There was heat building up between my legs, and my whole body began buzzing. I was drunk but didn't realize this because I had never been drunk before. I was sizzling hot, which was also a new sensation for me.

We finally left and arrived home. It was still early in the evening when Jack asked me if I would be able to relax more if I had some marijuana.

I perked up. "Weed? Yes! Can you score some now?"

"Sure, I get weed all the time from the kids in our church," he replied.

Within the hour, a young man came by the house and Jack purchased an ounce of weed. I was super excited that Jack was thinking of me and wanting me to have a good time, too! Jack rolled a fat doobie, and I smoked my brains out! It was great weed. I was happy and chill, forgetting about any discomfort I'd felt earlier in the evening.

He then invited me to get more comfortable and suggested I go put on the sexy robe he bought for me. I obliged, giggling uncomfortably.

It was soft and was sexy. I felt like a million bucks and damn grown up! Just what my uncle wanted me to feel—not like the fifteen-and-a-half-year-old innocent that I was.

Jack stood behind the couch and while I relaxed on the couch, he started to rub my neck and shoulders. It felt good. I was tense. His hands slowly crept down to my front, massaging all around my titties, then he touched my nipples. They immediately got hard. There was a tight, tingling feeling growing throughout my body. Jack was kissing my neck, my ears, and his hands were roaming all over my titties. I was feeling excited, really confused, stoned, and drunk. And bad.

Jack moved around to the front of the couch. He sat on the floor facing me. He was on his knees. His hands started rubbing very lightly the inside of my thighs. Tickling them. I was having a hard time keeping my shit together at this point as my eyes glazed over, sinking into the tingling that was growing between my legs and running through my body. Jack's hands were firm as he deftly moved my robe aside. My white, naked thighs were exposed, and his hands were separating my legs. I let him. It felt good. His fingers found the warm, moist, folds of my pussy and pushed in. Slowly his fingers moved in and out, and I closed my eyes. My whole body was buzzing. His mouth found my pussy. I felt his tongue probing the folds of my pussy, going in deeper.

Something in me snapped—shame filled me up. What the hell was going on?

I struggled. I felt extremely confused, with a black shame welling up in me because this felt great, and I was not stopping him. I liked this.

A huge pressure was building within. His tongue was way up in places I did not know existed. Finally an entire body shudder exploded along with liquid. I didn't think I peed. I wasn't sure what had just happened.

By now it was late in the evening. I was tired and all worked up. Jack thought I might enjoy reading some magazines that he had on the top shelf in his bedroom. I noticed that the master bedroom was the only room with furniture, other than the couch in the living room. I assumed I would be sleeping on the couch. When I asked where I was sleeping, he said I could sleep in the bed, and he would sleep on the couch. He reiterated that I might enjoy reading one of his magazines. Feeling twisted up inside myself when I ventured into the bedroom, tiptoeing like a little mouse, I couldn't stop feeling drawn to the top shelf.

Jack was in the other room, making himself another rum and Coke. I was on my tippy toes as I pulled one of the magazines from the shelf. In my hands I held a porn magazine on Family Lust and Love. I opened it. Blood was racing through my veins as my heartbeat picked up. I felt my heart pounding in my chest as I perused the magazine. I saw pictures of older men and really old men—like grandfathers— all with young girls, children. Boys and girls. There were boys screwing their sisters. Uncles screwing their nephews while the nephew ate pussy. There were all kinds of stories. I found one that I read. I started touching myself, getting excited, and got myself to experience the same full feeling. Then like in a heated race and crossing the finish line, the explosion of lust, ravishing sensations, and bodily fluid all melded into one big mess of confusing feelings. Guilt, shame, pleasure, and a huge release of tension. Now I felt relaxed and was tired enough to sleep. I rolled over onto my left side and wondered about what just happened during this whole evening. Self loathing and shame replaced anything pleasurable that I thought I had experienced. Mistrust of self and my body's betrayal weighed heavily as I tried to sleep.

Jack opened the door and walked into the room. I saw out of the corner of my eye that he was naked and sporting a huge cock. I pretended to be sleeping. He crawled into bed and snuggled up behind me, forcing his cock between my legs, which I try my damnedest to keep clamped shut. He was breathing heavily and whispering into my ear. Pushing his cock hard against my backside.

"It's okay baby. You know how good I made you feel? Well, this is how you can make me feel good! It's okay baby. I'm good at this. It's okay. Don't you want to make me feel good? Well, this is how I like it," he purred into my ear, getting my body to betray me, again, as he probed and touched me.

I was getting turned on. The buzzing between my legs started again. HELP... I didn't want this.

"I don't want this. STOP!" I pleaded with him. "STOP, or I'll call the police." The phone was sitting right next to the bed. I had no idea if it was turned on or not. I reached for it and dialed 911.

He stopped. Backed off and rolled over, telling me I could hang up. He wouldn't do anything.

I heard the 911 operator ask me who I was and if everything was ok.

"All is well. This is a mistake. I'm sorry." I quickly hung up, ashamed. This seemed to get the message across to Jack that I wasn't interested in what he wanted me to do for him.

Two days later, we were ready to drive home. I was dying to get on the road. I wanted to get home and get away from this monster. Every day, all day, I was fighting off his advances. Trying to act normal, as though I was fine. No big deal. I promised I wouldn't say anything. He continued buying me gifts, trying to get me to open my legs, willingly, to him again. But I knew what he wanted and refused him. I didn't want that huge cock inside me, and I knew that's what he wanted.

Finally, we were on the road heading home to Virginia. I couldn't drive fast enough. Jack told me we were not driving straight through. I argued with him. I wanted to. We argued some more. He won. That afternoon, as soon as we hit the North Carolina border, he had me pull into a motel.

"We'll stay the night here," he said.

I fought with him, yelled, and argued with him that I was fine to keep driving. I wanted to get home, and I could handle driving straight through. But I knew this argument was hopeless as he had other plans.

He registered us as newlyweds...a young bride, he joked with the manager of the establishment. I felt like that hideous Bride Doll Mommy bought me years ago. The manager looked dubiously at me while Jack had my small hand clamped tightly in his huge hand.

I was numb.

I remember being dressed up in a lacy, white dress, kind of like an after-wedding dress. It fit tightly against my body. I was so confused, because I felt really sexy, like a whore, though, not a proud bride! I was quiet. Not speaking. I felt mute and stupid. I thought my mom must be right about me—I was just a slut. Not much different than the whores I saw when I was little. They got paid. I wasn't. I got gifts. Unwanted gifts that had nothing to do with me and my desires! Maybe the gifts were the same as being paid money.

When we finally got checked in, Jack turned to me, undressing.

"Don't be shy, baby. I'll be gentle with you. I'm good at this, you'll see," he said, licking his lips. "Baby, there is not a thing you can do to avoid this. So, let's make it easy. You'll enjoy it if you don't fight me. Relax," he cooed in my ear as his arms encircled me. I felt like I was drowning in shame. "I want to make love to you. Be the first one, show you how it's done," he whispered in my ear, licking it.

You want to fuck me. It's rape, you're a sick bastard, I screamed in my head. But I stayed silent. Absent from my body. I knew it was going to betray me again.

And he did. Repeatedly for two days. We were on our way to our "honeymoon," and he just wanted to stay in the room to enjoy his "little" wife. Room service was ordered. I never saw the light of day for two days. Curtains were drawn, rum and Coke flowed, joints were rolled and smoked. I checked out, floating above my body, hovering around not able to stay in my poor, tiny body. I checked out as I was held against my will.

When I got home, I was different. I walked with shame, carried my head down, and felt guilty as hell because I couldn't stop pleasuring myself and thinking of what had happened the first night. It felt good, and I felt like a sicko for enjoying it.

I hate that I knew all these filthy and disgusting words. I grew up hearing them all the time when I lived in the Bronx. Common language was saying "fuck" after or before almost every word! "Fuck me, fuck you. Fucking A, man, are you for real?" And so on. Pussy was a common language, and using it to curse one's mother out, for the Puerto Ricans, was the worst insult.

I was a mess now. Uncle Jack had opened me wide to the world of G-spot orgasms! He had turned me on, and I wasn't about to turn it off. I wanted more, but not the intercourse or sucking cock part. I hated that.

Some part of me knew that what had happened was bad. Another part knew I was innocent and a victim of my uncle's. But I also wasn't sure about this because I was one of the bad P.K.s, wasn't I? Growing up I was always asked by other kids, "Are you one of the good ones or a bad preacher's kid?" It seemed this was a thing other people wondered about us, like we were some kind of a strange animal or an alien. And what about the part of me that loved having my pussy sucked on. Shit, I didn't know what that made me. I felt like there were many Mes and I didn't know which one to listen to. They were all fighting in my head.

I was burning up inside, keeping this hot mess a secret. I admired the hell out of my older brother, Greg. In my eyes, Greg lived on a pedestal. I thought he was gorgeous, and so did a lot of the girls, I had noticed. He had sexy, long, light brown hair to his shoulders that glistened in the sun. His eyes were a beautiful hazel color, which changed with his moods. He wore a fabulous deerskin, suede leather jacket with fringe that was a foot long on the sleeves and six inches round the bottom. Girls befriended me to have an invite to my home to hang out with my brother. Clearly, I had him on a pedestal in my mind, even though he treated me like shit, because he didn't give me the time of day. I admired him because of his maleness. He had freedom—no boundaries were set by my parents. I did not want to lose what little respect I believed I had of his. But I had to tell someone. Determined to tell my brother despite the terror I felt, I entered his room and looked around for the first time. Or maybe the shame I felt gave me new eyes from which I saw the world. Like I had new lenses over my eyes… As I looked around, I noticed one poster which stood out. The walls were covered with posters, but this one of a pregnant Girl Scout was the one I noticed. Greg shared his bedroom with our younger brother, Kevin. They had a huge floor-to-ceiling bookcase separating the young teen from his young, elementary school-aged brother.

Greg was the eldest sibling in my family. I wanted to tell Mom and Dad about Jack and what he did with me. Depending on how Greg reacted would determine if I told my nasty secret to Mom and Dad. I sat on his bed and shared my nasty secret in a voice barely audible. My head was bowed, eyes were downcast, as self-loathing filled me. Sadly, Greg freaked out on me. He told me I must have plumb lost my rocker to even think about telling them. He assured me that I would be blamed.

"They will tell you it's all your fault. Trust me on this. You'll regret it."

"Do you think it's my fault?" I asked him. It was important to me to find out what he thought.

He didn't respond. He bowed his head and just shook it. He didn't know what to say to his little, fragile sister. I knew he was sad. I could feel it in my heart. But he said nothing.

I didn't tell. I was ashamed. I felt completely filthy and disgusting, inside and out. I figured the filth that I had become must be able to be seen by others.

Next door to my home was a car dealership and next to that business was a funky-ass barber shop that the father of one of my school friends owned. Well, she wasn't a friend, really. I just knew the girl.

There was a sign that hung outside an old, beat-up barber shop. Frankie & Johnny's Barber Shop, this dilapidated sign read. The pole outside was painted with a red and white candy cane stripe but was faded and the paint was cracking and peeling.

I hated walking past these two businesses. The car dealership and the barber shop. The men would whistle, howl at me, and make derogatory comments to me. I had thick skin. Thickened up from living in the Bronx. I remember the same kind of experience when I was six of having to walk by men, holding my daddy's hand. I flashback to a memory: Outside of our church compound in the Bronx, on the other side of the spiked gates, there was a granite ledge which held the tall, steel spikes solidly in place. Sitting on the ledges were *emborrachados*, as Dad called them. Drunks.

I have this one vivid, horribly vivid memory of holding my daddy's hand as we walked to the entrance to unlock the gate and pass through. A small, black-haired, dark-skinned head popped up, like a jack-in-the-box, out of the trash can. Holy shit! What a surprise!

Daddy stopped. "Who are you?" he asked the pint sized, big brown-eyed child who was staring up at him, like a deer caught in headlights.

"Miquel," replied the small child.

"Where's your mama?" asked Dad.

"A whorin," said Miquel.

"How long have you been here?" Dad asked.

"All night. Mama pud me in here jist before you lock da gate, Father Curley. She tinks I'm safe here. She be here soon. I promise," Miquel said in a small, barely audible, shy voice.

"Okay," Dad said as he tousled the child's head with his big hand. And we walked through the gate which he unlocked.

Outside the gate were these poor, homeless men: "emborrachados." They stank of urine. Their nails were long and dirty, as was their hair. Their hands were filthy and clawed because of uncut fingernails. I shrank back from them as Dad began an enthusiastic greeting in Spanish. I followed along. I'm still fluent in Spanish because I learned it, along with English I was told, when we lived in Costa Rica. Dad was being himself, gregarious and friendly, shooting the shit with these guys.

He did not notice the filthy hands reaching out to touch me while I stood silently next to my daddy, my small hand, warm, in his big hand. My chest was pawed. I was at eye level with these men who sat against the fence. Unhoused. The man in front of me, pawing me, was licking his lips and salivating as his hand roamed up and down and across my chest. Dad was oblivious to this.

I shrunk away.

I was seized by shame at not wanting to be touched. I didn't like these men. Daddy did. I stood as a mute. Deaf and dumb to what was going on. Silent. Detached from my body. Judging myself in my head as I watched my father happily talk to these people. My father—God.

High Episcopal Church

Daddy finished his lively conversations with the guys, and we moved on. I didn't understand why I disliked those men so much when my daddy was perfectly comfortable with them. I was judging them. I felt really ashamed of this! I wasn't like Jesus at all. Worst of all, I wasn't like my Daddy-Father-God. I was a sinner for sure. My name started with the word "sin"... Is that why I was named this? I was born a sinner.

I was scared shitless. I just saw a child homeless, sleeping in a garbage can and my daddy did nothing. My body has just been pawed by disgusting, filthy, smelly men, and daddy did nothing. Mama was in a mental hospital. I hadn't seen her or spoken with her in a long time. My brother was at boarding school. My baby brother and sister were living at my grandparents' home in the country. And I was here. Stuck. Scared. And alone in this hellhole! No one was caring for me!

I wondered at night, alone in my bed: What if something were to happen to Daddy? Would I have to sleep in a garbage can at night, because I would have nowhere to live? Obviously, my grandparents didn't want me...

These men who I passed as I walked into town in Mathews reminded me of those homeless, stinky drunk men sitting on the stoop. The workers called out to me. They whistled "the cat call" at me and talked all kinds of shit to me. I had a hard time battling them off. I felt rude when I tried not answering them, to see if that stopped their shit talk. I engaged and answered them, oh so briefly, and kept walking, to see if that got them off my ass. But nothing worked. They seemed to get their rocks off by razzing me up into a complete flustered state of embarrassment. My cheeks became inflamed, my heart was racing, and my ears turned bright red. They must have known I was just a piece of shit. I knew they didn't yell and call out when my sister walked by. She was Miss Goody Two-Shoes. I couldn't stand my sister. She angered me with her straight As, her prissy-ass pink and yellow flowery bedroom, and the way she brought Mom tea and toast when she couldn't cope (with me). I hated her. And we shared a bedroom. It was the dark child and the light child trying to cohabitate. My half of the room was painted purple. I had a black and white, fuzzy, animal print puff on my bed and dark, purple sheets. I loved my side of the room. Her side drove me nuts. It was bad how opposite we were. I was so terribly jealous of her. We got into wicked hair-pulling fights with lots of screaming and yelling.

Finally, one day I was doing my usual walk into town after school, and I was feeling particularly dark. I sucked. My life sucked, and I was feeling black and filthy inside, filled with self-loathing. My uncle Jack had been around, visiting my family, boasting about his wine and cheese shop that he had opened in the next county over, in Gloucester, Virginia. He winked at me and told Mom and Dad that he wanted to hire me to help stock shelves. My eyes grew as big as saucers, and I tried to tell my parents that was not a good idea. They thought it was a great idea. I was going to Gloucester High School. I could live with my paternal grandparents, but that part of the situation wasn't bad. I loved my dad's mom, Mamma, a big-boned, English woman. She had long, white hair that she wore braided and wrapped around her head several times. She had a thick English accent and was quick to laugh, with her eyes twinkling bright. She had a great sense of humor, and she adored me. Papoo, my grandfather, was a different story. He scared me. Papoo had Parkinson's disease and was kind of cranky. I didn't blame him. He looked uncomfortable, all frail and slumped down in his red leather chair where he sat all day. He tried to be sweet and funny, playing word games with me and tricking me, making me laugh. I felt sad for him, trapped in his weak, shaking, and unsteady body. I was always afraid that he would fall when he tried to walk. His shaking had gotten so much worse after his son, my uncle, Clay, had been killed in Vietnam.

For me, living in Gloucester would be sweet and get me away from my damn parents. My mom was unbearably on my ass. She seemed to hate my guts. And I hated her. I didn't want to. But I did. I just couldn't help my feelings.

But this day, as I walked past the garage and then the barber shop, Johnny was standing in the doorway. Seemed like he was waitin' for me. I exhaled the breath I'd been holding.

"Hey Cynthia. How're yaw doon? You look awful perty today," Johnny observed and commented in his heavy Southern drawl.

I mumbled, "Fine."

Overwhelmed with shame, I froze in my tracks. He must know about me—this blackness inside seemed to grow daily. My eyes looked different to me when I looked at myself in the mirror. Deep, dull, empty eyes. I saw no sparkle.

Johnny stepped out from the doorway, making haste as he grabbed my arm. "I'm speak'in to you. How're yaw' doon, perty girl?"

My skin crawled where his hand was touching me—like those *emborrachados*.

In his drawl, Johnny got in close and said, "Come on in. Frankie is off today. I'm here. I'd like to talk with you. Git to know yaw a lit'le better."

I was trying to tug and wiggle myself away, but he had a big, strong arm with an iron grip around my shoulders, guiding me into his shop.

He closed the door. The shades were already down—as though he was planning/hoping for this opportunity. I had never noticed the shades down before, other than after hours. It was 3:00 in the afternoon.

I was scared. Petrified, frozen silent.

"Don't be frightened. I ain't gunna hurt yaw. I jist wanna talk widt you. Here, sit in my seat." He pulled up a chair and sat right in front of me. I smelled his nasty man smell of stale cigars, sweat, and that smelly, old urine was vaguely present. He stepped on his foot press and raised the seat. So that I was at eye level with him. I supposed that was to make me feel safer. Like his equal? It didn't. I wasn't stupid. I knew what he wanted. I had grown up knowing what girls were supposed to do. Obey, when asked to suck cock.

Obey was a commandment after all. So, I quickly thought up a scheme that I felt would make me feel stronger and better about myself. I told Frankie that I would suck his cock for $25.00. He, with lightning speed, complied and pulled his zipper down. His cock stunk of urine. It was purple and flaccid, hot, and sweaty. Disgusting to hold. But I had to. I had to hold it and put it in my mouth and suck on it, getting it hard. I gave him a blowjob and finished him off as quickly as possible.

I took his money and got the hell out of there.

I vomited at the end of it. Spitting the stinking, slimy, shit-cum out....

Goddamn it, I hated myself.

This began a whole journey of going to the neighborhood bar with my now one and only friend, Pricilla. She was a member of our church, and we became fast friends. I guess because we were both "fast" girls. Her mom owned my favorite clothing store in town. She lived in a huge mansion that was run down because of a lack of money. It was the family home and had been in the family for generations. Prissy, as I called her, had an older sister, Olivia. She was often away at college, I guess, but when she came home, we loved it. She was cute, sassy, and sexy. Olivia had bright blond hair, cut and worn in a bob to her shoulders. Prissy and I loved secretly going through her things. Beautiful, frilly, lacy underwear and bras. Her panties were a whole array of colors. Her nighties were pretty and sexy. She had shortie ones that were sheer and see-through and long, satiny ones. Those looked like they would just slide around in the bed if you were sleeping in it. I thought she was one hot lady. We found her stash of dirty novellas that she had in her suitcase. We then discovered a whole treasure trove of books in one of her drawers. Reading these would get us so hot we'd play with ourselves right there, when she'd be out on a date, or just gone for the day. No shame. Prissy and I loved to get each other off just as much as ourselves. It was different with a girl. Prissy was also my age and wasn't a goody two shoes. She wasn't Miss Prissy Pants like my sister and the other girls I knew. She'd had experiences, too.

We found a bar that we liked hanging out in, after school. It was on the same block as the garage and Frankie & Johnny's Barber Shop. I hurried past, never making eye contact, which meant I never turned my head left! I just kept walking. Johnny always was standing outside as he saw Prissy and I walking the sidewalk into town. Prissy wanted to stop. I refused. I grabbed her hand and said through gritted teeth, "Keep walking and don't talk to him. PLEASE!" I pleaded. "I'll explain later."

When we got to the bar, we quickly slid into a booth. I sat next to her so I could whisper to her about Johnny.

As soon as I finished recounting the mess I had gotten myself into, several times, the owner of the bar came to our table to take our order and introduce herself to us. Mary Lou let us know she was keeping an eye on us and said, "A bar isn't a place for girls."

I rolled my eyes. Oh please. I just wanted food.

"Can I order a Coke and hamburger?" I asked.

Prissy ordered the same.

The next day we returned to the same bar and sat in the same booth. We ordered the same thing. This time, two guys sauntered over and leaned their elbows on the table.

"Mind if we sit down?" the skinny one asked.

"No. Sure. Sit," I said, my eyes brightening with excitement.

They slid into the opposite side of the booth. I was pretty much a giggling mess, feeling self-conscious and dirty. I felt like my vagina had a flashing red light that attracted bad juju. Prissy had begun to talk with the guys. We found out their names were Billy and Bobby. They were friends, builders with hard, strong, sinewy bodies, and they came here every day after work for a Budweiser or two or three.

We introduced ourselves. Our food came, but I was no longer hungry. I was way too excited to be eating anything. We chatted away. I nibbled and picked at my food, moving it around my plate.

"Hey, how yawl go'n get home?" Billy asked.

"Prissy's ma, she'll come git us," I said in my heavy Bronx accent. "I live down dare, at da end of da block. In da rectory," I hesitantly replied, not sure how they would respond. I was afraid they would think I was Miss Fancy Britches from the North. People thought weird things in the South about Northerners. I'd found this out the hard way.

The next day we showed up again, decked out. The owner, Mary Lou, moved to our table before the guys could and told us to not get involved with those two. "They're no good for you girls," she said in a kind voice, looking me right in the eyes before I looked down at the ground. I hid the shame that was rising like bile.

What Mary Lou couldn't have known was that her words had just excited me more. Now I really was interested in finding out about these two characters. They moved on over to our booth, and this time, they just slid right in, each one taking the vacant seat next to one of us, so we were sitting properly, like couples should.

We sat for just a few minutes, ordering only a Coke for Prissy and me. The guys ordered a Budweiser. After the beers were sucked down and finished, they each took one of our hands and guided us out of the booth and the bar. As I left, I made eye contact with Mary Lou. She shook her head and rolled her eyes. I lifted my chin and gave her a big smile, like the Cheshire Cat that just ate the canary. Only I didn't realize that I was the canary.

We got to Prissy's house. Prissy had told her mom that she and I had a ride to the house and would go there after school. She was fine with this.

We don't even make it inside the house before we were making out with the guys while standing in the yard. The yard was planted with beautiful old oak trees and the majestic magnolias, so sweet I smelled their perfume as I sniffed the air. Reminded of Costa Rica, I closed my eyes for a second. A sadness welled up in me. I missed the brief life I had there. Seemed like forever ago.

There were also dead trees that stood, looking ready to fall. Prissy's family, no longer with their family wealth, didn't have the time or the money to take them down. Mother Nature would do the job with one good strong windstorm. They kind of added a haunted feeling to the place. Creeped me out. I got goosebumps on my arms. There were gardens everywhere. They were overgrown and hadn't been tended to in years. Sad looking.

Prissy led the way, holding Bobby's hand. We stepped into the big, wide hallway, which still looked like the grand old entrance it once was. It had stairs going off to the left and the right, wrapping around, with a sitting room farther into the house. We stayed in the hallway figuring we could hear any cars that pulled up or her father if he stumbled around, making noise. He was very sick with cancer of the mouth and throat and was scary to me. He looked incredibly skinny, a bag of bones really in his bathrobe, pulling a catheter along, with two stick legs sticking down from his robe. His mouth was twisted from surgeries, poor fella.

My body was hot. I was ready for whatever Billy wanted to do with me. Only he didn't want to do anything other than kiss me.

"Come on, man," I begged. "Wat's da matta? You tink I don't know what ta do?"

"Naw," said Billy. "It's jist that this don't feel right. I do this stuff wid my daughter. She 'bout your age."

"Well then," I said putting my hands on my skinny, little hips, "What's da problem?" I badgered him. "It's no different than wid me."

"She's family. It's different. She's my daughter," he said, his Southern drawl heavy. "I can do what I want wid her 'cause she's mine. Her ma don't like it. I told her to take to the highway then, if she don't like how I treat Annabell. Annabell loves me and likes it when we sleep together. But it's different. Like I said. She's my daughter. You're not. I can't do anything else with you but kiss you," Billy finished his sentence. We stood up. He got his pants right, pulling and pushing his big cock to the side, adjusting it, and was ready to leave.

I looked over his shoulder and saw a bare-assed Bobby jack-hammering Prissy on her knees, like a dog, with his pants around his ankles. Right on the floor in the hallway, Bobby was pounding away.

In the tenth grade, my brother and I changed schools. By doing this, Greg agreed to repeat his senior year. We lived an hour away, in Mathews, the next county over from our new school, Gloucester High School. My brother and I were able to attend the school free of the "across county line" fee, because Dad was beginning his first year teaching Spanish as an adjunct alongside his ministry work. We switched schools because it was known for being a better school. My curfew was midnight while my brother didn't have any curfew. For these "reasonable" people, my parents, to think that a friend was going to drive me home at midnight, an hour one way, was just a set up. It was not happening. So, it became a joke amongst my friends that every other weekend I would be on restriction because I didn't make it home by 12:00, when my carriage turned into a pumpkin. My brother, as I said, had no curfew and refused to bring me home. So, often I spent the night at a friend's house or lied and stayed with my boyfriend at "The Farm." I began smoking pot, I dressed in jeans which I recut to sit on my hip bones, and in the front, they were low and sat right at my pubic bone. They were purple jeans, and I LOVED those jeans. I got the nickname "Purple Rat." I have no idea where it came from. Purple was not an "in" color, but it was my color! My skirts were short. I was called a whore and a slut by my mom. Before I left in the morning for school, she'd have me stretch my hand down to see if the length reached the tip of my middle finger! It never did. I wore a jean jacket, which was entirely embroidered. I even embroidered a fire breathing dragon up the back. And my hip-hugging jeans had flowers, birds, and vines stitched up the sides. The huge bell bottoms had a heart chain embroidered around the edges. I thought I was pretty cool! A real hippie I was in my heart, soul, and adorned on my body!

In the beginning of my sophomore year, in my new school, I didn't really date one guy. We all went out together and then just ended up with someone. The thing about this was that I didn't want sex with any guy, just the guys I liked. I didn't know how this worked, and it seemed that the guys all just wanted sex. Not the kind of sex I liked. They liked "balling." What a strange word the guys used down here... I realized there was no choosing on my part—it was forced—if I didn't go along. Was this rape? I didn't think so. I didn't really know. It was what guys did. If I didn't stop them, then I was to blame. I'd get called names and that would be the death of me having any guys interested in me. There was no "rape." Sex was part of the high school journey, like it or not. Those were the days of "free love."

Submerging myself began at a slow and steady pace. My parents believed I lied, so I began lying. Sex was taboo. I became extremely sexually active. Thank-God one of our friends' parents, Jackie, cared about us girls not getting pregnant and took us to a free clinic for birth control pills. Jackie stood up for us and answered as an adult, for all of us girls. She was a cool lady. She had long, blond hair to her waist, which she pulled back in a low ponytail at the nape of her neck. She was quite large, a rotund woman who wore big, flowing mumus. She had beautiful blue eyes and always had a kind word of encouragement for us kids. Jackie was an easy person to talk to and welcomed my friends and I to confide in her. We knew she was a safe person whose trust we could count on and we could share our problems with.

By now I was eating every drug that was given to me. I did acid every other weekend when I was not on restriction. Yes, I had a stupid curfew of 12:00, but my older brother has no curfew. So what? It was a joke amongst my friends. I pleaded with my parents about how unfair my curfew was because there was no one to drive me home. If Greg didn't have to be home, then I had no ride. This didn't matter. Nothing changed. My life sucked.

What more was there to say? I became what I always had been asked as a kid, when other kids found out I was a preacher's kid, a P.K. That one stupid question: "Are you one of the bad ones or are you a good kid?" So ridiculous. It pissed me off. And given what was happening in my life, I had started to believe, one cell at a time, that I was one of the "bad" ones. And replied as such, shame and self-loathing filling me, turning my face and ears a burning, bright red color. I was so ashamed of who I had become. I didn't know where the other me, the real me, had gone! I felt shattered into bits and pieces. Some of me reacted to certain people and authority figures, another pretended to be happy, a smile plastered on my face, another was angry but silent, and somewhere a kernel of me existed. But where and how did I get to her? I was submerged. Hidden deep, safe with hope and my hidden faith, at knowing I'd come to know Jesus' love someday. Someday. I had forgotten what was said to me by the magical being that appeared using the Spirit essence of my uncle Clay. My parents thought I was crazy, and it upset my dad when I tried to share my experience while grieving my uncle's death.

I had learned how to embroider in our church as one of our Sunday School projects. My dad had a family service which was specifically for us teens. We had a guitar played by a beautiful Black woman who had joined our congregation, integrating it, at Dad's invitation. Lydia was like a gazelle and gorgeous. I really connected with her. Her skin was a beautiful shade of brown, she had almond-shaped eyes that sparkled when she got excited. She wore her hair pulled back into a tight chignon, and her clothes were colorful and sexy. Her eyes were painted with a thin outline of black accentuating them. She was a sweet, inspiring, haughty, proud, and beautiful, friendly Soul. She took a liking to me, and I loved her. I didn't know where Dad met her. She reminded me of Maria Carmona, my friend's mother, in the Bronx. Lydia invited my brother and I to accompany her with our singing. I loved this. I aspired to be a singer and dancer on Broadway. It was my dream. To be a writer and a performer! I dreamt of writing my own music and dances, and someday writing an autobiography of my strange life!

Dad made this family service friendly and inviting for my brother and me and any other "hippie" friends we had. This was how I met Pricilla. He encouraged us with folk music, newer prayers, and fun projects after the service in Sunday School. He had the services each week set up to tell one of the Bible stories. After the service, the girls were taught how to embroider by a parishioner in the church. Miss Lily lived on a tributary off of the York River in a beautiful, stately Southern mansion. Her husband's family had had a tobacco plantation which had long since been sold off. Her husband had died before my family moved to Mathews. She lived alone as a widow. Being a rich and vibrant character and full of stories, she adored my dad as he paid her a lot of attention, fascinated was he by her stories and she, his. It was a friendship made in heaven. Dad dropped me off at her home every week after school. I was greeted at the front door by her maid, who walked me through the living room, into the garden room. The garden room was a beautiful, huge glass atrium filled with plants. Her most prized plants were African violets, and the orchids were amazing and came in all colors and sizes, with beautiful, strange, and funny faces. The room was hot, moist, and smelled heavenly! Jasmine and the gardenia flowers were the freshest scent my sensitive nose picked up. It reminded me of Costa Rica and transported me to my happy place with the sugar cane and coffee bean smells. Miss Lily always had classical music playing, and her maid, Sally, served tea and cookies. Miss Lily was bombed on alcohol. I could smell it when she hugged me and sat close to me on her rattan, two-person, comfy sofa. But she was ok! When she was younger, she had been the head embroiderer for a museum in Washington, D.C., repairing delicate and important fabrics. Miss Lily had colorful, woven baskets filled with threads of all kinds, thicknesses, and colors: cotton in one basket, silk in another, samples of stitches in yet another basket. Then she had the scissor and thimble basket with miscellaneous items! I loved looking through her stuff, with her permission of course. I was in heaven and found that I loved the focus and peacefulness of women's traditional handwork.

We wore our jeans to church and sometimes I even went barefoot to the church service. The family service was in our parish house, which was adjacent to our home, so we didn't have to drive to get to the church service. We had two churches which Dad tended to. One in the north end of Mathews, and one on the southern end of the town. The one on the northside of town had one, old, sweet, Southern, Black woman. She had been attending this church, welcomed as one of the parishioner's maids, when she was a child. When the family matriarch and patriarch had passed on, she continued attending services. She and Dad became fast friends.

I loved this about Dad. He tried hard to be inclusive of everyone. He wanted our presence, his teenage children, and our friends in church. How we looked for the church services didn't matter to him, which was an improvement over what it had been my whole life, as a P.K., where the first pew was always ours. We were watched and whispered about as we walked in. We were watched and talked about endlessly in the small-town gossip mill. What we wore, how we kids looked, how we behaved, etc. I had my cheek pinched a lot. And I hated it. I wanted to grab the person's hand and stop it.

Mom's role as minister's wife was always a struggle for her because of the expectations which were unspoken but were very present and important here in the deep South. Mom railed against this. Courageous and bold, she stepped out and became super visible in church when she stopped wearing gloves and a hat to the services. That was a huge no-no. The next thing she did was to wear blue jeans around town with a tucked in man's shirt she'd worn for riding, and boots. She was a horse woman and felt comfortable in this attire. Well, this was totally taboo and seen as disrespectful to her role. Mom didn't care. After Mom had returned from the hospital, she was still manic and still the angry woman that she had been. She had learned some coping skills, though. One of her coping skills was collecting old, used pottery from yard sales, which she began frequenting. The boxes piled up in her studio, which she had set up behind our home in a little green shed. I'll never forget the first time I heard a loud crash and glass breaking, startling me, coming from her studio out in the backyard. I stood outside the door, listening. On the other side of the wooden wall, I heard Mom scream and crash, another dish shattering. I realized that she was throwing her yard sale dishes against the wall. Her therapy, she called it. When she came out of her studio, she always seemed lighter and happy again, like she'd emptied herself of unwanted, angry energy.

Our family's lives were the talk of the town. We provided a lot of gossip for this small, Southern town gossip mill. Like the one time we had a workman come to the house to do some renovating in Dad's home office. From one of the windows in Dad's home office, you could look right into my older brother's room and see all the controversial posters on his walls. My parents never dreamed that these "uncouth" posters would become a hot topic of conversation for the endless milling of other people's lives. As word spread through town, a huge controversy was created for my dad.

"I heard that Father Kelley has a poster of a pregnant Girl Scout hanging on his wall in his office," a parishioner finally whispered into Mom's ear as they chatted it up during coffee hour. "Is this true?"

My mom, horrified that this was what people were saying behind her back, told the woman that of course it was not true. She couldn't bring herself to say that her son had the poster in his room and that was where the poster was seen. Not in my dad's office. That night she read the riot act to my dad for allowing those disgusting posters to be in her son's room. "What were you thinking?" she screamed at my dad. Dad seemed oblivious to her rage and made a comment about the dinner we were eating. She regularly prepared meals from the "welfare" menu to save money. Tonight, we were eating one of those meals of lentils and raisins with rice and cinnamon. It was an interesting flavor. Not my favorite meal, but it was not bad, either. Just different with the raisins in it.

Dad had commented on her dinner. "Oh, I see we are having dog food again," he said. Next thing I knew, a glass of water went sailing across the dining room table. I shrank down in my seat, keeping my eyes on my plate, and I ate as quickly as I could so I could be excused.

"What were you thinking when you allowed Greg to put up those posters? From the day I saw them, I told you they were obscene and would cause you problems. But noooo. You never listen to me. They are obscene and shouldn't be in his room. Have you forgotten that our son shares his room with his little brother, nine years his junior?" She demanded that my father confront Greg and have the posters taken down immediately.

All the while, Greg sat at the dinner table, listening to the conversation and the rage in my mother's voice as it strengthened. Her face twisted up into what looked like another person entirely. A person demented. The veins in her neck popped out, spittle was spraying, and her face was bright red, and her eyes looked like she was possessed as she raged on. She looked like a demon.

I couldn't leave the table soon enough. I prayed to God to get me out of this crazy, fucking home. I fantasized about Mom and Dad getting divorced. In my fantasy, though, this had the dilemma as to who I would live with. God forbid I lived with my mother. We'd kill each other if Dad wasn't there to be somewhat of a referee, after instigating our fights by saying things like, "When you walk through that door you set your mother off." Or the favorite one I'd heard my whole life,

"You are just like your mother," which implied I, too, was batshit crazy. A mad woman. As Dad saw it, I was crazy, Mom was crazy, and her mom was crazy, too. And Dad was kind of a sadist. I hated to admit this, but he was. He was a bully. He derived pleasure from tormenting my mother. And me. Teasing her, ridiculing her, and basically beating her up emotionally. He never laid a finger on Mom. She also had her darts, which she threw at him with angry and vicious words. Here are some of my mother's real thoughts:

The Fuse Was Lit

The fuse was lit
when husband put himself on the needing list,
and awaited a turn to suckle breast.
His unfinished business affected his masculinity
and my sanity.
So that's my story—a child in the womb, a child on a tit,
a husband too,
with a child for each hand—
and me in the center
bearing the weight, keeping peace, preparing feasts.

If by chance a certain glimmer of my potential
happened to find its way into my numb and depressed mind-set,
a shriek rang out for humanity to hear
and insanity to fear.

My precious daughter—this started out to be your accolade.
Forgive me for digressing—but we are both women.
And that black phantom spirit hovering over you—
that one you said was me—"Ayla's Birth"
that kept you down and wouldn't let you be
was all that I abhorred and feared

repressed in me and absorbed by you.
No wonder your beautiful spirit had to vacate for awhile
and come haunt me with its energy,
wooing me into my sexuality,
so your tabernacle home could be safe for you again.

Gwynn Kelley - January 29, 1990

As I escaped to my bedroom and thought about Dad's very unnecessary comments to Mom about her cooking, I empathized with Mom. Why the hell didn't he leave her alone? Couldn't he see that she was sensitive and tried her best to cook, care for him, us, and take care of herself? She was an artist and wasn't doing her art. She never put herself first. If she tried to, Dad made fun of her, called her names, and basically silenced her. He did it in a weird, underhanded way, which seemed like it was a joke, but it was not. And it hurt. It hurt me to hear him talk down to her and to see her trying to fight back, but it was always through an enormous and dangerous rage, which got her nowhere and "proved" that she was unbalanced and "crazy," as Dad loved to call her.

Mom and I began to fight all the time. I felt like she hated me. Everything I asked permission to do, my parents believed I was making up stories and lying to them to escape the house. I remembered a time, as a junior in high school, when I had gotten a lead role in the school play. This was quite unusual because the lead roles went to the "thespians" who were seniors. But I was great and had landed the role! I was stellar in fact and very proud of this accomplishment.

When, on the first night of my rehearsals, I asked permission to use the car to return to my high school, I was refused. My parents didn't believe that I had gotten the lead role. They thought I was lying! How fucking dare they! I pleaded with my dad to PLEASE go and talk with the drama teacher the next day and ask her. "You'll see that I am telling you the truth," I tried to reason with him. Well, this set Dad off on a tangent about how embarrassing it would be for him to go and ask the drama teacher if his daughter had a lead role. He wouldn't go ask for himself. His own huge ego got in the way. So, I avoided the teacher, too ashamed to admit the truth. Because I knew that if I said something the drama teacher, Mrs. Howell, she would go straight to my dad and speak with him, which would piss him off even more, making my life more dismal. So, I kept silent and sulked around the school, going way out of my way to avoid the drama room.

I was feeling crestfallen and forlorn. I gave up and gave in, becoming what my parents already believed me to be, a deviant and evil child, requiring strict disciplinary actions. I became a product of the times, using sex, drugs, and rock n' roll to numb myself down, submerging my light completely.

Chapter 5

Submerging My Light

In despair and descending into a deep depression, I was taking drugs like crazy. Sex had become a part of everything, and I was sick of it all. I was desperate to find a way out for myself.

I remembered hearing about the private Episcopal schools in Virginia from my friend, Prissy, who was going away to school the next year. She told me that ministers' kids go to these all-girl schools. I did some research, called the school, and got an application mailed to me. When I tried to get my parents' help, I was told by my dad that I was not worth educating. My big hips, he reminded me, were good for birthing babies.

"You'll be getting married and have children, so no. No private school for you. It'd be a waste of money," Dad said.

I pleaded with him. "But there is *no* money involved. It's free to me because I am a minister's child."

"How do you know this?" he demanded.

"I fucking called to ask, like you could have done for me," I yelled at him, no longer afraid to curse at him.

I was beside myself with anger. What was I supposed to do?

The answer was final, no. I got my mouth washed out with soap that night before bed, by my mother. I stopped talking to Dad.

Dad stopped teaching Spanish at the high School at the end of my junior year. This meant he would have to pay to send me to Gloucester High School, across county lines. I was moved my senior year back to our town's high school, Mathews High School, home to the Blue Devils, which was free and far away from my friends.

I watched my sister excel. She had ballet and piano lessons. She got braces put on her teeth, which was good; Katherine, being a thumb-sucker, had bucked teeth. I had wanted to play piano and asked my parents if I could have piano lessons, too.

"No. There's no money for that," came the answer from Mom. I used to take riding lessons, but those had stopped a while ago.

So, on the days when my sister was in the parish house with her piano instructor, I snuck into the kitchen and stayed hidden, listening intently to the lesson going on in the main gathering hall. When they were finished and had left the parish house, I snuck out from my hiding place and ran over to the piano. I tried to replicate what I had heard. I did this for several weeks. But it was too hard. I couldn't really muddle my way along. I didn't know what they were doing. My sadness blocked my enthusiasm and desire to pursue my passion! So, I stopped.

Then I remembered that Dad had a guitar in his office, which he played occasionally. I went into his home office, closing the door behind me one day and picked it up. I was determined to teach myself to play guitar. I needed an instrument to play. I really wanted to be a performer, singer-songwriter, and Broadway dancer when I got out of this god-forsaken town. I was told it was just a silly dream; I'd been told this a million times when I brought it up. Now, I kept the dream hidden.

After a while I didn't remember the dream and got punished for touching Dad's guitar. What a selfish bastard. I was basically screwed and couldn't wait to graduate high school. There were no college plans being made for me. There was no talk of anything really for me at the end of high school. Guess I had to find a man to marry and soon, evidently. It seemed this was what my parents wanted for me, because like I said, there ain't nothing being planned for my future. Life was looking bleak at sixteen and a senior in high school, with perfect birthing hips.

I managed to get a job. It was a little over an hour away in Williamsburg, at the

Pottery Factory. I had to be at work by 4:00. I told my parents that I had to be there by 1:30. I got out of school at 12:00. I now had lots of time to get into all kinds of trouble. And I would have money to do so!

I met Rusty at the home of a new friend I had met in Newport News at Buckroe Beach. Rusty was older than me, nineteen. In his living room there were big, soft pillows everywhere, large, and small, and my new friend had a cool rug on the floor. It was cozy and reeked of pot, stale cigarettes, and beer. Rusty had brown, curly hair down to his shoulders. He was thin and wiry, wore faded blue jeans with a white tee shirt, and his Drum tobacco was kept in his front chest pocket, ready to grab and roll one. His eyes were glassy with a slight yellowish tint to the whites of his eyes. He had big dimples when he smiled and was jittery as a spider monkey. Rusty was kind of itchy and twitchy all the time, nervous. But I loved this guy. I didn't quite know why except that he was funny and had lots of stories. Sex with him was great. He was a Vietnam vet. Somehow, he reminded me of my uncle Clay, who was killed in Vietnam. What came back of him was a purple heart, and he, a dead hero. This guy lived and returned home a junkie. He was very different from the high school boys I'd been with and was sick to death of. This guy knew how to treat a woman. Well, kind of. He demanded to be the center of my orbit but gave me lots of attention when I was paying attention to him. He was jealous, and I took that to be "true love." He wanted me all to himself and didn't want to meet or hang out with the small group of friends I had made. I took that as meaning that we were "more grown up" than my high school buddies and had better things to do than hang out at the Dairy Freeze, circling it in our cars a thousand times. Round and round, we drove, what seemed like all night long, seeing who had come. Oh, we'd leave and go round the back roads to get high. But we'd always make it back to the Dairy Freeze and circle.

The night finally arrived when I had Rusty come to my home to pick me up for a real date. I was nervous and didn't want to introduce Rusty to my parents. What if they didn't like him? What if they wouldn't let me leave the house with him? Any behavior was fair game with them. I just never knew...unpredictable as they were.

But I was excited, and I really wanted my parents to like him. Rusty came to the door and rang the bell. Dad got to the door first and invited Rusty into the house. They shook hands. Rusty was nervous and was twitching like crazy, rubbing his nose constantly, and was jittery. He sat for a few minutes while Dad questioned him about his tour in Vietnam. I knew he was going to bring up his kid brother, Clay. He did, and Rusty was sympathetic, listening closely. I noticed his eyes tearing up, as were Dad's. They had a moment of bonding around Clay's sad death and his heroic act. Rusty contradicted the heroism. "I wish I had never come home. I live every day seeing my buddies being shot up and villages being burned, children and women screaming, running away from us, terrified. I feel like I became a monster." He looked sadly at my dad, sniffled, dried his eyes, and stood up. Mom was nowhere to be found. Dad seemed comfortable and friendly with Rusty. I think he liked him. I was chomping at the bit to leave. I wanted to get the fuck out of the house.

As we left, Rusty went out first. Dad drew me to him. I thought he was giving me a hug. Instead, he whispered into my ear, "Rusty is a junkie."

"What?" I questioned Dad in a loud whisper.

"We'll talk later," he said to me under his breath.

Out loud so Rusty can hear, he said in a friendly voice, "Have a good time. Be safe and get her home by twelve on the nose. I don't want any monkey business."

"Yes, sir," Rusty replied, with his head bobbing up and down. "I'll have her home without fail, by twelve on the dot." He was still bobbing his head up and down, like a dashboard doll with the head that wobbles.

Dad and I never talked later about what he had called Rusty. A junkie. When we lived in New York, Dad dealt with a lot of junkies. He considered himself an "expert" on the topic, and he boasted about his work with the hoodlums whose lives we had left behind when we moved south. Just like my girlfriends, Cookie and Gigi, used to taunt me when I first moved to the Bronx. They were skeptical of me being their friend for that reason. I'd leave, they wouldn't.

Rusty and I dated my whole senior year. We didn't have friends we hung out with. We just wanted to be together all the time. He and I didn't need anyone else for entertainment. Rusty's van was a comfortable pad with great sound, and the "balling" was great. I never did get comfortable using that word for sex. It always embarrassed me when he used it as an invitation.

Eventually Rusty trusted me, which took me into the dark and seedy world of heroin. I had my rose-colored glasses on which were like prisms. Splitting my reality into smaller triangles of perspective, all within my mind and wanting to be heard. I hardly noticed the dive down I had taken. The self-loathing was already so ingrained, its grip only deepened.

Rusty was sitting against the metal wall of his van, covered with psychedelic blankets, relaxing. The music was blasting "Truckin'" by the Grateful Dead. This was our theme song, it seemed. I was stoned, groovin', and rockin' it, sitting cross-legged. Nonchalantly, Rusty pulled out a rubber surgical tube about a third of an inch in diameter, and wrapped it around his bicep, putting one end in his teeth, and he started to take the other end in his hand, to pull it tight. He stopped and rolled his eyes up at me and asked me if I'd like to do the honors. I was instructed to tie it around his upper forearm so he could shoot up his junk. Yes, Dad was right. Rusty was a junkie. He got hooked up in Vietnam. I was fascinated with him shooting up and watching his eyes glaze over as his high kicked in. It was intriguingly sad. I wanted to help him but felt helpless. If Rusty was the kind of person Dad "counseled" in the Bronx, why didn't he do something to help Rusty? He knew before I did that he was a junkie. Why the hell did he tell me to have a good time and then let me leave the house with him? One of the trapped prism parts of me knew this was very dangerous and wrong, but I felt powerless and ignorant to do anything about it. If Dad couldn't do anything. How could I?

One day, after Rusty dropped me off, I dropped my shit in the hallway where my coat and stuff got hung up and ran upstairs to my room. I skedaddled as fast as I could up the stairs, two at a time. I didn't want to run into my parents. I was scared, angry, and confused. I slammed my door. As I turned around and headed to my dresser, I noticed on top of it a small, square newspaper ad, cut out, and placed there, almost shimmering with energy. My hands were shaking I reached out and picked it up. It was a hotline ad to the FBI for drugs.

If you know of anyone selling small amounts or dealing in large amounts of heroin, call this number xxx-xxx-xxxx, to give a confidential "tip."

The notice was right there. I wasn't imagining it. It was real.

And that was it. Nothing was said. Obviously, my dad had cut it out and put it on my dresser. His way of communicating with me about something so important, dangerous, and sad. I took that small newspaper ad and put it in my wallet for safe keeping.

Weeks went by, and life groaned on with the same old, same old. Rusty was getting high. He was not shy at all now. I was forever tying his bicep muscle off so he could shoot up. I was getting bored, never high like him. None of this was fun. Life had dulled, looking through my rose-colored lenses. The excitement of the danger had lost its shimmer. The well of empathy for Rusty's psychological wounding from his tour in Vietnam had run dry, and I was beside myself with despair. I was graduating from Mathews High School and the Blue Devils soon. I barely got through my senior year. Cheating on the algebra tests was a no-brainer. I had to pass algebra, this time, a second time, to graduate.

My sister had the class before me. Our teacher was an alcoholic, drinking vodka and orange juice all day long. By the time I had her, she was shit-faced. Katherine got straight As in all subjects, barely having to crack her books. I barely passed with C-minuses and Ds. An F in algebra, once, and biology I failed once and then passed it the second time. Teachers wanted to graduate me. Graduate me and get me the hell out of high school!

My sister handed me her papers and tests, which were all graded by the students in class, as she left and I walked in. We then, one by one, as she read out our names, walked up, showed her our test, and Miss Crockett (crotchety Crockett we called her) wrote our scores in her soft-backed, black teacher's book. This created little work for her to have to do at home. Miss Crockett looked ragged with sagging boobs hanging to her belly and her belts pulled tight, right up under them, wrapping around her soft, round belly. She spray-starched her hair stiff, and it smelled of hairspray. She had been teaching for thirty years. Her eyes were always glassy and bloodshot, her cheeks had small broken veins, and her nose was bright red. I felt sad for her.

I thought that maybe Rusty and I should just get married. That would take me out of my home. But yikes, marry a junkie. I was nuts, but I wasn't that crazy! At least I didn't think I was. Maybe I was. How should I know if I was nuts or not? My parents didn't seem to know what was going on, even though they thought they did. Just like me. I thought I did, too.

One night, Rusty was nervous and jumpy. More so than usual, his head nodded continuously. I got him to confide in me. I was good at that. I found out that there was a huge "mother lode," as Rusty called it, of heroin coming into Newport News. Rusty was the contact and the dealer for this area. I had no flipping idea about this, and I was starting to freak out. But I knew I had to stay cool and gather information about this. My mind wandered to my dresser, and I saw the ad sitting there that was now safely in my wallet.

Yes, I decided. I would gather information and then I'd call this in. Rusty had to be stopped before he got into deep shit. That I knew.

When I got home, I dug the newspaper ad out of my wallet. With hands shaking, I dialed the number. A male voice picked up the phone.

"FBI, Officer Scott speaking. How can I help you?"

I shared everything I knew. He asked for my name. I was afraid to give it, but I did. He said that I would never be identified and would remain anonymous. The FBI needed to know who I was so they could verify all that was happening and keep an eye on me to make sure I was safe. Over the next couple of days, Rusty was talking fast, all the time, about this upcoming "drop of the mother lode." He believed this was his ticket to freedom, to his financial independence. He started talking about marrying me if all went as planned. Rusty believed that he would finally have some real money. I don't know how much he was told he would make, but it was way up in the thousands.

Finally, the day came when we were going to meet the couple at the airport. I had noticed a chocolate-colored sedan showing up and hovering around me at different times. It unnerved me, but I figured it was an FBI agent, keeping track of me for my safety. He said they would.

We were picking the couple up in Rusty's van to make the exchange. I passed all this information on to the FBI agent I had been speaking with every time I had an update to give. I didn't want to be part of the whole thing, but I was told I needed to keep acting as though everything was just as it had been, to not trigger any suspicions. When the moment finally happened, I wasn't present. There was a window in time where I didn't make the last meeting with Rusty, intentionally. I was told at the last minute by the FBI to stay home. So, I did.

I never saw Rusty again after that. I graduated from Mathews High School and got a summer job at Eastern State Mental Hospital as a lifeguard, following a lifeguard course at the U.S. Coast Guard training center in Yorktown, Virginia. There was also talk that looked like a plan was forming to send me to Ecuador for a year, to live with Dad's best friend, Alfonso, the Episcopal Bishop of Ecuador. Dad had met Alfonso in Costa Rica when they were both young men and in the Priesthood. Alfonso was in the Catholic Church at the time. Through Dad's friendship and influence, he changed faiths and became an Episcopal minister, and eventually the Bishop of Ecuador. In honor of my dad, Alfonso had named his eldest daughter, Cinthia, after me, Dad's first-born daughter!

Talk continued for several more weeks.

My job at the mental hospital was ok, until one of the patients grabbed hold of me, fearing for his life, and basically sat on me in knee deep water, pushing me under the water. One of the orderlies pulled this big kid off me.

My next day working, as I walked across the campus to go to the beach where I was lifeguarding, a woman off in the distance closed the gap with me, quickly.

"You little fucking bitch," she screeched at me. "When I'm outta here you're a dead fuckin bitch." Her New York accent was thick, her long, black hair flying wildly as she closed the distance between us, fast. "I know you're the one who ratted us out. And I'm gonna git your ass when I git out. So be forewarned, you fucking cunt. You're as good as dead." And she spat at me.

I high-stepped it right over to the administration office after that encounter and quit.

The plan to send me to Ecuador solidified after I recounted this tale to my parents. My mother was super relieved to know there was a plan to get me out of her life. She'd have peace. Hopefully! She would no longer be my problem, nor I hers. I had a couple of weeks after I quit, until August arrived. I flew on the third of August and August couldn't come soon enough. I was scared shitless and wanted to leave the country as soon as I could.

My father got my passport expedited. It had a missionary classification, which meant I had a visa giving me a year abroad. I'd be working in the Episcopal church with Alfonso. Then my mother got the brilliant idea, and convinced me as well, to stop taking my birth control pills. She told me, "You are beginning a new life and can turn the page on your old life. You don't need these." She held up my packet of pills sitting on my dresser and waved them in my face, gloating, like the victory flag of an invisible battle she had won.

She didn't believe I'd need the birth control pills anymore. I was going to be a missionary and the Fairy Godmother was going to wave the magic wand. Poof! I was a new, clean girl! Did it make me a virgin again, too?

Oh please. Give me a break. I was going to turn into Miss Lily White Panties. She was convincing, though. My self-loathing was deep, and I desperately wanted to have my life change and head in a new direction. I was ashamed, felt like shit, and thought of myself as just an "easy piece of ass." It was not me. Somewhere inside this splintered self there was a part of me that wanted to have a life worth living. A Soulful and fulfilling life. So, giving up birth control pills started to seem like a good idea. I convinced myself that my compass had been set pointing in a new direction. A missionary. Who would have thunk it? I laughed hard at this when I was alone, thinking of all that had transpired. A good, cleansing, deep belly laugh. This just might be what I needed to get back on track.

A small glimmer of hope emerged.

Chapter 6

A Glimmer of Hope

The plane landed in Panama first. We were to board a smaller plane which was taking me to Guayaquil, Ecuador. I had a bunch of hours to wait before I boarded again. It was steamy hot, loud, Spanish music blared, and I was thrilled. I was feeling pretty grown up. Traveling by myself and waiting for the next adventure. Bring it on!

And here he came… Soon after we landed, a tall man, dressed in a beige safari shirt with jeans, long hair, and wearing a Panama hat, approached me. I sized him up quickly; he reminded me of my brother, Greg. He was handsome and wore lots of silver jewelry. He sat down close to me. I pretended not to notice him. Then he struck up a conversation with me.

"Where are you headed?" he asked.

"Ecuador," I answered.

"How long is your layover? I have some places I could show you, to see a little bit of Panama rather than just sit here, sweating!" He grinned, flashing a set of beautiful, perfectly straight, white teeth!

"Hmmm, I don't think I have time. I'm fine waiting."

He persisted, and said, "Oh come on," smooth-talking me with his British accent. "I'm not going to hurt you or make you miss your flight. I just want to show you the main drag. It's just a couple blocks away. You have plenty of time to spend two or three hours with me." He told me his name was Robert.

Oh geez here I go... I couldn't resist. Such a strong wave of "hell yes" took over any rational thinking. I flipped into the one I was trying to escape. She's still with me.

"Ok. What the hell. Let's go. I have some hours before I board again." I picked up my bright yellow backpack and headed out of the airport. It was sweltering outside. It felt like I was slogging through a thick, moist, dense sauna. I loved the heat. We went to a little car parked right outside the airport and jumped in. It was a convertible. There was music blaring in the streets. People were dressed colorfully, and I heard deep, loud, raucous laughter, echoing from one of the many bars. The air pulsed with energy; the rhythm, the heat, and music, the colors, and the scent of flowers, made its own vibe, and it was electric!

We stopped. Robert parked the car. We went into a bar that a friend of his owned. The place had loud Latin music playing. I swooned. Latin music made my body move! I started dancing, alone. I didn't care about having a partner to dance with. It wasn't long, though, before I had a couple of men who were vying for my attention. I ignored them and went to the bar when the music ended. I was raring to go. I didn't want to be cutting it too close. I found Robert talking to one of his buddies in the corner. I got his attention and began walking over to his table. He met me and took my elbow, guiding me out of the bar, carrying something. Fifteen minutes later, we are back at the airport. Robert took my backpack from me. He was checking it out, feeling all over the backpack. Then said he had a package he wanted me to take with me and mail from Ecuador.

I grabbed my backpack as he tried to open it.

"No way. I'm not going to take anyone else's packages with me. That sounds like a drug run waiting to happen and I'm the asshole mule who gets caught. Nope. Sorry, Robert. If that was your intention the whole time, you wasted time on me." I was angry and red in the face, surprised at myself for standing up to him.

"No. It's not like that at all. I just wanted you to take it with you and mail it safely from another country. I promise nothing illegal is in the bag."

"Open it then," I demanded.

"No, that's not necessary. You need to just trust me on this. I promise," he was begging now, sounding kind of desperate.

"Fuck you. I have a plane to catch. I'm not stupid." I turned to walk away as I heard my plane being called for boarding. Thank God. Get me outta there.

The plane landed at a small airport in Salinas, Ecuador. It was pitch black, except for the small runway lights set to guide the plane in. We had to change planes and board a puddle jumper to land in Guayaquil. It was deathly silent as we were all herded off the plane, following a stewardess with a flashlight. I was not understanding much Spanish at that point, and I was scared. I wasn't sure what was happening. I wondered if we were getting hijacked. Literally there was no one at this airport and it was pitch black. All of us passengers were being led from the plane into the airport by flashlight. I tried to ask what was happening.

"Shhh, nina, sigueme. It's ok," I was told by a passenger in broken English.

We waited for a bit for our plane to be readied or whatever they were doing. I just wanted to board and get out of there. This was too freaky.

As we entered the small airport, the desk opened with a glaringly bright, single overhead lightbulb covered in a big, white, cone-shaped shade. There stood a man waiting for us, gesturing with his hands as he spoke in rapid Spanish to one of the passengers. I guessed he was a passenger. Finally, we boarded, after passports were checked along with our tickets.

It was a short puddle jump to Guayaquil. I had to go through customs. The airport was quiet as it was so late in the evening. I saw the bishop standing on the other side of the chain link fence, holding up a sign in his bright purple bishop's shirt and white collar. He had a wide face, with a nose that sloped down, high cheekbones, and beautiful eyes that twinkled when he spotted me! Alfonso's face split into a huge grin. I saw him pointing at me and talking with a person at the customs window. Next thing I heard my name being called over the loudspeaker. I moved like a snake through the small crowd, all vying for their turn to get through customs, quickly. I felt hot stares on my back as I glided my way through the crowd as it moved aside creating a path, like Moses when he commanded the Red Sea to part. The bishop was my "Moses."

I whizzed through and was greeted by the bishop with a big, warm bear hug, which lifted me off my feet! Bishop Alfonso Diego was like a big teddy bear. He was of Inca descendants from indigenous Bolivian roots. When I finally met him and felt my hand held tightly in his warm, big hand, I was amazed at how soft his skin was. His skin was a rich olive brown color, which looked magnificent against the magenta of his bishop's shirt. The bishop was not much taller than I, but his presence was huge! All moved aside as he walked through the crowd holding my hand leaving the bustling airport, the heartbeat of Guayaquil. I realized I hadn't had my hand held since I was a wee little girl. It was a sweet gesture. I struggled with it, though. I was way too old to have my hand held. I was not comfortable with the bishop's kindness and gesture of affection for his best friend's daughter. The bishop was bubbling over with pride and joy!

The bishop, his wife, Sonya, and their four children were on holiday at the beach, in a small town called Playas, on the Pacific coast. It was not a long ride from the airport. An hour on rough roads into the backcountry, following the coastline. A ground rule was set immediately. The bishop would not speak English with me. I was to remember my Spanish from my early years as a child who grew up in Costa Rica. I was to learn to speak Spanish fluently. He lets me know that the children would be speaking English with me to practice, but I was to answer and speak only in Spanish.

Yikes, I was thinking. I didn't remember much Spanish, even though I spoke it as a young child in Costa Rica, learning it right alongside my English. I also took three years of Spanish with my dad in high school. I spent a month in Spain when I was fourteen. So, I wasn't totally stupid. But to speak only in Spanish, that was gonna be interesting!

We were staying in a concrete block house, across the street from the ocean, in the Episcopal Diocese coastal retreat center. The sand was black. It was volcanic sand, I was told. We were on the Humboldt, which was a current like the current that runs up the eastern seaboard, making a swath of the ocean warm, the Gulf stream. It was a strong current, and I was forewarned by everyone who swam to be careful. I didn't want to get caught in it.

The next morning, I awakened early. The house was silent. I was sleeping in my own cubby, where a curtain hung for privacy. We had no refrigeration, no electricity, and it was hot here. Once the household awakened, all the day's chores began. The first order of the day, I was told was that we must go into town to pick up our chunk of ice for our "icebox." Literally, it was an insulated box for the ice to be kept in with all the cold stuff. We had enough for a day or two of stuff. Everything was bought fresh and used that day. Eggs, milk, and fish, I found out, would be bought later in the day, when the fishermen all returned with their catch. Once we were ready to leave the house, we all piled into the old, really dusty, white jeep, and headed to town. The icehouse was in the center of the town, at the open-air market. It sat on the edge of the market and was a house. Inside the icehouse the blocks were huge and covered with sawdust. Sonya told the guy how big a chunk she wanted. He used huge tongs to grab a hunk about 2'x3'x2' that would be split in two. We would be taking half of the block of ice.

Next, we made our way through the market, stopping at different vegetable vendors. Sonya was so much fun to watch as she haggled away the price, chopping it in half, to begin. She had her favorite vendors, old women with their fresh vegetables from their small patch of dirt, on the edge of town. The women dressed colorfully, and most, I noticed, were barefoot, some with gnarly looking feet, thick with callouses from hoofing it everywhere. They wore the traditional woven, straw Panama hats, with their long, jet-black hair braided down their backs. Many had children playing around their feet or sitting in a row lined up one behind the other, picking lice out of each other's hair, biting them in half, spitting them out, all while chewing coca leaves. The coca leaves kept the peace. We finished up our shopping, and everything was put into Sonya's beautiful, colorful, hand-woven baskets and then put into the back of the jeep.

When we got home and finished unloading the car, I was excited to test the ocean's water and go for a swim. After lunch in the early afternoon, everyone took a siesta, and the entire small town shut down. Finally, I was released from the family and from my interesting and soon beloved duty of having to spend time every morning, after chores, sitting with the bishop, talking of spiritual stuff, in Spanish.

I raced into my little cinder block cubby, got quickly into my bathers, and headed for the beach. As I left the house, the bishop yelled that I might want to take my flip flops with me. I yelled back, "I'm fine. I don't need them."

As I began to walk across the black sand, I understood why the bishop told me I might want my flip flops. The sand was hot. It was blistering hot, and I was now bolting and hopping across the sand as quickly as I could to get into the ocean. I imagined the bishop laughing his ass off as he watched me skippity pap across the hot sand. I was right. He teased me mercilessly and imitated me hoping across the hot sand. It was hysterical to see the bishop hopping around from foot to foot, howling in playful laughter with me.

The ocean, once I was in it, was warm and luscious. It felt great to be lying on my back, floating. I looked up at the clouds and couldn't believe I was in South America, finally on my own. The clouds were amazing. In awe, I realized how much I loved clouds. I loved watching them change shape and imagined, through my mind's eyes, that I could make them change shape! As though on a hospital drip, my cells respond with tingling. I splayed myself on the ocean; arms out, legs open, my awareness expanded, as I took it all in. I was in Ecuador, South America, floating in the Pacific Ocean! I wondered what the night sky was going to look like in the Southern Hemisphere.

Later in the day, we prepared to go to the market to meet the fisherfolk as they returned with their catch. The beach was crowded with bystanders. All the seagulls were overhead, squawking, screeching, and wanting their catch, too! Sonya, my Spanish mother, took me by the hand and walked with me to the shore, where all the boats had come up onto the sand. Everyone was yelling, trying to outsell their competitors with their fish—"Aquí es lo mejor pescado en todo el mercado!"

Sonya spotted the fisherman she wanted to do business with and headed for his boat. I loved all the chaos: the noise of the squawking birds, everyone yelling, kids running around; it seemed the whole town was present to buy fish.

The only place that had electricity was the Humboldt Hotel. It was a big, old, majestic hotel that stood at the head of the town on a rise above the beachfront. People were proud of this establishment and the people it attracted for vacationing.

As I looked up at this beauty, I could see the twinkling of the lights as they began to come on, one by one.

Sonya began haggling with the fisherman. She had asked me to pay close attention to how she did it. She automatically cut the price in half. Lesson number one in haggling had begun! If the vendor wouldn't budge, Sonya crossed her arms, turned her face to the side, scanning for a new vendor, letting the vendor know she was dissatisfied with her body language. This signaled that she was threatening to move on to another vendor. This usually got Sonya what she wanted, which was for the haggling to begin! From there you haggled until you were satisfied with the price. At some point in the game, Sonya told the fisherman that his fish wasn't that great and that she could do better going to the next boat. Maybe he would want to sell his fish for a reasonable price. Sonya was brutal as she clicked her tongue disgustedly and began to walk away, with arms crossed and chin held high! The guy yelled to her the new price. She, happy, with a smug and satisfied look on her face, winked at me as we bought the fish.

This was a ritual we did every day as the sun went down. It felt like a daily festival of sorts. The waterfront was very colorful with all the varied types of boats painted different colors; some had symbols of fish heads, or mermaids painted on the bows of their little fishing boats. The fishermen wore battered clothing, using hemp rope as a belt to hold up their pants. It was a very exciting daily ritual, and I realized I looked forward to it. After a couple of days learning the routine, I told the bishop and Sonya that I wanted to walk home along the shore. They hesitantly agreed.

The next day after the ritual fish buying event, I headed up the beach. It was a beautiful evening. I was happy to be walking and stretching my legs. I had much to think about, and it was a good 45-minute walk home. This became my evening ritual as I relished being alone, sliding my feet along the cooling, black, soft sand. It made a squeaking sound. Walking along the water's edge, the cooled sand felt silky under my feet. I got lost in my own world of thoughts as I walked. I was feeling good, thinking about what a great decision it was to come down here. And to be living in such a beautiful place, with wonderful people. Every night the bishop and

I sat and enjoyed a rum and Coke together, going over the day's events. My Spanish got better and better each day. This drinking felt nothing like with my uncle Jack. The bishop, because I was his best friend's daughter, had a very special bond to me.

In one of our conversations, the bishop told me that it was time for me to make a *despacho*, with a fire ceremony, baptizing me with a new name. You see, his eldest daughter was also named Cintia (Cynthia), in English, after me. Well, not really after me, per say, but she was named in honor of my father and his first daughter. Since this was the bishop's first-born daughter, Cintia was her name, too. This led to name searching in the evenings, as he explained what a *despacho* was and why it was important for me to make one.

A *despacho* was an offering made in honor of our ancestors, Mother Earth, and all that our life involves, and from where all our gifts arise. Mine specifically would contain that which I was letting go of, or an aspect of me which no longer served my highest good. It was a metaphorical death of sorts and likened to a snake shedding its skin when the old one became too confining. The *despacho* offered us (humans) the same opportunity during the ceremony as a vehicle to connect with Source. The *despacho* was created with all the objects that were meaningful to me, placed within the folded paper. I blew prayers into it with my breath; my hopes and dreams. Most importantly, this *despacho* was identifying that which no longer served my true Self. Geez Louise, I was ready to do this, for sure, but what was I letting go of? I was not at all sure I could put my finger on it as "it" was who I had become. So, what if this was about allowing me the space to become my future Self. My true Self. Who was she, I wondered? My true Self, made in God's image, the bishop kept saying. *You know this Self*, he would tell me in his accented English. I wish I could converse clearly my thoughts and wonderings in Spanish, but I was not totally fluent yet. I'd only been there a week, and already so much had happened. It was all a bit overwhelming and then the bishop dropped the bomb on me.

"Your *despacho* will be an effigy of your old self. I see you wear your blue jeans and jean jacket like they are a badge of honor. They have symbols embroidered all over them that are meaningful to you. It is time to see these symbols clearly and their meaning, and to be ready to let them go, so that you can welcome new life, and with it, new symbols will be given to you. These new symbols will be filled with your essence when you discover their meaning," the bishop explained.

He continued, "We will make a fire ceremony, and you will make a mask of your old self out of, what do you call it, paper, flour, and water?"

"Papier-mâché," I responded, still listening.

"You will make a mask, and you will stuff your jeans, your blue jean shirt, and your jacket with newspaper, making a representation of your old self. As you make your mask and paint it, you will pray and blow these prayers into your hands as you shape and paint your mask. This is a very loving act and very healing for your Soul." He paused and looked me deep in the eyes. "I know you have suffered a great deal. I see it in your eyes. Your eyes are windows which allow me to see into your Soul. Your heart is broken, and your Soul doesn't like living in your body. It is unclean and has been hurt." He looked up. Took a deep breath, blew it into my face. I saw the twinkle in his eyes, and he continued, "Your Soul hovers around you—always near—but is not able to reside within you. Your house is unclean. We must burn your clothes—a symbol of your past—in this fire ceremony."

Holy shit... What was he saying to me? I was going to stuff my favorite jeans, jean shirt, and jean jacket with newspaper so they could burn. He was nuts. I loved these clothes. My jacket had a beautiful fire breathing dragon embroidered across the entire back. My jeans had flowers and ivy stitched up the sides. These clothes took hours of my time to create, and they were ME! I couldn't burn these clothes. There was no way; I couldn't do that.

Whoa! I *was* attached to my past. I knew I had to do this. I didn't know what this meant. It felt like I would dissolve and become nothing, like the Wicked Witch in The Wizard of Oz...I was afraid of melting. I didn't see the *true self* which the bishop kept talking about. I sort of knew what he was trying to say to me, but not really, not deep down.

Time to just jump off this cliff—gotta get 'er done!

I began ripping newsprint into strips. The kids helped me and were very excited about this. They seemed to know what was happening more than I did. It amazed me the way the littlest one, Anaite, chatted to me in Spanish so easily. She was only three years old. She talked both in English and Spanish and helped me out immensely. I saw myself in her when I was three and speaking bilingually. She didn't roll her eyes at me and get frustrated that I was not fluent yet, like the older kids did. They somehow thought I was just supposed to start speaking. I was getting there, but I was certainly not able to communicate everything I wanted to say that was in my heart. Certainly, while the bishop and I were enjoying our nightly rum and Coke, I struggled with my thoughts and trying to communicate them clearly to him. And communicate the depth of my feelings.

I finally accepted this effigy thing. He had given me three names to choose from: Inti, which was the Quechua word for Sun Goddess/God; Anna, which was too ordinary; and I don't remember the third name, Maria, maybe. The name that struck a chord with me was Inti. I liked the feel of it on my tongue.

Inti.

I finished my mask. It had a gruesome, red painted face with black eyes that stared vacantly back at me. I stuffed the jeans with newspaper, crying as I did it. I really loved these jeans and didn't want to burn them. I didn't really believe that this fire ceremony would change anything for me. I was who and what I had become. I was feeling very sad and scared to go through with this thing. My heart was grieving. For what loss, I wasn't sure. I had my doubts.

The shirt was stuffed. I finished stuffing the sleeves, and then I put the two pieces of clothing together. My beloved jean jacket I lovingly put on the dummy of me. I stuffed a head with newspaper made from a stocking of Sonya's and placed the mask over the head. The effigy looked gruesome. It frightened me. The bishop took a deep breath and let out a long whistle.

"How does this feel to you to see this effigy of your past life?" he asked.

"It scares me. It's ugly with the mask on. But I know I must do this, even though I don't totally get what we are doing," I answered quietly in English because I didn't know how to express this in Spanish.

Alfonso put his arms around me and said in his warm, sing-song voice, "My child, you are loved. You are God's gift and are love. You will see! I promise you there is a plan that God has just for you. We *must* clear the way for God's plan to be enacted," he finished emphatically, slapping me gently on the back, like I was an old friend.

On that day, we spent the day building the fire. The kids and I scoured the beach for driftwood. I had my flip flops on now, always, during the daytime hours. Didn't like burning my feet! We built a huge fire, laying the logs very specifically, building it with a triangle first, the Holy Trinity, as the bishop referred to this first layer, Father, Son, and Holy Spirit or in his mountain shamanism the Upper world (Hanaq Pacha), the Middle world (Kaypacha), and the Lower world (Uku Pacha) The next layer goes around beginning with the South, then the West, then North, and at last the East log is placed, standing on its end. These represent the four directions, I was told. Each of the directions represents some aspect of nature which we have available to us for guidance. Pacha Mama, Mother Earth lives in the South, and the animal is "Sacha mama"—the snake that represents shedding skins of the past. The West is the direction of our ancestors. "Mama Killa," Mother Ocean, autumn is the season, representing the great decay. The mammals are the dolphin (joy) and the jaguar (fierce and courageous) that represent the playfulness and mystery of our ancestors' stories, held in our DNA. In the West, we release patterns from our ancestors which impact us still today. In the West, the setting of the Sun closes the day. In the North, we go within. The winter is a time for going deep within one's Soul to commune with God/Goddess/Great Spirit. The eagle is the Spirit representation used to commune with Divine Intelligence/Great Spirit, because of its ability to fly high and pick a mouse off the ground from three miles up. This is the quiet place in the North, where winter urges us to go within; it's represented by this mighty and majestic bird! In the North, visions of (our) becoming are present; like the Bear we must slumber to rejuvenate when winter comes. In the East, Inti Taita, the sun, rises every day. The animal representing the East that metaphorically travels the epic journey on aerodynamically impossible wings is the hummingbird, Sewar Kenti. A beautiful jewel to remind us of the epic journey we Soul's travel in our human form, as experiences of our feelings! I've always imagined they hitched a ride on the back of a goose, nestled in their downy feathers, as they traveled South!

This ritual we were about to begin didn't sound Christian to me, at all. I remembered that the bishop was from Bolivia. He physically looked like he was indigenous. Had a broad, wide face, with nostrils spread wide and his nose was kind of flat. He had full lips and had that twinkle in his eyes. He was very mischievous and good-humored. Poking fun at me in a loving and playful way, getting me not to be so damn self-conscious about everything I did or said.

We placed the effigy sitting on top of the wood. It was kind of balanced on top of the fire with kindling sitting in its lap for a good ignition! The bishop began praying, singing his Quechua prayers and his Christian prayers. They were intertwined, blended beautifully, and sounded supernatural, echoing deep into the dark night, across the Pacific ocean. The wood and kindling were lit, and the sparks were flying high when the effigy of my past burst into flames. I began sobbing. I no longer had those clothes; my identity was going up in flames. I watched, feeling like my soul was being burned, the attachment was so strong. I felt seared inside and out by this ceremony. At the back of my eyes, I felt like I was being burned to death as my life flashed before me. So many frightening events.

After several hours, the family began to leave as the kids needed to get to bed. I turned to go, and the bishop took hold of my hand and gently walked me closer to the fire. "This is YOUR body metaphorically. This is your blood and bones going up into the sky and raining down upon you as ashes. This is Holy Communion in my people's, the old people's tradition, the Inca tradition. These are your memories burning up in smoke. Sit, my child, and enjoy this moment. Sit and listen to the voice within, God's voice, and to our mother's voice, Pacha Mama. Listen to him speak of his love to you. Feel Pacha Mama that you sit on and swim in! You must stay with this fire. This is your life you are asking to be healed transformed by Love. Stay and pray about this." And with this, the bishop heaved his body up off the sand and walked across the beach, with only the light of the moon, toward home.

I sat in the dark, black night, pondering, staring into my fire. I pondered all my actions and the choices that led me to the actions I took. I couldn't seem to see my way clear of being a sinner. Shame lived deep in my heart. It was an evil seed planted long ago, with, now, healthy, deep roots. I felt this truth deep in my bones but had no idea how to access the evil I believed myself to be. How could I tell the bishop this? All of this was just beautiful pretending. Deep within, I believed I was evil. The bishop was blinded by his love for my dad. He didn't see the evil in me because of his great love.

Finally, the embers died down and the last few fizzled out. It was pitch black, and the stars were amazing as I looked up. I hadn't seen so many stars. And there was not one constellation that I could identify. The night sky was totally different from the North American sky. This amazed me as I gazed up. My neck finally started aching. Reticently, I laid down on the beach and stretched my body this way and that, wiggling in the warm sand, still warmed by the day's hot, blazing sun. The sand felt good scratching against my skin. I got into this and began to wriggle and writhe like a snake getting out of my skin. It was so tight. I felt confined, suffocating with the identification I had come to know myself by. Mine was such a small, small, fearful world I had found myself living in.

I closed my eyes tightly. Squeezing them shut and letting out a huge belly sigh, which turned to a moan and then to a low deep growl as rage bubbled up, spewing out of my mouth, like the release of a demon. I vomited and lay writhing in the sand, clutching my belly, sobbing, finally, like a small child.

It was time to go in.

I crept stealthily across the sand, having cooled off now to the soles of my feet. Inside, the house was quiet. Only a candle lit up the room. Our concrete block house was one big room, with curtains dividing all the private spaces. One for Sonya and the bishop and Anaite, and one for the two girls. Ally, short for Alfonso, named after his dad, slept on the couch. I had a small room, with a single bed and a curtain. The bathroom was the only room that had a proper door on it. It was small but cozy. Below us was another big room, which was used for others who may be here for a church conference. It had bunks lining the walls and another small kitchen in the corner. We didn't use this. And there was no one else here except for us. We would be living here a month before we headed back up to the mountains, to Quito, the capital of Ecuador. This was where I'd be spending my year away from home. When we got back to Quito, the bishop and his wife would be leaving for the

United States for a month, to go to a conference. I was to oversee the house and the maid, I was told. This freaked me out. I was reassured and told by Sonya that I'd be fine. Sonya promised to carefully walk me through the running of the household!

The next morning, I woke up feeling pretty damn good. Maybe the fire ceremony and the *despacho* had worked! We went about our normal daily chores. Mine now was not a chore but a delight, which was to sit with the bishop and enjoy our coffee together on the little deck, which overlooked the front yard and out to the ocean. The yard was scrubby. No grass and lots of scrubby beach plants, cactuses and what not. This morning we drank our café con leche, made with black coffee, which was thick like brown ink, mixed with three-fourths of a cup of hot milk. Then sugar was added. And man, this was the way to drink coffee. Same as we had in Costa Rica. I wasn't allowed to drink coffee at home in the United States. Another fuckery and weird inconsistency in my life. As we enjoyed our coffee and I shared my experience of the fire, the bishop invited me to call him Alfonso.

"You are my true spiritual daughter, Inti. I love you as my own and will always care for you and have your best interests in my heart," he said. He took my hand gently in both of his big, warm hands, and kissed them. He smiled broadly, which lit up his whole face. His beautiful eyes changed color from a brown gold to a green then gold as they sparkled with his love. I allowed this feeling to seep into my bones. I felt its warmth trickling down through my body. It awakened in me the mimosa tree memory.

Today, we had a visitor coming to meet with Alfonso. He was one of the bishop's right-hand men at the church he ministered to in Quito. I was invited to walk, talk, and be part of all the discussions that they were having. Alfonso told Teodoro (Ted) that I was his new missionary and the daughter of his best friend, Juanito, little John, his term of endearment for my dad. Ted was to be my right-hand helper, while Alfonso and Sonya were in the United States for September, which was just weeks away. I was nervous about being left in charge of the household, I told my "brother" Teodoro, which was the name he invited me to call him. He was very reassuring with his sweet and friendly demeanor. I noticed that he was playful with the kids, and they loved him. He had brought the kids and me a gift. A box of mangos. "Estos son los mejores," I was told excitedly by the youngest, Tete (Anaite), as she grabbed one out of the box, and handed it to Ted so he could cut the end off. She then wrapped her little hands around the golden-colored mango, and sucked. "Chupa este, Inti. Como asi!"

She handed another one to Ted and he cut the end off and handed it to me. I grabbed a hold of the golden mango, like Tete had shown me, and squeezed the pulp and sucked. I sucked and squeezed many mangos. The meat was sweet, juicy, and dripped down my chin as it transported me back to Costa Rica, my sweet spot. I had never tasted a mango *this* sweet! I loved these. We each must have eaten four or five each day until the box Ted had brought with him was empty. The next morning, right after breakfast, Ted disappeared to his car and brought out a second box, much to our delighted taste buds. I got saturated on mangos until I couldn't eat another.

After Ted's visit ended, our daily routine started up again. We drove to the beach as a family and watched the fishermen come in with their catch. It was always a very colorful sight. Bright shirts, colorful boats, red, blue, yellow, green, and golden. Some boats had frightening faces painted on the bows to ward off danger. The bow-painted ones were little motor boats that came in full of the day's catch. Other men had canoes and came in riding the surf with their fish. It was an exciting time at the beach. I loved all the fanfare, the squawking of the birds and the fishermen yelling out their prices. It was a colorful pandemonium.

One evening, we all piled into the car a bit later than usual and headed for the beach. The day had been a busy one. We went into the small town with dirt streets, past the Majestic Humboldt Hotel brightly lit up, and continued into the town to buy some staples. All the women of the households—well, the maids mostly—were haggling for their family's fresh food and staples. There were also brightly colored woven goods, trekked in by the local indigenous people. Jewelry glittered in the open-air market, and the breeze felt lovely on my skin. Life was good!

Sonya began her haggling, insisting that I pay close attention to her as I would be doing this in Quito, at the big markets, with her maid. Finally, our shopping was done. We met up with the family and headed for the car and home.

By the time we put our basket of fresh goods into the car and gathered the children up again, it was later than we usually arrived home from the fish market! My evening ritual was important to me. Alfonso knew this, as did Sonya. They both instinctively had some reservations when I insisted on heading out to walk the beach home. I would be fine, I assured them. What could possibly happen? It was a 45-minute walk, and the last few minutes were close to home. It would be dark by the time I reached the house. They relented, and I headed out, walking along the water's edge. It was a glorious, sultry warm evening, and I was feeling relaxed and happy for no reason. Just happy! Life was easy here. Most important of all, I felt respected and important for the first time since the death of my uncle Clay. There were a handful of others who really saved my life in high school. I was wandering, musing about my most recent past left behind in Virginia, when suddenly my body started buzzing. My heart began pounding. Trusting the feeling that something was amiss, I turned around to see what I was sensing. Way down the beach was a person walking. I made note of this and continued, unconcerned. He was a speck on the beach in the far distance.

As I walked, my body continued giving me alarming signals, though. Signals I did not understand, as the person was like me, just walking down the beach. I turned around again, a few minutes later, as I was still feeling jittery, and noticed the person had closed the distance on me quite a bit. I picked up my pace while also trying to be casual, relaxing into a quick stride. The rhythm of my stride moved me faster. The tide was rising. The sun was sinking, and I still had a half-hour walk ahead of me. I needed to hustle up. I considered moving onto the road. There was a big ditch I had to cross, and there were no streetlights. The town had no electricity. But the street seemed more dangerous and ominous to me, plus the walk was longer by road.

I picked up my pace even more without running. I didn't want to let whoever was behind me know that I was scared. I heard him call out to me, "Oye. Pare. Yo quiero hablar contigo."

Oh shit. What was he doing so close to me? Did he have silver wings on his feet? "No hablo Espanol," I responded and kept walking, rapidly.

He caught up to me and grabbed my arm. I whipped around and told him again that I didn't speak Spanish. I really did understand what he was saying to me, but I didn't want to engage with him. I tried to pull away, but he was much stronger than I was. He was small in stature but with sinewy, muscled arms. A fisherman, by the smell of both fish and rank body odor. My heart was pounding hard against my chest. Blood was rushing through my brain, creating a haze in my thinking. I was buzzing with terror as I felt him grab my shoulders, tripping me, causing me to fall. I landed hard on the ground, and it knocked the wind out of me. He quickly threw himself on top of me.

I realized my head was facing the ocean, and the tide was coming in fast. With one strong arm placed across my neck, pinning me down, he was ripping off my tank top and had his zipper undone. I couldn't move as I struggled to get him off me. The tide was rising, creeping up. I felt it seeping into my ears as the tide rolled in and rolled out. The water lapped against my cheeks as I struggled, terrified I was going to be raped and then drowned. The waves kissed the sides of my cheeks, and I tasted salt in the corners of my mouth. The waves were very close to entering my nose. I became still as a snake readying to strike. I prayed and surrendered...

Suddenly, I was aware of a loud thundering in my ears. A rumble exploded from deep within, like an earthquake moving through my body. At the same instant, I heard myself call out to the Christ, Jesus: *Help me!* Simultaneously, a superhuman strength flooded my body, mind, and Spirit. I threw the guy off me and leapt off the sand, like I had springs on my feet and wings on my arms. I sprinted out to the road and didn't give him a second look. Here was this big, deep, wide ditch that I had to cross over. I imagined that it was filled with spiders that bite and snakes that slither and were probably poisonous. I couldn't stop. I leapt over the ditch and ran like the devil himself was chasing me. As a car came barreling down the road, I leapt into the ditch, hiding. I imagined the worst, thinking the guy had gotten some of his friends and they were scouring the roadside for me, to finish what he had started. I feared for my life.

I finally reached the house. Alfonso was worried sick, as was Sonya, sitting in the rocker, wringing her hands. Alfonso felt an extra special need to protect me because of his connection with my dad. Both Sonya and Alfonso knew something bad had happened but didn't press me to speak. They waited and cared for me, lovingly giving me space. Sonya undressed me. The whole time she was cooing to me, pampering me, bathing my body gently. The bishop was beside himself with rage. He was blaming himself for not trusting his intuition; instead, he allowed me to walk alone at dusk. Bad things can happen to beautiful young women, he knew. He was deeply remorseful and promised to go out with me the next day to comb the seashore when the boats came in, to find the bastard. I had never seen him so angry. He had steam coming out of his ears. I was ashamed and embarrassed at the predicament I found myself in. Not so different from the old days. Only this time I was viciously attacked and almost killed. I believed if I had not called out to my superpower, the Christ, I would have drowned after I was raped. I recounted to Alfonso about this superpower flooding my body and how I was able to throw the guy off, not just push him off. He went sailing through the air, which gave me enough time to bolt.

Alfonso closed his eyes as he listened, putting his head between his palms. He whispered, "The Spirit of Christ—God—our Father's son, saved you, my child. He filled you with his own power, as your whole being rang out—you were heard. He sent his never-ending love! Let's take a moment and praise God!" He bowed his head in prayer. Some power had filled my whole being, that's for sure.

I finally calmed down enough to go to my bedroom. I pondered Alfonso's words. Why did Father-God allow me to get into these horrible situations in the first place? I was beyond baffled. The *despacho* and fire ceremony were supposed to have magical prayers. It all felt like bullshit, this God stuff. Except that it did save my life. What was I going to do? The chances of finding this guy were nil. All the fishermen were indigenous and had beautiful, prominent cheekbones, dark skin, pointed noses, and sharp, dark, piercing eyes. To me, they all looked so similar, like all the fisherfolk could have been related.

Alfonso and I walked the beach the next day, into town at the allotted time of our shopping excursion. Sonya had the car and the kids. We walked, and he held my hand, assuring me all was well! I wasn't so confident. It was a nice walk. We talked about God stuff again. I shared with him my confusion and anger at God. "Why didn't he protect me? I'm told over and over in church that he does." I was really confused and questioning everything. And very soon I was going to be working in the church. What a freaking joke.

We never found the guy. I didn't think we would. The men all looked the same. I kept walking home on the beach, stuffing my terror, acting as though all was well. What else was I to do? Shelter and hide? Lock myself to the bishop's side and live in fear? No. That was not me. When I was told I couldn't, I did. This seemed to be the motto I found myself living by!

Finally, we packed up the little house on the beach and began our journey up to Quito. The month had ended. Quito was 9500 feet above sea level. It was a long, arduous journey climbing up into the Andes mountains. We had a jeep that was packed to the brim with all our luggage. The road was mostly dirt with rocks strewn across from rockslides. The turns were hairpin turns without shoulders to pull over onto to let other cars pass. The trucks that passed were topped to over the edges with everything from people, chickens, pigs, kids, bags, and who knows what else. Buses were the same. They were loaded to the brim with people and their farm animals just bought at the market or going to the market to sell their stuff. The road was terrifying when we met up with on-coming traffic. One car had to stop and back up, allowing the other to pass, just barely touching. Trucks were another story. I felt like we were going to run off the road several times. So basically, I shut my eyes and just hoped to God that we would make it!

We did.

We climbed from sea level up 9,500 feet to my new home in Quito. It was a beautiful city up in the mountains, nestled in a valley between two huge ridges. Beyond the ridges were three snow-capped mountains, and one was a live volcano, Cotopaxi. All stood majestically, like guardians of the city.

I was going to be broken in quickly as the mistress of the house. Sonya and Alfonso were getting prepared to leave for a month for the Episcopal Diocese of International Bishops Conference and retreat, with some down time at the end. I had the four kids who I was going to oversee. Sonya and Alfonso read them the riot act if they got wind of acting out any mischievous or bad behavior. I was taken to the markets with Sonya every other day to buy our vegetables, meats, fish, chicken, and condiments like rice, dried beans, herbs, and spices that were used in the kitchen. I was introduced to all the vendors and told to be taken good care of. Sonya explained to her favorite and consistent women and men who she had done business with for years, that she was going to be away for a month. She wanted them to help me when I came to the market with the family maid, Ana. They smiled big, toothless smiles, many of them, and nodded their heads, assuring Sonya that they would treat me well. Like one of their own!

The big city market was distinctly different and took up two entire city blocks, making it much larger than the small village market. I had become familiar with the noise of car horns blaring their driver's impatience, children squealing in delight, but the braying, mooing, and squealing from the voices of the livestock present was vastly different than the village fish market. In the country market, they had chickens for sale and maybe a pig or two would come to the village to be sold mostly to the Hotel Humboldt on the hill. The vendors yelling their prices to the people passing by on the sidewalks trying to coax them in was all music to my ears, like a choir with the harmonies all blended! I felt empowered and respected. I was excited to be entrusted with the responsibility of running the household for the month of September.

I was brought to the neighbor's home and introduced to them. Their families were best friends. They were considered Tia and Tio, the children's aunt and uncle. They didn't have children of their own, but they were very active in supporting Sonya with the raising of her family, along with the church work. Tia enjoyed the time she spent with Sonya immensely and loved volunteering at the church. She was thrilled to meet me and assured Sonya that she would take great care of the children and me. How difficult could running the house be when I had a maid who pretty much did everything? I had to be present overseeing the process.

Sonya and Alfonso left on September 1st, 1973.

I would be turning eighteen while Sonya and Alfonso were in the States, on September 25th. This felt a bit sad, as I had no friends to celebrate with. Besides, there was really nothing to celebrate. It was not like I couldn't drink already. There was no minimum drinking age here, same as in Europe when I went to Spain for a month back when I was fifteen. Teodoro got wind that my birthday was just around the corner and knew how important this was to a young person. Eighteen was a benchmark age. Ted arranged for his wife Beth to take me out shopping. My trunk was coming in soon, and Ted would take me to customs to pick it up when it arrived. He wanted me to have something new to wear now, for my birthday!

Beth and I went to the market. I found some beautiful shirts that had embroidery on them of flowers and vines. They were peasant style—a traditional blouse—and I liked them. I bought some earrings and some new blue jeans. I was not willing to live without a pair of Levi's! I bought a knitted wool sweater because it got cold at night. These sweaters were all hand-knitted and were the traditional colors of the alpacas, whose beautiful, soft wool they used. Brown, gray, a creamy white, tan, spun by hand with a traditional drop spindle into rough and nubbly wool, which they knitted into beautiful, warm, water repellent, patterned sweaters. I literally had no clothes as they were all packed away in my trunk. And I loved my big, chunky warm sweater. I loved all my new clothes and felt very feminine in them.

That night, we had a wonderful, traditional dinner at a local, small, family-owned restaurant. The whole family came, plus our neighbors, Tia and Tio. A big cake was brought out, and the whole restaurant sang "Happy Birthday" to me, in Spanish. It was a great night. I was overwhelmed with the love I was receiving. The joy I felt expanding in my chest started to leak from the corners of my eyes. I was happy and felt well-celebrated. I was eighteen! I had made it to adulthood.

Across the street from my home was the National Mounted Police Academy. I walked by it all the time as I caught the bus to go to my Spanish classes at the Universidad Catolica. I became curious and walked over to the fence where there was a big hole from a knot in the wooden fence, having fallen out. The board was broken away. I peered through and saw a young man walking his horse. He spotted me and came over to speak with me. His name was Gabriel. He was Ecuadorian, and his father was a government doctor and kept several horses here at the Academy.

Gabriel was tall, with sandy brown curly hair and a dimple on his right side when he smiled. Gabriel invited me to come visit the school the next day. He was finished riding for the day and was cooling his horse off. He said it would be better if I came tomorrow in the morning.

I was excited. I had ridden horses in Virginia at our friend's home. It was the only thing I was allowed to do for lessons. I had shown in a couple of horse shows before. I didn't do that well competing against girls who had lots of money and connections to the judges and expensive, well-schooled horses. Family ties are thicker in small towns, like blood! I also rode in Costa Rica when I was four and five years old.

The next day, I got up and got all the family's chores done. I gave the maid, our wonderful Maria, the plan for the day of our meals. She always polished the floors by putting Brillo pads on her feet and shuffling around the floors in a systematic pattern. She'd have music playing and be scuffling along, dusting as she moved past the furniture. I loved watching her and learned a great deal about how to have fun cleaning and cooking while running a household. I headed out the door to the Academy. Dressed in my blue jeans and a tee-shirt, I met Gabriel at the entrance. I needed someone to get me in. He took me into the stable area, which was huge. It was a big square arena, with stables going around the entire perimeter. There was a stablehand room, off in the corner of the arena next to the huge tack room that held a hundred saddles. When the entire police force was mounted, there were a hundred strong officers and their subordinates. I was astounded at the size of this Academy, hidden behind the long, tall row of bushes, in front of the seemingly small entrance into the Academia de Caballo de la Policía Nacional. This was where the mounted police were trained for the entire small country of Ecuador. The country had ninety mounted police officers and several hundred more subordinates. Not all the officer's rode at this school. There was another school at the other end of the city. This school also had other privately-owned horses that were boarded by people who worked in the government in some capacity. The doctor, Gabriel's father, was one of these people, as was the only other woman who had a horse here. Her husband had a position as a government lawyer. Otherwise, the school was all male.

There was a dormitory above the entrance, like the top of the letter "T", with the entrance being the horizontal part. This was also for the guys who had long shifts, through the night or worked two-to-three days in a shift before having a day off. I was flabbergasted and impressed to say the least. Gabriel introduced me to his teacher, Fausto Salinas, a lieutenant in the mounted police force. He had slicked back, shiny jet-black hair, super high, sharp cheekbones, a pointed regal nose, and jet-black eyes, with dark, olive-colored skin. He was an indigenous man, for sure. By this time, I'd learned, though, that not everyone was comfortable acknowledging their indigenous blood. Spanish blood was revered here. Most of the people here had roots to the indigenous ancestors of the proud and magical Inca Empire, known for its energy medicine practitioners, and the Shipibo Kneibo jungle people, known as the master herbalists. I loved all the different dialects of Quechua and the sounds of Spanish being spoken so quickly; I was beginning to catch on and able to speak more comfortably. I was still not fluent, but I was beginning to hold my own. I swooned at the strong, sweet smell of the horses, their dung, fresh hay, leather saddles, and sweat.

Fausto caught my eye and winked at me. He immediately thrust out his hand to shake mine.

"El gusto es mío, Señorita Inti. Vamos conmigo y Gabriel a hablar."

He nodded at Gabriel as he led me into the groomsman shitty little hole in the barn, with a bed in the corner and lots of other things; clothes hung on pegs on one wall, boots were lined up against the wall, all well used, and it smelled of horse. Pungent, strong horse smell. And of body odor and dirty dungarees. I was in heaven. I could've done without the strong, rank body odor!

Gabriel translated for me; basically, I was told I could lease a horse that I would care for as my own. I would pay for his feed, which was $60.00 a month. I wasn't sure I could find the money. I told them I would have to come back another day with my answer. Fausto was willing to take me on as his student when I was ready.

Every day I went to the stables and watched Gabriel have his lesson with Fausto through the broken, wooden-slatted fence. I was beside myself with excitement but wasn't sure what the bishop would think and needed to wait until he got home. I also needed to talk with my parents to see if they were willing to increase my monthly allowance. I was also going to begin working for the church when the bishop returned and gave me my assignments, now that I was comfortable and familiar with everything. And with my Spanish, I was seeing improvements every day.

Everything went smoothly, considering I had no idea what I was really doing. Maria, the maid, was great. She basically ran the house, checking in with me for my permission before she began her next detail. I watched her dance happily around the house with pads of steel wool on her feet, shining the beautiful, hardwood floors, clearing the wax off. She said it was faster and easier on her body than being on her hands and knees. I agreed with that! She then would put fresh wax down every week and rub this into the floors on her hands and knees. She finished up with soft buffing pads on her feet, to buff the floors into looking beautiful and new again. This was brilliant creativity at work!

Finally, the bishop and Sonya arrived back home, and the household returned to the new normal.

Chapter 7

Beautiful Pretending

The bishop and Sonya returned home. All was well and in order. The children and I had made a pact not to tell Alfonso and Sonya that Josie, the middle child, had run away from home the second week after her parents had left. She was very strong-willed and didn't like me "ordering" her around. I didn't think I was being Miss Bossy Pants, but maybe it felt like that to her.

I began excitedly telling the bishop and Sonya of my plans to ride next door at the national Police Academy. The bishop was not happy. We argued about this. He said, "You're here to work in the church as a missionary. You are not here to ride horses, Inti."

I disagreed and let him know that he wasn't going to control me like my parents had tried to do. He was livid with me that I was speaking to him in such a way. I didn't care. I'd had a taste of freedom, where I was in charge, and I liked it. I wasn't about to give this up. After three months of arguing every time I left the house to go ride and a fight ensued, the bishop finally gave up and told me I worshiped the horse rather than God. I rode on Sundays because the entire barn saddled up and rode across the city, high up into the majestic Andes mountains. The forests we rode through were tall eucalyptus trees, not native to Ecuador. The smell that filled the air was intoxicating and cleared my sinuses with every inhalation. It was exhilarating through my nose down to the tips of my toes and out through my boots as I hunkered down into my saddle, galloping up a hill in a group with forty riders, tight on the hindquarters of one another. The school ride was a four-hour trek. This was my church experience, being out in nature.

I was starting to realize that being a missionary, for me, was a joke. It was a way for me to leave the country, buying me time with a visa for a year. I still worked at the church. I enjoyed my church work with the kids. But I wasn't a committed missionary, like Dad was.

The bishop was preparing to go to the *oriente*, the jungle, to visit the missions that were along the Rio Napo, a tributary off the Amazon River. I thought that I would be accompanying him. We discussed this, but he put his foot down. "No," was his definitive answer. It was final.

But why? I pestered Alfonso. Finally, he told me that if he brought me with him, the chief would consider me a gift, and I wouldn't be able to return with him. He sighed, his eyes twinkled, and he said, "Your father would kill me. I can't break his heart, Inti. I know their ways. You would have to stay. You will not be coming on this trip, my dear Inti. I am sorry. I truly am." I felt he was genuinely sorry that I wouldn't be traveling with him. I knew he loved me to accompany him on his visits to his more rural missions, way out in the countryside.

One night, after the bishop returned from his *paseo*, I was told by Alfonso that a certain minister was struggling with loneliness and he wanted me to be his friend and accompany him to dinner, giving him some female companionship. He was British. His wife was Ecuadorian and had just given birth. Her husband was feeling quite depressed as his wife was struggling with postpartum feelings of despair. He asked me if I would be ok entertaining him for the evening. "You'll be taken to a nice restaurant. He'll take you dancing if you want. I want you to be a good friend, and good dinner company, and give him good conversation. Ok, Inti?"

"Sure, I'll do that, for you, Alfonso." I figured we'd go to dinner, maybe dance, but I found most Anglo men didn't enjoy dancing the way I did. Maybe he'd just talk about his struggles. I had no idea what his "struggles" were, just that he was unhappy, which wasn't how the bishop wanted his missionary to be feeling.

Unhappiness caused problems within the clerical community.

I got driven to what I believed was Father Phillip's house. But it was pretty much unfurnished. I was puzzled, as I knew his wife had just had a baby, so this couldn't be their home. And if it wasn't, where were we? Why were we meeting here and not at a restaurant?

I was confused when I was dropped off by Father Ted, a person I trusted, and was greeted by Father Phillip, a stranger. I wasn't feeling safe, but I remained silent, with a fake smile plastered to my face. Ted told me that Father Phillip would bring me home after we were finished. Finished? That felt like a strange word to use! Finished eating dinner, at whatever restaurant we would be going to, Ted must have meant to say.

He asked me to call him Phillip as Ted was leaving. Still standing in the dimly lit apartment, I was struggling within because it didn't seem like Phillip was intending to leave anytime soon. He reached for me and drew me quickly into his arms. He whispered into my ear how long it had been since his wife had been pregnant and now had just given birth. "It's been forever, and I feel like I am going to die from this need," he said, his voice husky. His cock was rock hard against my body. He began kissing me.

I was not into this. I struggled to get away, pushing on his chest to separate us. But he had an iron grip around me and squeezed me hard, making it hard for me to take a breath. He was panting and struggling with one hand to open his zipper. He then fought me to work one hand around my waist while the other pulled my panties off. I hadn't worn my jeans tonight.

"Wear something feminine tonight, Inti, not your favorite blue jeans. Something more appropriate," the bishop had smoothly and tenderly requested.

I came dressed in one of the pretty peasant dresses purchased on my birthday shopping spree. It was not hard to get my panties down while pinned up against the wall, feeling like I was going to suffocate from his weight against me.

What was the point in fighting? I knew I wasn't going to win this fight.

I finally surrendered, making it easy for him. I left my body and hovered above, leaving my body weightless. He lifted me effortlessly up as he braced himself, placing his legs solidly in a semi-squat position and placed me directly above his sword, sticking out from britches that had been dropped to the ground but were still around his ankles. His cock was stiff as a rod. He plunged me down on him and began lifting me up and down as he raped me. It was over in minutes. He pulled out and ejaculated all over the floor. I was disgusted, irate, and ashamed. I ran into the bathroom and washed myself for what seemed like thirty minutes.

What the hell just happened? What was this night about? A damn set up to "pleasure" this poor priest because his wife hadn't in months. I was pissed. I couldn't tell the bishop about this. He couldn't have possibly known of Phillip's intentions. Could he have? Had the bishop's opinion of me changed since I had insisted on riding? Did he see that as a "slap in the face" from me? I was shaken to my core and horrified. I felt dirty and black as the night enveloping me, inside.

Now Phillip, the asshole, was ready to take me out to dinner. I was still feeling sick to my stomach and didn't have an appetite. He spent his money, pleading with me to not say anything. "This is just a special little something you and I experienced. No need to tell anyone else about it, right?"

He was so pitifully grateful to me for relieving his pressure. He didn't know how he was going to manage much longer and was frustrated with his wife for taking so much time to "heal." He said the last word in a mocking tone. I sat silently through the whole dinner, moving my food around the plate from one side to the other. I said nothing. If I had spoken, I would have spewed fire on his sorry ass. And then I'd be the one to get a "bad" report from him to the bishop.

What was this game I was embroiled in? I always felt like a victim. But wasn't I giving permission just by going out, as was requested of me? It seemed like that was some sort of permission. Why did the bishop ask me to "be his friend"? And was there an intention in that request that went over my head that just men understood? I was twisted into confusion and burning up inside with rage.

Somehow, I faked it and acted as though nothing had happened. I didn't know what else I could do or who I could talk to. I thought about mentioning this incident to Teodoro, as he had been appointed as my "guardian" of sorts. So, I decided that was a good idea.

I invited Teodoro to go out to lunch with me one day, to talk about church stuff. I wanted to start a new program for the kids, I told him. We met at a small, local bodega, owned by one of the families in the church. They'd turned their dining room into a small restaurant of six tables and usually fed the bishop when some of his missionaries came into town. The food was delicious and inexpensive. The family was super friendly to us.

We sat over in the corner. My back was facing the wall. I had a bird's eye view of the restaurant and always felt safer when sitting in the corner. For some reason I never sat with my back to the door. I wanted to see everything and everyone coming and going.

I began by asking questions about Phillip and his wife to find out a little more about him and his life. Teodoro spoke candidly and said that he had a hard time with fidelity. His wife seemed cold, a bit of a prude possibly, and she was uptight, while Phillip was a bit of a wild card. A party boy and a hell of a good priest. But he did have a wild hair that got up his ass, and when that happened, he couldn't keep his pants zipped up.

So, I told him about my little encounter. He looked at me with a blank stare.

"Damn. I feel awful that you fell prey to him. I can't imagine the bishop knowingly setting you up like that. But how can the bishop not know of his indiscretions? We all do. But maybe Alfonso doesn't or didn't think he would bother you," he replied, apologizing profusely to me. He was sad to admit that he wasn't surprised at all. Nothing else would be done. It was never to be mentioned again to anyone. It seemed there was simply nothing I could do. Teodoro said if I didn't like his attention, then I was to steer clear of him. "Don't engage with him, and don't give him any attention. He will find another, more appropriate woman. You are not her!" He finished up his lunch and seemed to be about ready to leave. "I'm really very sorry, Inti. It is really shameful that nothing gets done."

Teodoro then confided in me that he was gay and not happy in his marriage. Oh shit, I thought. This was going to cause a major problem. Ted was the right-hand man for Alfonso. If he was not happy and was thinking about getting divorced, that would devastate the bishop.

Ted talked with Alfonso a few weeks later. He didn't share with him that he was gay. This was taboo and as a priest it wouldn't be good PR for the church's diocese, at all. Beth, Ted's wife, was totally freaked out and distraught. She was returning home to her family to give Ted some time to think about all of it. She didn't want to get a divorce but couldn't stay and live with Ted. Beautiful pretending was not Beth's game. She was honest to the core, loving, funny, and a great mama. But she wouldn't just sit by with this as her new reality. She wanted Ted to be happy. He needed to choose, and she needed to leave for a while. Maybe she'd be back. At this point, she was not sure of anything. I would miss her. She had been my ally! I wondered if I should disclose to her what happened between Phillip and me? I thought better of it. She would break my silence and tell the bishop and then proceed to tell Phillip off, right in front of his wife. Nope. I couldn't cause that kind of an explosion. There was already enough chaos. Why did this shit always feel like it was my fault? The adult world was so convoluted and a confusing world to navigate.

Chapter 8

Am I an Unpaid Prostitute?

My interest in church activities and my job as a missionary began to feel threatened. My deeper Self (was this my God Self?) was really loving the horses and all the barn activity. I was happy and believed I was thriving, having made the decision to lease a horse and put myself on a limited budget to buy feed for my horse. Gabriel was angry with me because Fausto had committed all his teaching time to me. He told Gabriel that he could ride on his own and compete if he chose. He would still coach him, but he was good enough to ride and be committed to his own journey, checking in occasionally with him, as needed.

When I first began riding, my Spanish for the language of the equestrian world wasn't fluent at all. So many new words around riding and the horses, the drills he wanted me to do, the proper leg position, and pressure of the leg. And then there were my hands and how to position them. It was an exciting time for me, and I was soaking it all in. Fausto spoke no English and didn't understand squat. Neither did the barn hand, Roberto. My horse, Garua, was huge. He was eighteen hands, which meant I came up to about the middle of his belly. I needed a step up to get on his back. He was jet black and gorgeous, with a white star on his forehead. A big gelding! He had a wonderful gait which felt like a rocking chair, and he was a "pacer." The saddles were different. The "balance" seat, keeping your ass in your saddle, glued to your horse was new to me, as I had been riding a classic English "hunter" seat.

Gabriel got over his anger eventually and translated still for me. I met with him once a week to go over the new words I was learning and asked him to clarify drills that I was being asked to do. Gabriel and I became good friends, and he didn't let his hurt feelings get in the way. I was sensitive to his ego getting bruised being displaced by me. That couldn't feel good to a young man in this Latin culture where men rule. The women were revered, don't get me wrong. But it was the accepted norm for men to have mistresses. The wives seemed to accept this, justifying their husbands need to satisfy their virility. They were happy to have sex go elsewhere if they were good fathers, husbands, and good providers.

It wasn't long before I was riding every day for several hours. We gave the horses and ourselves one day of rest on Sunday. Since it was Sunday, I could go to the church, run the Sunday School program and show up, supporting the bishop. The bishop was happy to have me back in church on Sundays. I was sad that the Sunday Academy ride had stopped for some reason, unknown to me. I missed the terrifying thrill of clinging to the neck of my horse as he followed close on the tail of another, galloping up the steep eucalyptus-forested hills. We still had school rides across the wide-open fields on our "fox" hunts. Zorro, the one we chased with a fox's tail attached to his saddle, was dressed in black and seen off in the distance as a silhouette on the ridge, cape flying as he galloped across. Veering our horses as someone spotted Zorro, we'd head off in a different direction, chasing the illusive Zorro. It was great fun, and we never caught him.

Fausto began to groom me right away to become his mistress. I didn't realize this, but other officers must have. Gabriel must have known this, too. Maybe that's why Gabriel was so angry at Fausto. But no one said a word to me. I found out that the dormitory was also used as a "safe" place to take their mistresses. The officers would spread the word that the dorm was in use, and all stayed away. I didn't know any of this at the time. I later found this out by becoming part of the scene. I believed I was an innocent woman with intentions to ride. Anything else was not on my radar. It should have been, with the life I had lived so far. But it just wasn't.

• • •

One day, as I was walking home from my classes at the university, I felt a car following me. I had ten blocks to walk to catch my bus. I loved walking and being enveloped by the cacophony of sounds in this busy city. I also loved people watching and clothing looking, noticing the variety of colorful clothing people wore. It was much livelier here than what I remembered about the USA and our big cities. Black was the color worn by many in big U.S. cities. Well, I knew New York. The slums of New York. And everyone seemed to wear black. Except for my beloved, Maria Carmona. I felt the prickles on the back of my neck and the hair on my arm standing stiff. My breath was shallow as I became increasingly frightened. Unsure of what to do and beginning to panic, I walked out into the middle of the thoroughfare and stopped at one of the many police podiums placed in the middle of the road with an officer in it, directing traffic. I told him I was being followed by a car full of men. He shrugged and said, "If I were off duty, I'd be in that car following you, too."

Oh, that filled me with confidence! I couldn't even trust police officers to protect and serve! They wanted to just "service" their needs.

After the last episode, I took a side street thinking to avoid being followed. Well, that didn't go as planned. I was walking fast, enjoying the hot sun, the stucco and adobe homes, the vegetation around me was lush and colorful, when again my heightened awareness felt a car stalking me. Sure enough, a car full of men was coming in and moving at my pace beside me. One guy jumped out of the front seat just as it rolled to a stop. He tried to grab me by the arm. I somehow managed to slither away and veered to my right, running up to the closest front door. Furiously, I rang the bell. The door opened. Lo and behold, standing in the doorway was my history teacher from the Universidad Catolica, Jim. What a miracle! He took me into his home. The car roared off. And I was safe. I recounted my experience to him, trembling all over as I shared my story. My body felt like a volcano boiling over as the shudders got huge and shook my body uncontrollably. I was sobbing. Years and years and years of mistreatment burst free, like a torrential downpour, saturating the dry, parched land. I cried my heart out. Poor Jim. He probably didn't know what had hit him…

I finally pulled myself together after a nice, hot cup of coca tea to soothe my wounded heart and settle my nerves. It tasted great, with its slightly bitter taste and slippery feel on my palette. It relaxed me. My teacher, Jim, drove me home.

I rode the next day at the Academy. I told Gabriel about my ordeal and this story he recounted to Fausto. Fausto, livid, then assigned me a police vehicle with a driver who picked me up from my home—the bishop and Sonya's home—and drove me to school.

When the police car arrived the first time, the bishop saw it through the window and looked at me askance. "WHAT ARE YOU DOING TO GET THIS KIND OF SPECIAL TREATMENT?" he yelled at me, very uncharacteristic of this gentle warm, caring soul. I said nothing. My heart felt like it was going to pound right out of my chest. When I calmed my nerves and tamped down the imploding anger, I told him about getting accosted, twice, and miraculously, the second time, being right at my history teacher's home. Fortunately! Which was why he drove me home yesterday. I then told the bishop that I shared the incident with my instructor, who was furious with his officer's response and relieved that I had the good fortune to knock on the right door and get to safety.

"He offered to give me a driver to keep me safe. That's it. Nothing else is going on," I explained to the bishop, trying to maintain a forced, calm composure.

He didn't buy it and assured me I would be expected to repay him for this kindness. *What does it matter,* I wondered. *You set me up with that asshole minister who raped me. What does it matter if Fausto has this in mind as well?*

I didn't speak my truth. Having been so long silenced I automatically chose not to vocalize what I was thinking.

By this time, I have been in Ecuador for three months. I needed to move out. I couldn't stand fighting with the bishop. I loved him and Sonya so much and felt awful. Their kindness and warmth wasn't being respected or appreciated by me. I was not the missionary they had hoped I would be. I felt ashamed of myself, perpetually.

During my time at the University, I had met a few women and made friends with them. Three of us decided we were going to rent an apartment together. I dropped this bomb on the bishop and Sonya, and he said nothing. He turned back to his reading and didn't acknowledge me at all. I got the "evil" eye from his twinkling eyes, and he gave me the silent treatment until I moved out. I walked around with what seemed like a rock in the bottom of my stomach. I had become invisible to Alfonso.

Our furnished apartment had three bedrooms. I somehow got the master bedroom, at the back of the apartment. There was a living room at the front, and we lived over top of a little bodega, which opened at 5:00 a.m. for the workers. We had a small, adequate kitchen, and two bathrooms. I had one in the master bedroom. I shared this since it had a big double sink, which kept all our rents evenly divided.

One of my roommates was a sweet, caring, gentle soul. She was from the Midwest, had long, brown hair, was a good student, and had a steady, happy personality. She was neat and always helpful and pulled her weight. The second woman, Heidi, was engaged to an Ecuadorian oiler working for Exxon. He was down in the jungle for the year. She was bored and lonely and I found out she was like a wild cat, uncontrollable, and lived a precarious, high risk-taking life. I don't remember where I met her. Maybe in Spanish class. She was a flake. She had a wide, open face, and was always smiling and laughing. She was a party girl to the max and, evidently, it didn't matter that she was engaged. Just no sex was her rule... even though she figured her novio was having affairs in the jungle, knowing how Latin men were. I had to agree with her on that one. Heidi was a slob and had little respect for others' boundaries. She'd eat everyone's food and laugh about the "mistake." She never cleaned up the messes she made in the kitchen. And it was a big mistake to share my bathroom with her. She was disgusting, leaving her menstrual pads just lying in the trash can, open, not wrapped up. She was a pig, really. And I was no neat freak myself. But her filth was disturbing, and I was disappointed that she was my roommate.

Oh well! That's how life went!

Three weeks later, Jane's father died. She had to take an emergency flight home.

I was sad and was going to miss her. Now it was just Heidi and me. She was a wild card, I was discovering. She went out all the time, had guys constantly coming back to the apartment with her, and didn't seem to give a shit about the fact that she was engaged to her honey in the jungle, Jose. Jose would shit his pants if he knew about his woman's behavior. My mouth was closed. I had never met him, and it wasn't my problem. I had my own.

I was still in contact with Sonya. But Alfonso never acknowledged me again. I had let him down, and it weighed heavily on his heart, because he felt like he had let my father down, his best friend. He was deeply concerned for my Soul, I found out from Sonya after having a heart-to-heart conversation with her. She was kind, understanding, and I always felt she was respectful of me and my boundaries, even when I messed up.

I was invited over for Christmas. I received a beautiful piece of hand-woven, wool fabric Sonya bought for me. The children each made something for me, and I had gifts for everyone, too. I wrote a poem for the bishop, as his gift. I had it framed and gave it to him. He received it graciously, and I was grateful for this.

I hadn't spoken with my parents since I had left on the first of September; that was our agreement. The calls were too expensive and Christmas time was the agreed upon first call home. My parents and I exchanged long letters to one another. I looked forward to receiving their letters as they responded to mine. My letters were colorful and descriptive and were six or seven pages or longer as I described everything in vivid detail, so curious was I about life here, the differences, and the similarities.

I dialed their number. It was great to hear their voices. For a few minutes, the call was great. Then Dad got on the phone alone and started in on me for moving out and making his friend so uncomfortable. How dare I be so disrespectful to them having welcomed me into their life when I had made such a mess of my life back in the States? This trip and job as a missionary were supposed to give me a new lease on life and get me on a better path. He was disappointed that his plan hadn't worked. He was embarrassed for himself. It felt like he didn't care one iota about my feelings. I was sad. Nothing had changed back home, it seemed.

The call ended. I was sick to my stomach and had no appetite for the delicious meal Sonya and Ana had prepared together. The table was beautifully laid, with garlands, candles twinkling, and the traditional, handmade bread dough figures decorated a small tree that sat in the center of the table. The table was laden with a beautifully prepared meal of roast goose, various meats, potatoes, and vegetables, but I had no desire to eat. The dinner conversation was stiff as the bishop wasn't acknowledging me. Sonya tried hard to make light of it all.

I returned home to my little apartment and to a hot mess of a roommate. She had gone down to the jungle to be with her *novio* who had a week off from the oil drilling rig. She came home, and life continued in the routine I had set for myself. I continued riding and had my first big event coming up. I was riding all the time, several hours a day, practicing flying over the jumps, and using my body weight and leg pressure to work with the "flying changes," which meant the horse changes leads in midair, landing on the opposite foot, and ready to change directions, making it the "flying change." At one point, Fausto put me up on his horse, a big, chestnut gelding who was a powerful jumper. He was jumping five-foot jumps, with no hesitation. Fausto wanted to see what I could do with him, as I was much lighter in the saddle. He was considering me riding his horse in the upcoming show.

I cantered around and around, feeling into my horse's gate, until I was ready and we were in sync. I then urged Rojo, using my leg pressure, with a kick to his side, moving my hands to shorten up the reins, rising out of my saddle to give Rojo his head, legs pressed tightly against my horse's flank, as we headed for a monstrous jump. We flew over the jump, effortlessly. Around, and around again, and again we cantered. Each time clearing the jumps with no problem. It was a steamy hot day. We rode dressed in full riding gear. Our boots were spit-shined every day, I had my breeches on, and a hack riding jacket. My brain, encapsulated in the black helmet, felt like it was melting from the heat. No jeans and tee-shirts were allowed, and dirty boots were a big no. It was hot under my helmet.

One more run around the course was asked of my horse and me. Midway over the jump, I fainted and fell off the horse. I landed hard. Miraculously, the horse's hooves landed pretty much straddling my body. From the distance, from where

Fausto was standing and the angle he watched from, his breath caught in shock as he thought I was dead. He later told Gabriel that it looked like the horse's hooves had landed right on me and he thought I was dead.

When I came around, I was told to get back up on the horse and do it again. So that I wouldn't "grow fear." If I didn't do this, the seed of fear would take root and stop me from ever jumping again. I was jumping five and a half feet! Those jumps were taller than I was, at 5'2".

He was right. I was scared. I climbed back into the saddle, getting a leg up, and began circling again, getting the horse and I synched up. I only had to jump the course once, and then I was done for the day. Fausto was trying to decide if he was going to put me on his horse or not, for the upcoming show. My debut!

To ride in this competition, I had to have my formal riding gear custom made for me. Down through the narrow city streets, Fausto and I were driven to a hole-in-the-wall shop, down an alleyway, to the police tailor. This was where all the uniforms for the officers were custom made. The shop included several rooms with several seamstresses sitting at their machines, I saw as I poked my head, curiously looking past the main measuring room. It was hot. The women who were handling the dark, olive green, wool gabardine for the uniforms were sweating bullets in their stuffy work environment. I was measured, shown fabric I could use, and picked out what I wanted for my coat and breeches. These would be finished in a couple of days. When I returned to pick up my *vestidos*, I had to try on everything before I left, to make sure no adjustments were needed. When I put on my custom-stitched clothing I swooned and felt like royalty. Decked out in my stunning cherry red jacket with a black velvet collar and white breeches, I was looking in the full-length tailor's mirror at one hot tamale. She was staring back at me, feeling full of excitement at the V.I.P. treatment I was receiving. To finish my formal gear for the upcoming show, I had a white blouse with lace cuffs and a front lace insert, completing my riding habit. And of course, my knee-high black boots were spit-shined and glistened in the sun.

The day of my big event was exciting. The National Academy was filling up with spectators filing into the school's formal arena. I had never ridden in this arena, up until a few days ago. We were allowed to do practice runs, to see what it felt like to be in the big arena.

My show day had arrived. My heart was pounding in my chest like the steady beat of a drum. I thought I was going to implode with nerves and excitement. My palms were sweaty, and my armpits started to stink. There was a buzz racing through the throng of people, entering the arena, jostling, and pushing to find seats. The arena had bleachers, but people preferred to sit up close, and it felt personal! As I was walking to the barns to check in, a diminutive, beautiful, dark-haired woman holding a child's hand in each of hers approached me. When she got right up in my face, I tried to excuse myself as I was headed to the barn to get ready to ride. She blocked my leave and asked me if I was Fausto's American student?

"Yes," I answered her, looking at the two small children she had in tow. "I'm Inti. Who are you?"

In the next moment, she filled with anger. I saw it in her eyes, welling up. She basically spat the words out at me, "He told me you were short, fat, and ugly. You are beautiful! He lied to me!" she said rapidly in Spanish.

I was a bit confused as to why he would blatantly lie about my looks to this woman. I now assumed that this was Fausto's wife and kids. I knew when I asked him if he was married and he continually said "no," that it was odd for a Latin man, at his age, thirty-three, to not be married. I'd been lied to by him, but also by all the fellow officers, because I had asked them the same question. It just didn't make sense that he was single. But a lie was a lie, and I had believed them, against my better judgment.

I was rattled by this. Soon Fausto came looking for me. As he approached me to prepare me for my competition, I challenged him with the episode I had just experienced. He waved his hand and spit. "Eso no es nada," he said. He told me she would be jealous if he told her the truth. This would cause him a headache that he didn't need. "Todo esta bien," he finished.

"Now take this shot of whiskey," he told me, "to calm your nerves, and then get your ass on your horse and focus. You are about to represent me, and our school, as the first American woman to compete here, nationally, for Ecuador, on our team.

Focus. Get on your horse and focus." He pointed his two fingers at his eyes to emphasize the "focus" word.

I was weighed in. Two bags of sand were added to my saddle's blanket. I had to weigh in at around the same weight as my competitors.

The show was on. My name, "Inti Kelley, la Americana," was called, and I trotted into the arena; all eyes were on me. I was feeling nervous but confident in my ability to be a good competitor and give the guys a run for their money. I had a good round in the beginning. I heard someone yell at me. It broke my FOCUS. I took the next jump the wrong way and had to circle back around to finish the course heading in the right direction. That cost me precious time, as we were competing against the clock. The rest of my run was excellent. That mistake put me into fourth place. Still, I was happy. It was my first major show, ever. I had relearned how to ride in the short time I had been training under Fausto. When I first got up in the saddle, he yelled continuously at me that I didn't know what I was doing. I had to forget what I had learned in the U.S. about riding English. This hurt my ego in the beginning. But I soon realized that the balance seat was different. I was sitting in the saddle, moving my hips (like sex, as my instructor had shown me the movement while on the ground). Front and back the pelvis moved, staying in the saddle with the horse's gait, as if glued to the saddle. It really was different than in the States, where I was jumping and riding "the hunter" seat, where your ass is out of the saddle as you canter. Posting was the same. But the leg communication was totally different, and much more directed to the horse, joining in union. I felt the difference and was becoming a great rider. I was a natural.

By now, Fausto was becoming way more intimate with me during our training sessions. I remembered one time he told me to tell him when my period began. I was mortified. Why on Earth would he need to know that? When I challenged him with my question, he simply replied, "A woman can't ride when she is bleeding. Her legs are weaker, and the horse knows this. She could get hurt." Wow! This was news to me, but I obliged and skipped my next couple of lessons when my period started. I had already been riding for several months mind you, and my muscle strength was growing, not weakening. But what did I know about the finer details of a horse's sensitivity?

When I returned to my lessons, Fausto was happy to see me. I did not know this at the time, but Fausto had calculated in his head when I was able to have sex without a pregnancy. Ecuadorian men knew these things evidently... I sure didn't.

The first time Fausto took me to the dorm rooms to show them to me, he also managed to get me onto the bed that he said was his. It was a little cubby hole of a room. It did afford a bit of privacy, as he was an officer, not a regular cadet. Fausto didn't have to fight me. I wasn't up for the fight. I had surrendered to the fact that I was an unpaid prostitute, who got "favors" instead of money, like Fausto having his patrol car pick me up and drop me off anywhere I wanted to go. I also knew this was Fausto's way of keeping tabs on me, as I had become fearful of just being out on the streets. My blond hair and blue eyes seemed to be a neon light. I didn't know this at the time, of course. Another underlying factor, which I didn't know at the time, was that my "victim, shame, and guilty" girl was in control with a neon light flashing.

Fausto grew in his amorous and preferential treatment of me. The other officers knew me as "his woman." It was hands off to all of them, and they respected this. I loved my time with Fausto. He and I took long rides through the countryside, crossing the city proper, and rode up into the eucalyptus forests. The strong smell of eucalyptus was intoxicating. Arriving at the top of the ridge, which surrounded Quito, we looked down into the next valley over. It was an amazingly beautiful and exciting time for me. I felt like I was on top of the world sitting astride my horse under a crystal, clear, blue sky. Sometimes we'd undress and make love right there in the field full of blooming and aromatic flowers. Every now and then a sheepherder would happen upon us, humping like two rabbits. I loved being on the horse for hours and hours, riding to our destination and home again. Often, we'd mosey down at a slow pace, enjoying the air-infused eucalyptus, nostrils flaring, like my horse, from the strength of the air being inhaled. Fausto knew many people and we'd stop, tie our horses up, and eat in small, local bodegas where the food was cooked and served from the family's kitchen. No Federal Food and Drug administration here, regulating for cleanliness and sanitary conditions, but the food was savory and delicious. Simple meals prepared with love and intention, and whatever food was local. I promised myself that I'd try everything once before I decided if I liked something or not. I was also not told ahead of time what I was eating. My taste buds expanded greatly during these educational and thrilling rides.

On other *paseos*, Fausto had access to a jeep which was there for the officers to use on their off days. On these days, we ended up in some weird little motel with a garage, which were mostly booked for a couple of hours. The car remained hidden during this time, parked in a closed-in garage, making it all discreet and private. Payoffs happened. It was a way of life for the people here. Mistresses were no big deal if the family was cared for and provided for. The prostitution of women was accepted. I grew in my understanding and saw women's roles as "mistresses" as "sacred," as they were evidently needed and fully embraced by the social system of their country. At least it appeared so. I never talked with a native woman about this and would have loved the opportunity to do so! Men had mistresses, so what.

The next big event that was coming quickly at the Academy was a national parade celebrating the president. All the horses and their riders would be transported by train across the countryside to be in a parade. I was to ride at the head of the parade, leading the School of Officers and their subordinates, as a mascot. Whew... this was going to be a trip to remember, of this I was certain.

The train arrived at our destination. All the horses were unloaded, fed, and tended to before we tended to our own needs. After this, we went to a big government hostel of some sorts. I was rooming with Fausto and his superior, Coronel Domingo. He was a big, burly man, and was enjoying thinking of me as his "roommate." Oh my God, this was awkward for me. Was he expecting something from me? And knowing that he had the power over Fausto, would nothing be done to stop him? Was this some new scene I had to deal with? I had become good at beautiful pretending, acting as though all was well, when clearly it wasn't, and I wasn't. Thankfully the night was quiet, and I slept deeply snuggled between two men snoring loudly.

The president's parade went well. I was quite the "looker," causing heads to turn as we paraded through the city. We passed by the stand where the president was sitting and stopped. The national anthem was blaring, the Ecuadorian flag was flying high and snapping in the wind. The president stood while being saluted by his mounted military police force. There was a formation that was flanking out around me, allowing me to be at the head. I stood stock still, sitting on my horse as officers and their horses moved into formation. It was beautiful. I felt amazingly proud and filled with a sense of self-importance. I wasn't really an important presence. But I believed I was. I wasn't stupid; I knew I was a beautiful, sparkly ornament. And on that day that felt just fine with me! It was a feeling I'll have forever!

That night, we were invited to a formal dinner and dance in honor of the president and his military, which, at that time, was the National Police Force. The dinner was for officers only. I went on Fausto's arm, dressed in a beautiful, long burgundy evening gown, with a peek-a-boo collar right at my collarbone, leaving my cleavage exposed. I exuded femaleness, finishing my dress wearing a stunning antique brooch at my throat, gifted to me by my grandmother, Mamma. It was delicate, with finely braided hair wrapping around a circle of itsy bitsy seed pearls, set into a beautiful filigree case.

During these events, I was told, the president also gave out commendations and promotions. Fausto was honored and became a *capitan*! He was a proud boy strutting his stuff like a cock in the hen house! All his buddies congratulated him and had a party in his honor that night. In the several days that we were in this small city, showing the country's forces to the president, Fausto disappeared, returning only for the events he had to attend, now in his new position as captain. He was not around during the daytime hours, except to ride when we had some place we had to show up with the horses. I was "assigned" to two of his buddies, to be watched over. They did a good job of it, taking me around and making sure I was ok, happy, and seeing the sights. His buddies told me Fausto was off visiting another mistress he had in this city. I didn't care. This had become so normal and ordinary to me—mistresses, sex, whistling, and hearing comments made about me and at me, all the time. I had grown a thick lizard's skin and was also a skilled chameleon.

Shortly after returning home, Fausto drove me out to the country on his next day off. We arrived at a beautiful piece of land, which overlooked a valley, about thirty-to-forty minutes out of the city. The land was a bit out of the way but had lovely, soft, rolling hills, with a view of the valley below. Fausto was telling me he had recently purchased this land and was going to build a home for me to live in. By now I was fluent in Spanish. *No, I will not live here,* I heard my Self say to myself.

"If you expect me to be your mistress and live here alone while you are away playing with your other ladies or spending time with your family, you are sorely mistaken," I said to him in smooth, fluent Spanish. I continued, "I can be happy living alone while you are away. I can take a lover, just as you can." I watched his black, piercing eyes narrow as they flashed anger. "No soy Ecuatoriana. Soy Americana." I took a breath to settle my fear and continued, "En mi país es diferente."

He did not agree with me. He was angry and hurt. Why did he feel so betrayed? I wasn't committed to him. There was nothing in the relationship for me, other than to service him. I was angry and insulted. Flattered on some level maybe, as this had stroked my ego and made me feel wanted. But I knew myself and there was no way I was going to sit in a house in the country twiddling my fingers and playing with myself, waiting for his return. Nope! Not happening!

I continued to ride. He continued to teach me, but I was no longer his mistress. I had made that clear. I was done playing Miss Mistress. He adjusted and was cordial with me, flirty, and still protective. I just didn't go any further with him. And he didn't press me. Surprisingly.

Inti jumping Garua in her first show

Chapter 9

I Think I've Met My Twin Flame

My crazy roommate, Heidi, was all excited one day after I had returned from the barn. She was chattering away about how she had met a guy who was wicked cool. He was a producer of new, young musicians and was sponsoring a show soon. This guy had invited Heidi to go. She, of course, had said yes, and then he asked her to bring a friend along, as his business partner was also going. Heidi immediately began pestering the shit out of me. Bugging my ass, following me around the apartment, and pleading with me. I reminded her that she was "engaged" to be married... She said that her man was fooling around and so could she. Oohh! I said, knowing this was total bullshit, that it was okay for her to be prowling around and sleeping with any guy. Her *novio* would flip. Even if *HE WAS DOING IT*, it didn't matter! She couldn't. Finally, after two days of relentless pestering, I gave in. We would be flying in the morning on a small private jet to another city in Ecuador. Ok. I was getting excited to go hear some up-and-coming great musicians and to see another part of Ecuador. I was uneasy with the guy/girl set up. It was obvious what was expected of me... I could only imagine what Heidi had promised...which obviously created a connection to whatever friend Heidi brought along. Me! We'd see about that.

• • •

The day we landed it was warm and balmy. We landed in the coastal city of Ambato. The air was claustrophobic, with steam rising off the sidewalks. But I was excited to be there. The two guys were nice enough. They were both super good looking and well dressed. Their hair was greased back, as seemed to be the style, and they were polite with Heidi and me.

We got to the theater early to make sure all was well with time to kill. Heidi and I walked around the streets for a little bit and checked out the shops, etc., while the promoters saw to their singers' needs. The show would start at 8:00 p.m.

When we returned, we were led down to the front of the majestic, old theater, where front row seats had been reserved for us. Heidi and I were thrilled. I couldn't believe our good fortune. The singers came on, one by one. They did short sets of three to four songs, and then there was the finishing act: Sergio and Julio, a duet. The blending of the two voices was in perfect harmony. The energy these two gorgeous young men created was palatable. I was swooning. They wrote their own songs, which were songs of romance and love, songs of the heart. I completely melted in my seat as I stared at Sergio. I was not able to take my eyes off him. I tried. Heidi tried to talk to me. I'd answer, but my mind was elsewhere. I was awe-struck by this gorgeous man and his voice. He had brown, wavy hair, big brown eyes, and a beautiful smile that lit up the place. His songs were so tender in their seeking to know *love*. Real, true *love*.

Midway through Sergio and Julio's singing, I began to feel my body get super-heated up. Sergio was staring right at me. It was not an optical illusion I was seeing because of the lights... He was staring right at me, trying to make eye contact with me, I believed.

Heidi elbowed me and said, "I'll bet you fifty dollars that you can meet him. He has been looking right at you for some time now!" The singing continued, and my heart was melting. I didn't know what was happening with me, but I felt like I had been hit with a bolt of lightning!

Finally, the evening ended. Sergio and Julio came out again onto the stage for one last song. Sergio looked right at me at the end of his show and invited me to the bar where he would be. He raised his eyes and his arms and invited everyone to come to the *bodega* and gave the name and the address to the crowd of mostly women. All seemed to be Hispanic women except for Heidi and me!

We found our hosts and told them we'd meet them at the club. They agreed as they had last minute details to tidy up before they made their way there. Our taxi arrived, and the place was packed with women of all ages, shapes, and sizes. Everyone, it appeared, was clustered over on the other side of the bar, clamoring to get closer. I knew Sergio was in that corner of the bar! I made my way, snaking through the throng of women, dying to get closer to him. He finally saw me struggling to make my way to where he was, like all the other women. Only I was *not like* all the other women. He got up and made his way over to me and put his arm around my shoulders, pulling me in close, and he pushed his way forward, ahead of me. We sat down at the bar, and he ordered me a... You guessed it, rum and Coke. My favorite drink. Soon he took my hand and led me to the dance floor. He was holding me close, and I was swooning. He danced smoothly, leading me with gentle pushes and tugs on the palms of my hands and my waist. I felt like I was going to pass out because it was super crowded in the bar and my body was hot. I told him this, whispering into his ear as the song was finishing. He took my hand, walked over to the bar counter, laid out money, grabbed his jacket, and we exited. He held my hand as we walked down the street. I was not at all sure where we were headed, but I was good with that. Feeling the cool night breeze on my inflamed body was sweet! After a delightful walk filled with the sound of our laughter, we made it to his hotel room, and he unlocked the door.

The room was nice. Not fancy but clean and pretty. There was a double bed, some bottles of rum, Coke, and something else, a native drink, Aguardiente, a licorice tasting local specialty that he liked to drink, were all sitting on the side table. He made us drinks and sat down on the bed. I sat across from him in the easy chair. He started talking to me in a soft-spoken voice as he was unbuttoning his shirt, letting his curly chest hairs be seen. He was relaxed in his demeanor and was sharing stories with me about his childhood in Uruguay. He was a young, musical star, beginning his career in childhood, with a loving father promoting him. He told me how he and Julio found each other and that before Julio and him, he was in a well-known band called Los Tios Queridos. He shared how much he felt his heart calling to me, and mine responded in kind, having been touched by his love songs.

Was this for real? Had he sensed this correctly? I was stunned. I didn't know what to say with my heart about to explode, so I leaned into the moment and to my surprise, kissed him. When I pulled my face away, he looked into my eyes and tenderly touched my face. It was damp with tears. And then it was over. Our clothes came off, and we jumped under the sheets and stayed there all night, making love and making out. My body rose and fell like the tide reaching for the shore in ecstasy! Every time we kissed, I felt myself surrendering into oblivion, melting into the tenderness of his touch as though I were clay, the pads of his fingers leaving soft impressions upon my heart. Never had I felt such kindness expressed with such loving care being offered to me. Parched and cracked like a desert which hadn't seen rain in forever, my heart soaked it up.

Waking from a satiated slumber, I remembered that I was to catch a 9:00 a.m. plane to fly home to Quito with my hosts. I began searching the disheveled sheets for my clothing and again remembered the plane I had to catch.

We quickly got dressed, walked out into the fresh city breeze coming in from the ocean, and began scouring the small city to find the hotel where I was to be meeting up with Heidi and the guys. The intimate loving moment that had caught both of our hearts off guard and ensnared us, much to both of our astonishment, had come to an end. I felt like an idiot as I was totally confused. I had no idea where I was staying! It was a strange city, and we basically just walked to the theater after shopping. We stumbled upon the hotel as Sergio remembered it was the place his sponsors had told him they were staying. Surprised to see their number one man standing in the doorway, they razed he and I, questioning me and poked fun at me. They knew damn well where I'd been and with whom.

Several days later, Sergio showed up at my apartment. I was baffled as to how he had found me. I had been kicking myself for days because I hadn't given him my

Cynthia, 1974 from Sergio's scrapbook

*Sergio in Esmeralda, Ecuador (left) Julio, Maria, and Sergio at 0 degrees
longitude and 0 latitude, Ecuador (right)*

address. I hadn't remembered him asking for it. If he had, I am sure I would have given it to him. But there he was, standing before me in the flesh and blood. He had found me easily, simply by asking his sponsors where I lived because they had come to my apartment to pick Heidi and me up. I had forgotten that!

I invited him in. We sat in the living room, and he began to tell me his story. He and Julio had a falling out of sorts, as far as being a duo. Julio was getting married; his wife was pregnant, and he couldn't be traveling all the time. So, he was bowing out of their contract. It was offered just to Sergio as a solo performer, but he was homeless now and wondered if I could put him up for a week or so, until he found himself a place to live.

Of course, I agreed to this. I had the master bedroom, so space wasn't an issue. My heart was thumping hard against my chest, like a drummer beating out the rhythms for the sacred dance about to begin. I was dizzy with the excitement of the moment flooding my sensory system. I felt lighter, and the air seemed to crackle and sparkle as love flowed between him and I. At around the same time, Heidi found out she was pregnant and had to tell her *novio*. He was livid. She said it was his baby, of course, from their last visit with each other. "Whose baby do you think it is?" she fired back at her *novio* when he doubted her story. He would marry her immediately, unfazed by Heidi's protests. I stayed silent, saying nothing. She moved out and went down to the jungle where Jose was able to keep a close eye on her and their baby.

Like a revolving door in a fine hotel, as she moved out, Sergio moved in. We went to visit the place where Julio and Maria were living and were with them as they talked about their plans to get married, which was happening over the weekend. They lived in a Spiritual community. A Hari Krishna community—all love, peace, and happiness...blah, blah, blah. It was interesting when we visited, but it was not for me, nor was it a place for Sergio. I was relieved. The language and the perspective I witnessed was too flowy and dreamlike for me to believe it was real. We parted, saying our goodbyes, and wished the newlywed's good luck. Sergio and I headed back to my apartment, which meant going up and over the valley, back into Quito. Each of us sat silent, lost in our own musings.

Sergio had an orange Volkswagen Beetle. It was a good car, a bit older, but it ran decently. We had many sweet adventures together in his little beat-up Volkswagen Beetle. But the one adventure that was most vivid in my mind was the night when he really wanted new headlamps. The bulbs in the headlamps were blown out. I wasn't aware of this, and I'm not sure if Sergio was either. We had just traveled over the mountain from Quito into another valley in the morning, where the music studio was, and were headed back home again. Twilight had passed, and the night had enfolded us in inky darkness. There was not a light in sight, other than the gazillions of stars twinkling above in the night sky. My eyes grew big as saucers as Sergio told me, "Mi amor, Parece que no tenemos faros."

We drove up and down the switchback mountain roads, following cars ahead of us, by way of their car's headlights leading the way. Since our headlights were out, what we had for light to let other drivers know we existed was the shitty little interior light, barely bright enough for us to see inside the car, let alone others who were supposed to see us! That was it for light, driving on a pitch-black, switchback mountain road that neither one of us knew. There were no guard rails on these switchback roads that have sheer drops thousands of feet down. There were no street lamps lighting the way and no homes that I could see were built along this mountain road, other than the indigenous mountain folks who lived and hiked these mountains; they knew the pathways by the memory in their cells...ancestral memories of walking the very same footpaths. I reminded myself continuously that I was in South America. Car inspections, guard rails on dangerous drop offs, etc, were nonexistent. Folks put their faith in God when these mountain roads were driven. And I sure as hell was praying fervently to God to save my ass from any potential catastrophic event! And Sergio', too!

Upon returning from our harrowing ride, Sergio had a hair up his ass and made a promise that he would replace the headlamps before his next recording gig took us back over the mountain. He was on a mission. He scoured the city for days and found a Volkswagen that was a few years newer than his. The headlights were newer, the color was the same—orange; the headlamps were a fit. Sergio and I stole into the folk's driveway one night, by foot, parking a block away. The fencing system at the house Sergio had chosen was easier to scale than others' because it didn't have shards of broken glass glued to the top of the wall or guard dogs. I stood watch while he gathered his tool bag and began creeping stealthily through the night and over the fence, with only a headlamp guiding him and his hands once he reached his destination, the car! Sergio took the headlamps from the newer Volkswagen out and replaced them with his older ones. The next day he had the lamps in, and the car was golden at night. I felt horrible about the person whose car we had vandalized. Sergio justified it saying, "I gave them my headlamps; they just needed new light bulbs. They'll be fine." After that comment, I never gave it another thought.

We had some wild and crazy adventures. His guitar and his voice went everywhere with us. He loved to sing and play his guitar. I loved to hear him sing all his own music. He sang love ballads to me at night or in the wee morning hours, if he couldn't sleep, or upon waking. He sang anywhere when the love bug hit, and God had a new song to give him! It was an exquisite way to wake up or be romanced into being ready to make love, or my favorite was being serenaded to sleep. I had fallen deeply in love with this man and believed Sergio was the love of my life.

I remember one night he didn't come home. He'd been at the studio, over the mountain and in the next valley, recording new material with a female group, Las Tias. They were collaborating, featuring Sergio's new music, with their trio of vocals backing him up. He didn't return home until about 6:00 in the morning. I was so angry. Whew, how my jealousy flared. Quickly, I realized this was my issue and veered my energy away from these strong and destructive emotions. His work involved these kinds of late nights at times. Part of his job was socializing with people who he needed to work with and that included beautiful, flirty, and talented women. *Get over it, woman*, I scolded myself, in harsh, unloving words. *This jealousy won't be tolerated.* I slammed that inner door shut.

He invited me one time to the studio to be a backup singer. Thrilled and terrified I accepted. Sergio had heard me singing in our apartment and thought he'd like to give my voice a try. This was a dream come true for me, because as a child I had always had a secret dream to be a singer and dancer on Broadway! But I wasn't a confident or trained singer. I was painfully shy to sing in front of anyone, but I'd give it a try and do some beautiful pretending!

I was asked to sing from the rock opera *Jesus Christ SuperStar*, the song "I Don't know How to Love Him"—a song that I was personally moved by. My only experience of singing had been singing in the church choir and singing duets with my brother in our family service as a teenager. I froze. My voice croaked out sounds between super tight vocal cords. It sounded terrible. I didn't know how to warm up my vocal cords and relax into my body through my breath and singing! Even though he had heard me singing at home, in front of him and the sound guy, I couldn't make the cut! I had no voice. It came out sharp and unstable as I attempted to hold the higher notes, or timid and flat with the lower notes that were to be belted out. I was embarrassed and ashamed of myself. I somehow led Sergio into believing I could be his backup singer, a dream I had held near and dear to my heart my whole life. To be his lover and musical partner was beyond my wildest dreams, but I snapped back into my painful reality. What was I thinking? But then again, I really didn't remember initiating any conversation about this secret desire I had. Maybe Sergio had felt the desire in me being sensitive and an intuitive person.

Mom was preparing to come to Ecuador for a month's visit. She would be living with me in one of the extra bedrooms. My dad and younger sister, Katherine, were coming at the end of Mom's month and staying for two weeks. The plan was then for me to fly back home to Virginia with them. I was sad about this. I wasn't ready to go home. I didn't know if I ever really wanted to go back to Virginia. It frightened me thinking about it. So much was left unresolved, especially the woman in the mental hospital who had threatened me. She knew I was the one who had ratted them out.

I asked my parents to buy Sergio a harmonica with a head piece as a gift from me. And at Sergio's request, a 12-string Gibson guitar. It would be paid for, with a reimbursement, when he received it. Dad agreed and was thrilled to be tasked with this! Oh, and two pairs of Levi's, size 32 waist, 34 inseam. Levi's were a hot commodity and hard to come by in Quito.

I was still riding at the Academy and had arranged for Mom to lease a horse for the month, as well as an instructor also for the month, to be at her beck and call when she arrived. That's how they did things down here! Mom was a great equestrian in her own right. She had trained her half-thoroughbred half-Morgan, named E-Bird, for years, taking her on long rides through the woods, jumping her over small jumps in the fields below Christchurch School where my family had moved, a month before I left for Ecuador. I was excited to be able to share with her the riding that I was experiencing. I had written home long letters, detailing the adventures I was participating in with the Equestrian Academy and alone with my instructor, Capitan Fausto Salinas. I described in my letters how in Quito we had three seasons every day. Cool in the morning, warranting a jacket, rainy mid-day, and then steamy hot sun in the afternoons. Many days when we started out from the school, crossing through the city with as many as thirty or forty riders, we'd need jackets. By the time we arrived and headed up the mountainside, the rain would be drenching us in its daily downpour. The path became ruddy, slick, and muddy. The saddles, bridles, our boots, and leather gloves got soaked. The horses were not comfortable slogging up a mountain in the mud and instead galloped up the steep, wooded mountain side, clumped nose to tail, running as a herd, almost bumping into each other. If a rider lost control or one horse lost their footing, stumbling, and went down, the whole bunch, especially the horse and rider closest behind, were vulnerable to being seriously injured. Horse and rider both had to be in sync, and I prayed like hell, hanging on to my horse's neck, my nose buried in Garua's mane, eyes open wide, peering out from under the helmet, scrutinizing the situation, that I was in sync. Breathing in deeply, the cloying scent of the eucalyptus forest and the scent of his mane and sweat immediately calmed my nerves. Feeling the heat from his body and seeing the steam rising from it due to his exertion was exhilarating. My sinuses were tingling and clear on those days. Breathing deeply was euphoric.

Mom and I were looking forward to sharing a wonderful time together. I had never experienced this kind of rugged riding, and I hoped Mom would be invited on one of the school's outings! The instructor that was available was the *coronel* who was

Inti riding Garua (left), sister Katherine (right)

the head instructor of the Dressage Academy. As a young man, he had been trained in Austria, on the famous Austrian military horses, the Lipizzaners.

Mom was a "looker." She was a big-boned woman, with beautiful auburn hair and burnished red highlights that she wore pulled back in a long ponytail. She had a beautiful smile, slow to move across her face, and brown, shy eyes that retreated if she was noticed for too long. She was attractive, and the *coronel* did not waste any time putting the moves on her. I was horrified when she told me this. She, on the other hand, was quite flattered. I tried to warn her, but her ego with the flattery she had received won, and she giggled like a schoolgirl, assuring me she could handle herself. So, she welcomed his attention, but the tradeoff was that she had to constantly fight off his advances, even with her setting and enforcing her boundaries. She was not going to end up in bed with the *coronel*, of this I was both certain and relieved.

A week after my mom's arrival, I began thinking I might be pregnant. Ha! Boy that might be the biggest cosmic joke of all! The timing was ironic. It couldn't have been more perfect or worse. Karma was a bitch. Mom was the one who made sure I was off birth control when I'd moved to Ecuador, almost a year ago. But I'd made the choice to listen. I was horrified, scared, and didn't know what to do or where to go. Sergio was clear that he was not ready for a baby. He couldn't jeopardize his career at this early stage. He was also very gentle and kind about the whole mess we were in. He suggested that I go to Fausto. "They have women on their staff precisely for this purpose, for themselves," he explained, logically.

I knew Sergio was right. The police pretty much had an abortionist on staff. I was mortified to have to go and ask Fausto where I could get an abortion. But I knew I had to suck it up, put my big girl panties on, and ask. I was relieved that Fausto had no reaction. He gave me the name that the officers use for themselves with no drama. I told Mom, and Mom, of course, told Sonya. In their eyes, I was really looking bad. I received no sympathy, and all had to be very hush-hush, as abortions were illegal in Ecuador.

Go figure with all the mistresses the men had...

No pregnancy test was taken. I had just missed my period for two months. A pretty good sign I was pregnant. The day finally arrived for my appointment. Sergio and I went together. He was tender with me and very concerned for my safety and wellbeing. We climbed a dark stairwell on these rickety steps that creeped me out. Hand in hand, we walked down a barely lit, long hallway, and stood knocking on a door, which hopefully was the right door. The woman who answered looked like a witch. She had long, wavy black hair, wore a black jumpsuit that clung to her body, sported red lipstick and red nail polish. She scared the shit out of me. This wasn't feeling like a real medical procedure but more like someone with a hacksaw, ready to dive right in.

She had me unclothe myself and lie down on the table. She brought out a long envelope and pulled a narrow blade out of it. I was reminded of an old-fashioned razor blade, sharp on one edge, after being slapped along a piece of leather on one side then the other to sharpen it. She proceeded to maneuver the blade thing up my vagina, and gently swirled it around, scraping my insides clean of embryo. It didn't take long but felt awful. I had sharp, pinching pains as she worked to clean me out.

When we were done, Sergio handed her an envelope, which she opened and counted out the 150 *sucres* it cost him. We left quickly with his arm protectively around my shoulders, and I leaned into him. It was a simple process and ended the day with us getting back in time to make dinner for Mom. She had been riding all day, so I thought she'd be in a great mood. Unless she was harassed again by the *coronel*. Mom was in great spirits until she saw me. I got the silent, "pretend-I'm-invisible" treatment, which was fine by me; it gave me a wide berth.

The weeks flew by. The month was coming to an end, and my dad and sister were arriving before we knew it. Sergio was still living in my home. Mom had accepted that there was nothing she could do, short of her moving over to Alfonso and Sonya's, which she didn't want to do. She didn't want to have to pretend with Alfonso that all was well. She was not good at hiding her moods or curbing her tongue.

Sergio proposed to me after the abortion ordeal. We had gone away for the weekend to Esmeraldas to have a break from Mom and before my family arrived. While standing on some rocks, which seemed to be undulating, I noticed upon closer inspection that this was a sunning spot for what seemed like millions of octopus. They were wiggling around, making weird suction noises as they lifted their tentacles, suctioned, moved, lifted, suctioned, and moved. We were taking funny snapshots of this odd circumstance we found ourselves in, surrounded by octopi, when Sergio took a hold of my hand, sat me down on a rock clear of octopi, and asked me to marry him. I felt like the heavens had opened as a deluge of emotions flooded me like a downpour of rain; love saturated my body, mind, and Spirit. My heart was touched by what felt like a golden ray of light. I said yes, of course. Relieved that I was as madly in love with him, and he was with me. This wasn't a one-way street.

When we arrived back home, Mom, on her warpath, insisted that Sergio move out. "Your father is arriving with your sister. Sergio must move out. He can't be living here. I have not told your father this. I won't tell him all that we have been through—but Sergio must move out," she finished, spewing her anger. Her face was bright red and the veins in her neck were popping out, she was so damn angry with me.

When she ended and my heartbeat slowed down, Sergio took my hand, looked Mom in the eye, and said, "We are engaged to be married. I love your daughter, and I will ask her father for her hand, as soon as I meet him."

Her mouth dropped. Stunned. For a moment, she was speechless.

"What?" she screamed at me, Sergio becoming invisible. "This is way too much for me to handle. A pregnancy, and now you're telling me you're engaged to be married. I can't handle this. Wait until your father arrives. We'll see about all of this."

Sergio was stunned. A look of horror knitted his eyebrows together. I was blown away by her lack of empathy and her outright disgust of me. I was mortified for Sergio to have witnessed this. She showed no excitement for me whatsoever, just thinking about the hassle of my being pregnant and what an inconvenience for her and an embarrassment for her, with Sonya. The two women decided not to tell Alfonso or Dad. And I was happy and engaged to Sergio. I loved this man. I believed I would travel to the depths of my Soul discovering the nature of unconditional love with this man. He was kind, gentle, thoughtful, believed in God, was handsome as hell, and had a voice like an angel. His creativity was astonishing to me. And he knew he was living the life of his dreams, creating a rocking music career for himself. I was animated to be a part of it.

Dad brought the guitar, the jeans, and the harmonica, and a headpiece for the harmonica. Sergio was delighted to have a beautiful 12-string Gibson guitar, the love of his life! And how he could play it!

During my family's two weeks, we took a trip higher up into the mountains to Cuenca, a beautiful Colonial city nestled in the Andes at 8,400 in altitude. It took a ridiculous number of hours by bus to get to Cuenca, and I was sick as a dog. Dad wanted to see the cathedral that Cuenca was famous for. It was intricately built and was an old Colonial Catholic cathedral. Sergio didn't come with us; he was in the studio working on his first release.

My vagina stunk. I wasn't sure what was happening, but I was not smelling healthy. Something was up with the abortion I had just gone through. My pussy felt swollen and infected. I saw a doctor right away when I got back to Quito, with Sonya. And yes, I did have an infection. I was put on antibiotics. It was assumed I'd be fine. We went out to dinner to celebrate our engagement with the bishop and Sonya. Alfonso was still sore at me. I'd never met anyone who could hold a grudge for so long. He did like Sergio, and through the evening's passing, Alfonso warmed up to him and saw that it was a good match for his Inti! Alfonso warmly congratulated us at the end of the evening, with a toast. "Que tengas una larga vida, muchos hijos, mucho amor, con mucho dinero para disfrutar tu vida."

Two days after we had our simple engagement party at our favorite local restaurant, my family and I were flying home. Sergio would be following me in a month. He'd first go to Miami, and then he would be flying to New York to fulfill his recording contract. After that, he would be visiting me in Virginia to experience my life. We figured we'd be seeing each other in about three months' time, around Thanksgiving or Christmas. I hated saying goodbye, until we saw each other again... My heart was being wrenched in two. I wanted to stay behind and fly to the USA with him when he came. I didn't want to be separated, and my parents were scaring me again as they forbid me to stay. They believed it was best for me to return home, gather my thoughts, prepare myself to welcome Sergio into our home and life, and then fly back to Ecuador, married, after a year of waiting.

They won, as Sergio hated seeing us fight and me upset. Quite frankly, he had no concept for understanding the fighting that ensued between my parents and me. He assured me all was well. "Mi amor, esto me dará mucho tiempo para extrañarte y escribir más canciones de amor." Keeping a happy demeanor and a stiff upper lip, he went on to say, "It will only be a few months that we will be apart. You'll see. Time will fly!" This gave him lots of time for his heart to miss me and for the songs to flow!!! My body rose to meet his embrace like the sun rises to greet the day! Heaven and Earth joined, as I melted into him. It was settled then. I would be seeing him in a few months at the most. Certainly, by Christmas.

Chapter 10

The Betrayal

It was the end of August, 1974. That was the last time I ever saw Sergio. He never met me at the airport the next morning as planned, to say one more farewell. He never wrote to me when I returned home. I never saw my beloved again. And I've never forgotten the love we felt for one another. The lack of closure and the mystery around his not showing up was a constant wound, leaking energy, drawing more abandonment and betrayal experiences to me, until I chose to seal and heal the wound. This opportunity showed up in my mid 50s, 2006. A man I was dating at the time spoke big words about his capability at being a computer wizard. He boasted that he could find anyone on the internet in less than thirty seconds! This was astounding to me. The internet was still quite a mystery to me. I asked him to find Sergio. He did, in less than thirty seconds. I was floored. I sat down, stunned, imagining the day when I connected with him again and asked him why I never saw, nor heard from him again. I was still mystified with an open wound, seeping, from the experience.

Precious Sergio responded immediately to my email, with a completely different story to share than what I had been told and through the years had come to believe. But the first thing this sweet man asked was, "Am I a father?" This caused me to remember those horrible weeks following my return home to the States.

"No," I wrote to him in Spanish. "You are not a father. But when I returned home, I found out that I was five months pregnant. The abortion I had with you didn't work. I thought I was dying from a tumor I had growing in my belly. Cancer. Never did I imagine that I was still carrying our child. I had a window of two weeks to make my decision."

I recounted to him how my father had made an announcement at a faculty meeting about my "condition" and asked if I would have everyone's support to have a baby and raise it without a father. I had *not* given him permission to do this and was mortified, humiliated, and most of all devastated to feel my broken heart shatter all over again.

I continued writing my email in Spanish: "My mother, on the other hand, told me that if I wanted to have this baby, I was to move out immediately and raise it on my own without their support. She was done raising children and wasn't about to raise mine."

The next thing that Sergio wrote blew me away and brought the memory of my shattered heart, now beating rapidly, right up into my mouth and into the foreground.

As I read his words, my eyes filled with fresh tears, as though I had fallen and a new wound was open and bleeding. "Your father told me you never wanted to see me again. Your father asked me not to come to the airport because he said it was too painful for you to have to tell [me] this." I continued reading as I crumpled in agony. "So, you had asked him to deliver the message, as I was leaving your apartment, when your dad walked me downstairs." I remembered Dad had walked him downstairs. I thought it was a future father-in-law thing. It was then that Dad told Sergio this lie, which altered the course of our lives, forever.

Sergio's words continued, "I searched for you for a year. I wrote letters to you every week up until Christmas, hoping to hear from you soon about our plans. I never heard a word from you. I was heartbroken. For that year I wrote many love songs lamenting my heartbreak, all inspired by you." I believed I heard a deep, sad sigh breathed into his words.

I was speechless and horrified. The anger I felt was beyond my wildest dreams.

My volcano, Irazú, I peered into you as a child. I felt you rumbling, bubbling up, imploding. I didn't even know what to write, the devastation of my father's betrayal was sharp and so deep. All consuming. I felt a chasm had opened, and I fell down, and down. When I landed, I felt like I had been smashed to smithereens. How dare he have interfered with my life as he did. I couldn't believe what I was hearing. I was so very, very sad, as was Sergio. Two lovers lost to each other through no fault of our own. Was it really meant for us to meet for only a split second in time? I've asked to understand this. And for what purpose? To have a love so totally and thoroughly shattered?

My God, what had my father done to my life? How could he have betrayed me so completely? I was devastated and livid with him. I felt like the Earth had just swallowed me up, so incomprehensible was my rage. I felt the rage running thick through my blood of eons of women whose lives had been altered by their fathers, or some other patriarchal decree. I was blind with fury. A red, hot, wild, unhinged fury. A wounded and wild thing in me was unleashed...

Tempering my rage to a simmer, I called Dad that night to talk with him about this new discovery I had made. He denied everything. Flat out denied his involvement at all. He put Sergio down as a typical Latin male, which got my dander up my ass even more. If he had been standing in front of me, I'd have punched him in his face! The fucking bastard. How dare he. And how dare my mother be complicit in this... No wonder she wanted me out of the house if I had chosen to have the baby. She didn't want to be reminded of what her husband had done to her daughter's life. All but destroyed it!

I was relentless in my confrontation with my dad. Finally, a light bulb full of wisdom exploded in my brain. All was made clear! I understood that I must confront my dad in Spanish. When I called him next, my conversation was in Spanish and an hour before his Sunday service began when I knew I had his full attention. This time he recalled having spoken to Sergio the night before we left Ecuador. He started crying and admitted in Spanish to having taken all the letters he had written to me and destroyed them, without my knowing it.

Holy shit, how had he done that? It was a federal offense to tamper with mail.

It was tragically easy where we lived. He had been able to talk to the postmistress on our private school campus, a major fuckery, and asked her to give him all letters that came to me that were in Spanish. He told her that he needed to translate them before he passed them on to me. And the dumb bitch didn't stop to think...duh, I was teaching Spanish at the school! Of course, I didn't need my father's help. She was his unknowing accomplice in this, along with my mother, who knew. They all kept silent and watched me grieve and go through an abortion as a public spectacle.

The thing about this silence was that my mother had decided, before she came down to Ecuador to visit with me, that a man on campus named Ivan was the targeted man of her choice as my potential husband. He had already befriended my parents, being a teacher on campus himself. Ivan became best buds with my youngest sibling, Kevin, and my mother adored Ivan. Ivan paid my mom a lot of attention. He was lighthearted, playful, and really fed my father's ego as he loved Dad's stories and never tired of hearing them, several times in fact. Ivan was lively, vibrant, and a wildly talented creative, and to top it off he was a great person with a soft, easy-going way about him. He was friends to all and immensely enjoyed and known for his sense of humor. Ivan created a stellar Art Department for the school, coming down from Toronto, Canada, at the invitation of his good friend and his former art teacher from Brewster Academy, in Wolfeboro, NH, Bill Koen. Ivan was the first true friend I had when I returned home, devastated and still grieving at not having seen Sergio the morning I flew home to the United States. I was pregnant but didn't know it yet. Ivan lived on campus, next door to my home, and was about my age. We hadn't met one another, even though we ate dinner in the dining hall together and I walked past the Art Department at least two or three times a day to get to my job as the first-year Spanish teacher. Until one day, as I was walking across campus when the art director—a large, rotund man, gruff in his mannerisms, harsh in his criticisms, wearing ragged jeans and a blue jean shirt, sporting a huge, grayed beard—Bill Koen and Ivan's dear friend, called out to me, "Hey, Cynthia, come here. Ivan, come here. Ivan this is Cynthia. Cynthia, this is Ivan. Now it's done. You guys have been driving us crazy avoiding each other. Why?"

Ivan and I looked at one another and shrugged our shoulders, who knew?

And from then on, Ivan and I became inseparable. He was a kind soul. Damn good looking, gentle, and a hell of an artist. I loved his apartment, which was filled with cool antiques, beautiful handmade pottery, dinner plates and bowls, and hanging plants in the windows and lining the old fashioned, deep window sills. I was intrigued as I hadn't met a man so refined as to love plants and hand-made pottery dishes who was my age! He was a good listener, too. He didn't turn me away and shame me, or silence me, in disinterest, because of my situation. I was desperately in need of a friend. I thought for a long time he was gay. He didn't seem sexually interested in me, which was shocking to me. All men were interested in sex, but Ivan was different. He was very sensitive to me and to my deep well of grief. He was really upset with my father for making such a private situation so damn public that it made it embarrassing to meet me, which is why it took him so long. He was embarrassed that my pregnancy was like the elephant in the room, which no one wanted to talk about.

I found out on my nineteenth birthday, September 25th, 1974, that I was five months along. During my examination, Dr. Petri, at the Medical College of Virginia (MCV) had found thick scar tissue dividing my vaginal wall, giving me two vaginal openings. I remember him asking me what had happened to cause this thick wall of scar tissue. I had no idea. There was no memory of anything hurting me inside my vagina. I mentioned the clearing of the fetus from my uterus I'd had done in Ecuador, but this scar tissue was not newly formed. The scar tissue he was talking about was old.

Before the abortion, though, I had to have a "vaginal septum removal." Because this was done in a teaching hospital, there were a whole bunch of medical students encircling the operating table above in the observation room, looking down at my private parts splayed open.

It was gruesome. The most horrific choice I've ever made, and the experience was a living hell. Two weeks after my surgery, I was induced with saline, which put the baby into convulsing in my uterus as it struggled for its life. The saline solution was killing the fetus, and I felt every cell in my body surging with death as the fetus struggled to live in its toxic environment. The struggle finally ended, and then the work of my body having to expel the fetus began. I had bad contractions and rang the buzzer many, many times to get some pain medication. My soul was in agony, hovering. My human self was in agony emotionally and physically. My brain was splitting in two not being able to fly away from the horror of the choice I had made.

Sometime in the early morning, I gave birth to my dead fetus. I was distraught with grief, still grieving the loss of Sergio from whom I hadn't heard in several weeks. The emotional grief was far deeper and greater than the physical pain as I detached from my body and watched from above. Until the body was out of mine, I rang the buzzer relentlessly, to no avail. The baby was lying between my legs, a bloody mess. Its skin was translucent. I saw veins, muscles, and arteries through the thin veil of skin, once the protection for vital and thriving organs. My heart shattered again. And again, as I reached to touch this little being. I wanted to hold it so badly but was afraid to pick it up. Damn it, *where were the nurses?* Maybe the buzzer was broken. Buzz, buzz, buzz, again and again. The baby was a little boy, I saw, as I uncurled its fragile little body to check the sex.

Early in the morning, Dr. Petri arrived, starting his rounds. I was his first stop. What Dr. Petri saw when he walked into my room was an exhausted and emotionally distraught wild woman. My face contorted in agony as I rocked back and forth, keening at the losses I had suffered. Sitting cross-legged on my bed, while in my lap was my dead baby.

Dr. Petri noticed the bloodied sheets I was sitting on, and his eyes got big as saucers as he registered in his mind what had taken place. The anger rising in him was visible as he quickly went to work to clean me up and offer me comfort. He tenderly picked up the fetus, wrapped it in a towel, and left the room carrying it. I heard his voice roar for his staffing nurses to attend to Room 206, like yesterday.

I hadn't heard a word from Sergio in several weeks. I was alone with this decision to abort. I was so grateful to have Ivan with me. He brought me to the hospital, visited me, and he picked me up at the end of the ordeal.

My parents had nothing to do with me. They didn't come to the hospital or pick me up or visit me while I was there, nor were they speaking to me. So freaking weird. Would you treat your daughter this way? I sure as hell never would and never did. Disgusting disrespect and betrayal again, on so many levels.

I remembered my mother telling me that she believed with all her heart that she had to be the first one to hurt me, to prepare me for the wounding I was to receive as I grew up and became an adult. She believed she loved me so much that it was her duty, because I was so precocious and sweet with my beautiful blue eyes, strawberry blond hair, and quick smile. She feared for me because of my innocence. This belief drove my mom to demean me continuously as her example for how much she loved me.

Whew—twisted stinking thinking if you ask me. But she lived her beliefs and acted this out through emotional abuse, never laying a finger on my body. She wounded my self-esteem and self-love, supporting the re-wiring of my energetic system, during the Ritual Abuse Torture (RAT) ceremonies I would come to remember.

Ivan was my knight in shining armor. His tenderness super-soaked my heart. He cared for me as a dear friend, never belittling or making fun of my situation. I dedicate this book to you, my dear Ivan, father to our most wonderful children, and grandfather to our children's children. I will always love you.

Like I said to him on the beach the first evening we were on a date: I remember telling him we were going to be together the rest of our lives. At that moment I had no idea why he didn't run like hell, because he had no idea what he was getting into when he said I was either the craziest woman he'd ever met or the sanest woman he'd ever met. Ivan believed he had to stick around to find out. I think now, if asked, he might say I was touched by a little bit of both! In June 1976, Ivan and I married. We had a Colonial-style wedding in honor of the 200th anniversary of our nation's birth.

Chapter 11

Spirit Had a Plan for Me

And so it was that Ivan became the father of my children in a bizarre twist of fate or destiny, because while I was in Ecuador falling in love, my parents were, Mom in particular, focused on Ivan being the perfect match for me! One made in heaven!!! So when I came home from Ecuador Mom had sweet, funny, handsome Ivan on her radar and was hoping beyond all hope that he and I connected. You see, she needed me married. That was the woman's legacy in our family. Married and having a family...serving our men.

Winding my way back through the past to 1988, I remember my Near Death Experience and that leaving the church of my birth was a very scary, big, painful choice. I had been born into the church, raised in the church, and indoctrinated by its prayers repeated by rote memory, every day of my life. Not having church services to attend to on Sundays became a day of mourning and floundering as my metaphoric sails flapped in the wind while I searched. I searched deeply, asking hard questions of myself.

I was given the plan upon returning from the NDE, which was to discover the truth as to why my body had a "death wish," so I had a task before me, not so different from the journey which my ancestors set out upon to find the Holy Grail!

The language I had grown up with from the Bible and the Book of Common

Prayer was an exclusive religion, written by men, supposedly inclusive of me, and it was making me sick. During this time, I was guided by an inner wisdom, a strong feeling that tingled and buzzed through my body, to be flat on my back, horizontal—as my mother fondly referred to a need to be flat on one's back. This was easy. Exhaustion overtook my body, and I collapsed from living a lie for thirty-three years. I spent the year in bed, horizontal, which allowed my body, mind, and Spirit to reintegrate the unbound emotions flooding me, and the new information which came during the trauma of the Near Death Experience.

Family Photo

• • •

My daughter turning seven triggered the unresolved and buried memory of my abandonment, which happened to me at around the same age. Literally any mothering instincts I had relied on, went dry. Zip, gone. I had no memory of being mothered as a six, seven, and eight-year-old child. And it was frightening. Old grief moved into my heart as it had when Joselyn was an infant; I was afraid to hug my daughter. Old fears surfaced again and told me, as voices screamed in my head, that my love would kill her. While I allowed my love to flow into her being, as I hugged her or just gazed at her in awe, I felt love fill me and flow out through my eyes. Harsh, fearful beliefs took over, spewing ugly, toxic words in my mind that taunted me and said, "Your love will destroy her."

Jesus Christ. How was that possible? I was so sad and tired. I wanted my past done. I needed to figure out why I had these sick thoughts in my head that did not allow me to love as I knew was needed and how I wanted to love my children.

While curled in a ball, I screamed into my pillow at my father's God, "What happened to me? What truth do I need to discover?" In the dead of night, lying wide awake, I shook with night terrors. I requested to *know*. I needed to know to stop this cycle of violent thinking churning in my mind continuously. It was driving me crazy with sorrow.

Desperate to remove the DNA imprint that my vulnerable daughter might well be inheriting through me—of the mad woman—I stole into my daughter's room in the dead night, every night for weeks. I remember seeing shadows dancing on the walls, frightening me at times as the trees swayed and gyrated wildly outside, seeming to taunt my sanity.

When all was still and quiet except for my breathing and the pounding of a hundred horses running my heartbeat, I sat open and pleading. I was guided by an inner Source of strength, inspiration, and a deep well of love to place my hands above my daughter's body. I was to allow myself to fill with energy and pray. I prayed for whatever karma, family lineage history from the past, or present that was projected onto her, I owned and recalled back to myself. Night after night I did this and watched my daughter who had become withdrawn, shy, very sad, and frightened— open like a flower. A flower starved of water when suddenly the little delicate flower felt a trickle seeping through then finally a deluge of rain poured. The parched flower drank greedily and bloomed, strong, sure, quickly, and beautifully. It was like watching a slow-motion movie.

This presence which instructed me to pray over my daughter was not the God of my father's church. It arose from deep within—like the imprint of the volcano in my cells was bubbling, speaking through me. Jesus was a friend imprinted in my heart and understood by me as unconditional love. This superpower I shall name SourceLove!

This presence and the growing truth I had welling up within was growing stronger as I remembered snatches of my early life in beautiful, sensual Costa Rica and the connection I had had. The beautiful early imprint of a childhood lived in sweet, rich, vibrant, Costa Rica laid the foundation for me to have a place of refuge when the horror show began playing. A place where my olfactory system remembered not being assaulted.

My Soul remembers my human self, buying the metaphoric tickets on the bus, headed for this Earth journey. "Whoa, a ten. I'll take that trip!" This sinks in. "I choose to learn all I can about love and growing love as big as I can in my next incarnation on Earth." After some thought, the Soul adds, "I am going to be in service to love. That is what I desire...to help humans love more and see their own amazingness!!!"

"That's the highest level of forgiveness and love one can achieve. You sure you want a ten?", Source asks. "That's huge work, not for the faint of heart, I assure you, my dear."

"I'm good with it. And I'm ready. The Earth needs more love to evolve!"

Disturbing thoughts swirled through my mind, tormenting me. They were becoming more frequent, and I was unable to hide them any longer. Ivan was always ready to hold me when these commanding thoughts surfaced. At night sometimes, if in a deep sleep and he reached for me, I'd awaken screaming at him to stop. I was in such a state of distress, caught in a triggered night terror memory. I did not recognize Ivan as my dear husband and best friend. I felt stuck in terrifying episodes that continued, relentlessly growing in strength and demand for my attention.

I shared these frightening and disturbing episodic events with friends who suggested that I go to a Yuwippee healing ceremony, which was being hosted on the up-coming weekend at a friend's home. The Chips family from the Rosebud reservation in South Dakota were of the Lakota Sioux tribe and were hosting the ceremony for a woman who had breast cancer. She had asked the community to pray for her.

It was a full day's event and lasted late into the evening. I arrived and felt totally out of place. I was shy. I had no idea what to do or what was expected of me, a white woman and a former Christian who was raised to believe all this stuff was heresy, opening me up to the evil that existed in their uncouth ways. I barely knew the family who was hosting the ceremony. Basically, I felt like a fish out of water.

I was told I needed to make four hundred prayer ties which would be hung in the sweat lodge for our protection and for the personal petitions, we would be sending up through the smoke. These prayer ties were to be made from 2x2 squares of red, yellow, black, and white, 100% cotton fabric, each containing a pinch of tobacco placed into the center of the square. With this intention, I gathered my thoughts, honed my prayer, and blew a prayer into each square, and twisted the string around it, then moved to the next one. Each one needed to be done with mindful intention, and my attention focused on the task at hand, to create the result I desired. That was a whole lot of praying. Probably more than I'd ever done. I got started making my bundles and tying them together with cotton twine, doing as I was shown. I found this to be very satisfying work and I was content, sitting in the grass, making my prayers to Great Spirit, another new word for SourceLove. I blew my thoughts and quiet musings into my squares, sharing dreams of what I desired, held deeply in my heart and shared with no one, for a long time now.

Finally, hours later, the sweat lodge was ready, having been built while I was busy with my prayer ties. The sweat lodge was run first for the women, with many rounds of the flap opening and more rocks being shoveled in. We were in the lodge for what seemed like many hours, doing rounds of hot rocks, purging, sweating, praying with our voices in full song, all as one. I liked this. No one prayer or voice was heard over the others. We were all one and the same. We were jam packed in the lodge, three layers deep with bodies. Within the group, each one of us was trying to stay in the lodge for its duration and were instructed to put our faces on the Earth if we needed fresh air or got claustrophobic. It didn't take me long to feel claustrophobic, and my face went down as I crumpled like a pretzel into my lap. I placed my cheek upon the Earth, so cool she felt. My heart burst wide open and tears flooded. I wept, sobbed, and cried as I had never wept before. Purging dark, vile poison put my vulnerable body into shaking and trembling uncontrollably, like the volcano Erazú had erupted. I felt wrung out like a dishrag when we finally finished and the lodge flap opened for the last time.

We all slowly made our way out, crawling crab-like around the circle clockwise. I was barely able to move. I felt so spent. Still no speaking was encouraged. Once out, I crawled over to a nice spot in the field. I laid my body out flat on the moist, cool, Earth, palms down and pricked by the grass. My eyes wide open and staring up at the millions of stars above. I felt blessed beyond words and so grateful to be there, lying on Mother Earth, cradled by her solid body. I was amazed and in awe. My mind was curious and requesting more! Wanting more...starved for more.

The men began filing into the sweat lodge for their opportunity as we rose, one by one, off the ground and slowly made our way to the huge spread of food that was laid out on the table in the house. It was a beautiful spread with all the potluck dishes that had arrived and been placed on a lovely table, with a traditionally woven blanket for a tablecloth. The food was blessed. It was to nourish ourselves after the purging and cleansing sweat lodge. We were ravenous and ate heartily and joyfully! Never having tasted venison before, I found it savory, tender, and delicious, seasoned just right. As we satiated our body's appetite, the ceremonial room was being set up, where the sacred Yuwippee ceremony was to be held. The men finally came out of their sweat lodge, ate, and we all waited until we were invited to enter, quietly.

The host family's garage was turned into a sacred ceremonial hut. The windows were covered over. There was an altar set up in the center of the room on the floor, encircling the Medicine Man, Brother Chips. He had been bound with a blanket wrapped around him, from head to toe, like a sausage skin. Around that, he was wrapped with a thick hemp rope and looked like a mummy. Symbolically, he was representing the binding of the woman's cancer as it grew in her body. He metaphorically invited the cancer to be present. He chose to take on this fight for her, to release the cancer from her body.

It was fascinating, scary, mind-blowing, and triggered deep, Christian beliefs of evil spirits, and the heresy surrounding the destruction of my own indigenous roots. Yes, I said my indigenous roots. My roots are Celtic and of Viking ancestry. These are strong, vibrant roots which connect me to my ancient ancestral lineage. But the Episcopal Churches and the Catholic Churches, and many other Christian churches have called these people and their practices savage, heretical, and demon worshippers.

The ceremony began...drumming started and the candles were extinguished. Bodies sat in three rows, behind one another. We were squashed in like sardines. The prayer chanting continued with the drumming, becoming a constant, background drone. This continued for quite some time, lulling us all out of our rational, thinking, judging minds, and into the sensing, feeling, creative mind...the one that guides us back home. All sense of time and space dissolved.

Suddenly sparks began to shoot about the room. Pinging here and there, flying about, challenging our torpid minds to "wake up!" See the unseen with your God eyes! *Wake up*, these sparks seemed to be saying as they were dancing and flitting around. It was a magical and mystical event that I couldn't explain and will never forget. I felt what was happening in my body but had no words to share what I had witnessed. I was good with this. This silence was golden!

The ceremony came to a close with the sun slowly creeping into visibility, awakening dawn... As the sun rose lazily in the east, a new day was upon us. In the east, a harbinger of new opportunities initiates every day! As our eyes adjusted to the faint light seeping in and the window coverings were taken down, I saw that our Medicine Man, the Shaman, was unbound. He was sitting peacefully, cross-legged, in the center of the room, as though in a trance. When he spoke, all he said was, "Thy will has been done, Great Spirit." His eyes flew open, and he peered deeply and lovingly into the eyes of his client. "The rest is up to you, my child."

Fazed, dazed, and wide open to SourceLove, I got into my car and headed the short distance home. When I got home, I sat quietly in my living room, enjoying the breaking of the dawn light. I lit a small fire in the sweet, little Rumford fireplace to warm my bones, pondering what had happened as I gazed into the fire, mesmerized. Then an amazing thing happened. In that moment, I had to decide whether I was in fact crazy, as was told to me my whole life, or not. I chose to believe that I was not crazy. Simultaneously with this choice, I met a Spirit.

I felt the hair on my arms stand up. My body was buzzing, and I felt a presence. I became frightened, not sure what to do or say. I quelled the warring voices in my mind and traveled within.

Guided by SourceLove, I remembered my Christian roots and asked:

Are you a Spirit of the Light?

I waited.

I felt a buzz rising in my body from my toes to my fingertips. My nipples hardened. And I heard the words in my mind:

I walk in the light of Christ, but I carry darkness, too.

Oh—oh. Damn...

What do I do with this?

I asked SourceLove for guidance.

I sat. I waited.

Who are you? I was guided to ask the Spirit as the hair prickled up on my arms.

I am your grandmother from five generations past. I have come, daughter of my blood, to ask if you are the one who has come to free the voices of the women of our family, daughter of light? Is it you who has chosen this clearing for our family? For all humanity?

Yes, I answered. *I am the one. I have chosen to be in service to this journey. I seek to know why my body has a death wish, rather than seeking to enjoy life and allowing my love to flow freely. I have a death wish. I seek to know the truth. Why?*

And so it was that my journey into the past, tracking the family stories like stepping stones, to discover the wounding which had traveled through generations, repeating itself, had begun.

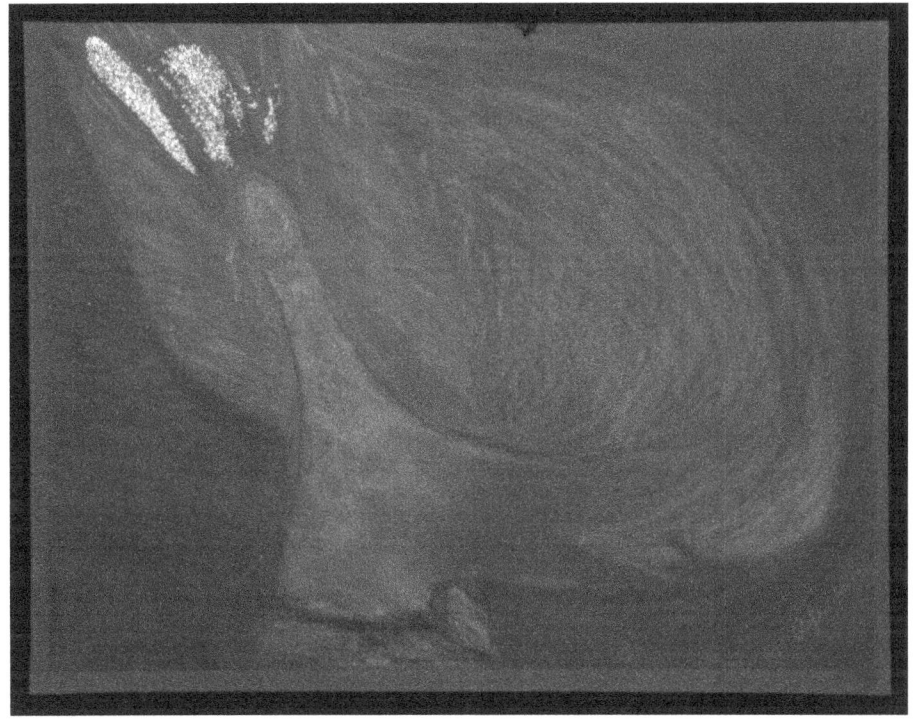

I met an ancestor

My first assignment was to decide whether I was bat shit crazy or not. As I said, I chose to believe that I was not crazy. I also had chosen to believe that there was a curse within our lineage, attached to the first-born woman of every generation, as told to me by my maternal grandmother. Christina, the spirit of my great-great-grandmother, told me she was the one who made the curse. Only her heart's desire was not to create a curse. It was a prayer that a daughter of her blood, in some epoch, would choose to free the voices of the women in our family by listening deeply to our Soul's voice and share the stories.

In a flash of inspiration, I realized *I am the one*. I felt this "truth" in my bones. Somehow, there was a connection to the "evil" root planted in me, devouring my love, through FEAR. The *plan* that was shown to me during my NDE was connected to this story. You see, I grew up hearing from my mother's mother that Christina, this great-great-grandmother, five generations back, was a *mad woman*. You know, the ones we read about in Victorian England, the women who needed to be silenced and were treated for "hysteria." The inquisitive, outspoken, creative, or the witchy-bitchy ones were the one's silenced in Christina's world, the patriarchal world of logic and reasoning, where violence and abuse of others, the Earth, and her peoples, were the accepted cultural norms. Women were objects, seen but not invited to speak, subjugated to serve (their) men. Women wore tight corsets that physically suffocated them to support the suffocating that was happening emotionally and spiritually during my great-grandmother's era.

During this time of great exploration, I had a dream: *I am leaving the family in which I'd been living. There is a ceremony with the High Priest. I am standing before the High Priest, naked. SourceLove places a crown which shimmers in the light and glows in the dark upon my head and speaks. "I give this crown of wisdom to you; may you always seek within to find your answers and follow your Soul's truth!*

Next, I am given a shield, brightly painted with symbols I would come to know, understand, and use. The shield is to protect my heart when fear and love collide. This is where courage grows! May the power of unconditional love be the law of the land, as it is woven through my peoples' subtle bodies.

Next, I am handed a sword. The sword is to slice away all untruths that wound and blind people. It is the sword that defies fear with the courage to choose and stand in LOVE.

This dream foretold the moral courage beginning to grow within. It was a magnificent representation of the three years of growth I had undergone, and it was the closing of my therapy, in contrast to this dream I had when I first began recording my dreams:

As a young, newly married woman, I take an elevator up to the fourth floor in an old building for a family gathering. When I step off the elevator and proceed to walk into the room where the large family gathering was happening, all conversation stops. All eyes turn and are on me. I am welcomed in. As I step across the threshold and into the room, my mother-in-law throws a huge bag of marbles onto the floor. I try to navigate across the floor, with a smile plastered on my face, acting as if everything is fine.

I discovered, with these metaphoric tools—the crown, the sword, and the shield—that I was prepared to fulfill my Soul's choice and destiny, to free the voices of the women in my family and reconcile the wounds which shattered my family to pieces during the mid-1800s to the late-1800s, and forward into present time. This integration, as I continued, taught me to trust my intuition when I received guidance, surrendering, and acting on behalf of my highest good. Living in this trust and unconditional love released patterns from seven generations back, reweaving the fabric for the generations moving forward in time. I was shown this was, is, and always will be, the way we change our world and create a New Earth, rooted in authenticity, unconditional love, and to raise people who understand and have the wisdom to act accordingly. Energy is neither created nor destroyed. It can only be transformed. And that can only be done by us! By choosing to do the work.

My work of freeing my own voice was a metaphoric pebble dropped into the ocean of potentiality and possibilities. Its impact reverberated from shore to shore as the ripples have gone out and the tides come in. We all, those of us who are Light Workers, are doing this work. The clearing of heavy, dense, fear-driven karmic debt was done! My family's lineage was unraveling the energetic roots of betrayal, deception, and abandonment. I am Woman who brings my light to the Earth.

Things got even a bit more weird as I had a bizarre experience while sitting on the toilet in my guest bathroom. The only way I can describe it was as a whole-body orgasm. Every chakra—of which we have seven—spinning energy wheels was jolted into awakening! My neurons were stimulated into high alert. My entire body organism was put into a state of heightened awareness and the feeling was euphoric and other worldly. This also meant that my vulva, my sex, being the basin for the feminine energy center, called the *Kundalini*, exploded with sensation. My vulva grew exponentially huge and was dripping wet. Honestly, it's what happened. I didn't wear underwear that day as I was just way too sensitive and it was uncomfortable to have fabric clinging to this flower in full bloom! An intense tingling, shaking, vibrating, twitching, and sensitivity within my body went on for the day. A *kundalini* awakening is a powerful experience of enhanced self-awareness. According to tradition, an awakening can create great changes like states of blissfulness and enhanced psychic abilities. It can also awaken DNA patterns imprinted and unfinished ancestral lineage business, which the Soul has chosen to clear. It was the deepening of my desire to know the truth and to clear my ancestor's betrayal and abandonment! And wham-o!

Chapter 12

Paint

A deepening of the vibrant relationship with a force known to me as SourceLove happened through the *kundalini* energy present to me now. Personally, the word God no longer was a comfortable word for me to use. I felt like an imposter using our indigenous people's term "Great Spirit." I argued with the Source about the buzzing being triggered... It still frightened a part of my brain.

Paint, said the Source.

I don't paint, argued I.

Paint spoke as Source through a vibrational language I couldn't see or hear but could feel the answers!

Damn it, I don't paint. I don't like to paint. I can't stand the smell of paint. And I am not an artist. I'm not painting, I argued. Being an artist was for other people in my family. The men.

PAINT. I felt a vibration, a strong pulsing which was growing stronger and was uncomfortable. The pulsing buzz oozed through my nervous system from head to toe. Surrendering, finally my mind gave up its fight. My will had collapsed, no longer up for the fight.

Ok. I'll paint. To be honest, I'm frightened of the images that I am seeing in my mind's eye. Bizarre, sick, and scary images, I shared with the Source voice.

The vibration said, *You are always safe. You are protected, my dear child. Nothing will harm you on this journey. I promise you this. You are worthy. The harm is done. You are strong and grow stronger by the day in your relationship with your inner compass. The implicit trust needed for us to work together is building. I am strong within you; be not afraid, my child. Your moral courage has been deeply rooted and grows daily with every choice you make, saying yes to unconditional love!*

Be not afraid, for I am always with you, continued SourceLove. *You have the name of the ONE who will always empower your physical body with superhuman strength, if need be. Superhuman eyes and heart and answers are yours, and are there when you ask. You know to call out my name through the power of the Christ, the Holy Spirit dwells within, flows through, and guides all patterns of life force. This is the truth, the way, and the Light of the world. Choosing to love and being authentic is what is being asked of your physical self, by your Soul for its progression of growth and learning.*

YOU KNOW THIS! I EMPOWER YOU TO REMEMBER!

And I did! Slowly.

I began painting the bizarre images I saw in my mind's eye. The very first painting to emerge was of a bright, wide open hole of light pouring through a dark space, surrounded with black. The title was *Innocence Pierced*.

Innocence Pierced

The paintings reminded me of, and I was inspired by, Georgia O'Keefe, with natural, vulva-like shapes and colors of bright purples, deep rose shades, midnight blue, and black.

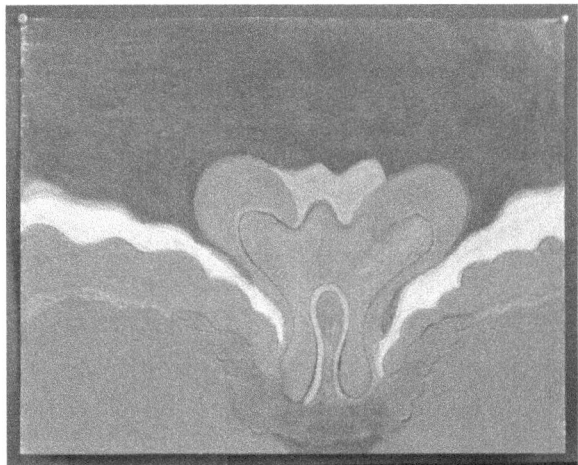

Innocence

As a painting emerged, so did the body's memories. I painted.

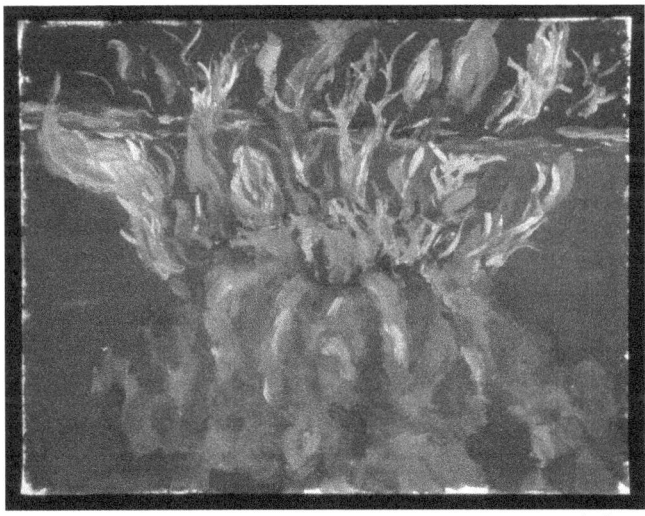

Emotions Explode

My body was then seized with a memory that buzzed, shivered, and shuddered through my being, like an earthquake shaking the Earth to its core. It felt like the job of a winnowing basket being held up to the wind while lifted up and down, gently, allowing the chaff to be blown away, leaving the rich, golden kernels of wheat! This shuddering through my body opened a channel, allowing the paintings to come faster. Almost like an orgasm when I was held in the throes of the creative flow.

I was painting on my dining room table. Paint and brushes, large sheets of paper, and gesso to coat the paper first, were all spread out before me. I had no idea what I was doing, but this I knew—I was frantic to capture the imagery as I saw it emerge. Sometimes as I finished one painting, another began to emerge on top like the peeling of an onion. Layers were being released from horror locked in my body for years. Horrible images appeared. An image of a corkscrew winding down my spine, emerged as pain ripped through my vagina up into my uterus, doubling me over. In this painting called *No See*, the spine with the corkscrew energy was undulating within an ocean, symbolizing my emotions. All the eyes that had watched in silence but didn't offer me protection were flying out of me from the winding energy, releasing stuck, hardened, black goo.

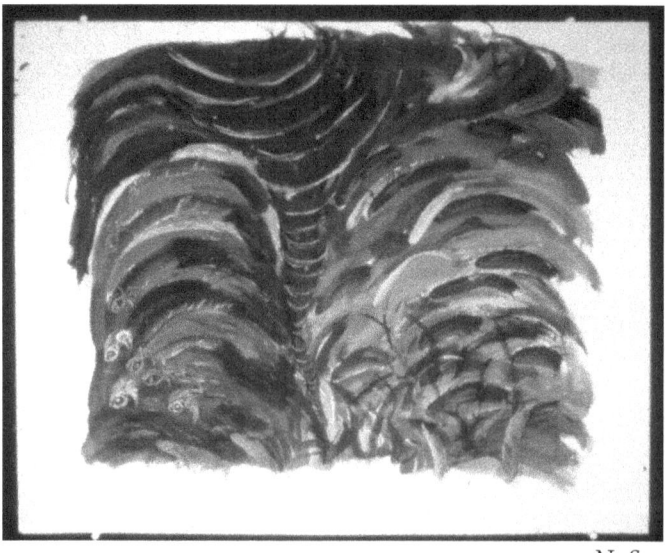

No See

My next painting was of a golden light pouring down from the heavens, flooding my vagina. My body's bed was a bed of spikes. The legs are a spread eagle. Then this painting emerged, separating itself from the others. It was a black monster, cat-like with eyes that looked human. The face had blood dripping from its mouth. When this emerged, it scared the shit out of me. I recognized this image with feelings of hatred wired into my body, replacing unconditional love with utter self-loathing. This monster's presence was the root of evil, sucking my sweet life from me. A vampire.

Self Loathing

Paintings were coming faster; paint seemed to be flying everywhere as I tried to capture the kaleidoscope of visuals emerging. My mother's presence emerged in *Ayla's Birth*. In the painting, I am lying on the ground, naked, surrounded by an angelic halo. Enveloping the outside of the halo is a swooping, hovering presence of hatred with cruel, piercing, yellow eyes splashed onto the paper.

Ayla's Birth

The battle lines were drawn. The war was being waged in my psyche. Spilling onto the paper was the purging of hatred and fear. Afraid of love, afraid to be loved, and I was afraid to give love. Love was twisted into a cord of denial and lies and had kept me hostage for decades. I feared *for* my life if I surrendered to love.

As my memories continued to flood me in the mid 1990s, a total of forty paintings emerged as I slowly remembered being ritually abused in the basement of St. Ann's church. The truth I sought was unraveling, revealing my story.

I noticed these images had become darker, more bizarre, and sinister. Deeply disturbing to my sense of self. Images that made me question my sanity again. What were the motives driving these paintings? And why would I be painting such disturbing images? Memories of the abuse I had received kept emerging and being pushed down as I struggled to accept.

My fear told me constantly: *You can't paint.* "Was this stuff connected to anything real?" my poor, unbelieving, frazzled mind questioned. I felt sick to my stomach and needed to vomit. I purged. I was a sick and twisted bitch to see what I was seeing in my mind's eye. I felt such black, ugly, heavy feelings being carried around in my body, like rocks from a riverbed moved from a human-made disaster forever changing the river's natural flow.

I picked up my paint brush again. I felt like I was stepping down into another dimension. The deeper, more obscure unseen world of my unconscious mind. These paintings had power behind them, extending into and then out as tendrils from my fingers. The first painting in this next series was of St. Ann's church in the Bronx. The "high" Episcopal church was painted as it looked to me, through the eyes of a seven-year-old. It had the graveyard humps painted as I stood looking at it from the courtyard. The church, with its bright red painted doors and black wrought iron hinges and doorknobs that aren't rooted to the earth. On the other side of the painting, I painted in the tall, spiked steel fence which surrounded the church and my home.

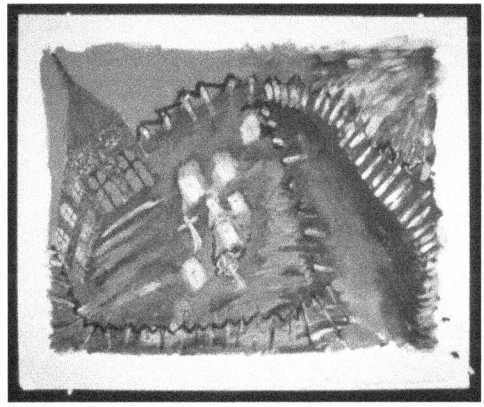

High Episcopal Church

Next came a painting of a female hung on a cross; half her face is light infused, the other half is dark. *The Sacrificial Lamb* is the title. The woman, whose private area is represented with a V, and whose breasts are exposed, hangs on a cross, encased in a glass box. A desert Earth, dry and scrubby, with soft mountainous contours in the horizon can be seen through the box, in the background. It is a small painting, 8'x10', painted in acrylic, which my dad bought and hung in his office.

Isolation

Then came a painting of a vagina in vivid colors with a crucifix plunged into it up to the cross bar. The body of a child, encased in a bubble, floats outside the violated body's vagina and is surrounded in light, divinely protected.

An eerie painting then emerged of an altar with candlesticks on it, painted in a skewed and strange perspective. A heart lies on the altar. Blood is dripping down the front of it, staining the pristine, white altar cloth. Such a contrast to putting my face on the Earth during the sweat lodge and praying as I smelled Mother Earth's dirt.

In the corner of a blackened room, drawn with charcoal, a child is depicted. Her knees are pulled up to her chest. Her arms encircle her knees. Shadows of adults in black robes hover around her. Everything in this painting is elusive and hazy.

The Black Crows Watch

These paintings saved my life as horrible deeds were done to my body. I am remembering myself to be a thriver after having experienced Ritual Abuse Torture, or the acronym R.A.T. These ugly memories were released from my cells through the voice of my emerging and powerful creativity. Talents unbeknownst to me broke through the prison walls of fear held in my locked mind. The paintings told the story of how the Bride Doll shed her smallness and grew into her authentic greatness. The paintings became more detailed and mature as trust builds and confidence rewires itself between the *vibrational voice of Source* and me, my human experiencer, empowering my true, authentic, Soulful Self.

My parents must see this body of work. I was bound soulfully to present my story to them. But how? I talked continuously with Source, trying to figure out how I was to share this body of work. My voice had uncovered ancient wounding in need of attention. I understood that I had to offer this gift of my work, to my parents without needing anything in return. That means I am not to hope that I get their approval, or their validation, or even their love. I was understanding that I must look within to forgive myself first before I am able to share anything with them.

Forgiveness was a struggle for me to understand. I was angry with my parents. With their lack of awareness, their assumptions, their inability to trust or believe in me. I was seething like a fire-breathing dragon. I also loved the creative journey I was on and felt like it was a gift. The most amazing silver lining! I was split in two—warring within as I struggled with this concept—a very Christian concept.

Split in Two

I had witnessed people using forgiveness to justify poor behavior one day, seek forgiveness on Sunday, then turn right around and do it again on Monday. So, forgiveness in this fashion didn't cut the mustard with me. I was puzzled. I asked for clarity, answers to know how I was to forgive because I was at a loss.

As I was driving down the road one day in Keene, NH, I remembered the street was busy. My ears began to ring loudly. I felt like I was having a mental explosion— a breakdown, or breakthrough, or melt down, as I tried to keep my shit together while driving. Luckily, I was alone, and the kids were at home. I couldn't pull over as I was caught in traffic—I saw an image of "the mad woman" appear before me, in my mind's eye. She was screaming...

I'm losing my mind. I'm losing my mind to my body
cause I can't go on any longer.
No, I can't go on any longer like this.

The Mad Woman

I heard music in my head; a melody came with this screaming mad woman image searing herself into my brain. When I arrived home, I was frantic to paint who I had just met while driving. Scrambling to spread the gesso, a face emerged. Her mouth was open wide in a scream—her eyes were wild—and I painted her out of me. I found a beautiful antique, hand-tatted lace collar that belonged to my great-grandmother, Emma, and attached that to the paper, around *the mad woman's* neck. I was amazed that I fell in love with her immediately, no longer a threat to me. She was free to be an ally to me now. *Great-great-grandmother Christina, you are free to leave now. I've got this!*

I felt deep sorrow and anguish well up from within as the extent of the silencing penetrated deep into my bones. I found myself relating to her story. I felt the anger of my mother for the first time, conscious of how terribly hard it was for her to have been silenced and rendered useless by the church, her husband, and ultimately by her roles of wife and mother. I understood why she resented her children so much. I was remembering the lonely days in the Bronx when my family life shattered; Mom decided she had to go away to care for herself.

In need of fresh air, I stepped outside into a beautiful, crisp New Hampshire fall day. Inhaling a breath all the way down into my belly, I whispered, "Great-grandmother, Christina, dear love, you are free to leave now. You are forgiven." Through my breath I gathered her essence several more times, whispering to her Spirit, "You are loved. You are forgiven. You are worthy and always were. You are loved. All is well. I am so sorry. Thank you for showing me your truth. I see you, love. You are loved and you are forgiven. You are free to fly free." *Whoosh*, blew in a rush of air and stirred up the leaves on the ground, sending them flying in all directions as she went on her way.

The cords to the past unraveled seven generations back and seven forward when this energetic release happened.

Metaphorically, I was swimming in an ocean at night as memories continued to flood my consciousness and hijacked my languid body. I remembered being ritually abused in the cold, stone room in the catacombs of St. Ann's. Candles encircling the room flickered, creating wild shaped shadows undulating on the walls. Dark shadows moved through my mind's eye as though floating; the men dressed in black appeared as crows. I heard the droning like angry wasps. It flooded my senses.

The Weeping Christ

The Weeping Christ emerged on paper. My "brother" was so sad. His teachings were grossly misunderstood. Fear was rampant, mistreatment of women was rampant, and his words had been misconstrued by men in power who wanted power over people to rule with greed and scarcity as their means of control. Through my new eyes, in the center of my forehead—called the Third Eye or Pineal gland—I perceived a deeper, sinister past; the Earth was as an object to be plundered for her resources—raped. Just as women and girls were treated while shoulders shrugged.

After *The Weeping Christ* emerged, I gained insight into forgiveness and what I must do. Forgiveness had nothing to do with what I was spoon-fed in church—to forgive others. That was not MY job. That was your job, SourceLove. I must forgive myself for hating myself, for calling myself a stupid bitch, a dumbass, and worse when I made mistakes. I must forgive myself for the years and years I caved in and believed the false perception my parents had of me, which I finally believed as well. I was stupid, not worthy of educating, I was filled with self-loathing, and I pondered this. This made sense as to why there was so much violence in the world and numbing tools; if self-hatred was at the core of my belief, then treating others' as I would have others treat me was a no brainer. In this paradigm, hatred ruled.

That was the Soul's plan. I was born carrying the past ancestral lineage of business left unfinished, carried through my DNA and my own childhood experiences of betrayal and abandonment, triggering the path which was set, to lose my way, forget my beauty and grace-filled self, and to hate everything about me! How was this complete betrayal to my Self done? I chose the exact people as the "teachers" I needed, for my Soul's evolution. I have never seen myself as a "victim" but rather an experiencer of life looking for the silver lining in what it takes to be happy and live a meaningful life!

The perfect "energetic" match for me, which triggered hidden patterns to be released, presented itself as I was groomed to be silent, waiting on the men dressed as the little Bride Doll. Dressed as they wanted me to present myself in my little frilly apron and shiny black shoes, so when the dark rituals happened, I knew to be silent. While I was alone in the Bronx, living with my dad, the head priest had access to me pretty much all the time. I was frightened by his boldness towards me and didn't like his fondness of me. I felt his eyes devouring me and then how he enjoyed me squirming in his lap, uncomfortable when he caught me between my apartment and Dad's office and insisted that I enter his office and closed the door behind me.

Laid upon a cold slab of concrete, which served as an altar, it was believed by my perpetrators that I was unclean because I was a girl/child. I had the power of the Light within, that was the problem, as they saw it. God's light, as they saw it, was only to be acknowledged and accessed by means of a priest. Anything other than that meant heresy! I was a wild card to them and needed to be silenced, altering my path and submerging my authentic voice.

The dark services began with chanting. Shadows danced on the walls in the catacomb, seemingly to the vibration of their unified sound. It was loud and sounded like a hive of bees busy at work serving their queen. As my body lay naked on the altar, traveling in my mind's eye up, I saw a set of golden stairs which descended from the right hand of God. My Soul rose out of my body and ascended these stairs, placing me in the lap of the Christ. This was easy as I visualized myself in the large mural behind the altar, up above in the Sanctuary of St. Ann's. As I watched from above, surrounded in a bubble of light, a crucifix was inserted into my vagina to "cleanse and purify" me, ripping my vagina to shreds.

The body felt nothing.

Numb Family Chaos

• • •

The mending of my vagina created scar tissue, making two small vaginal openings. During these "cleansings" I was repeatedly told I was unworthy to "gather up the crumbs from under my Lord's table," a part of the same prayer from the Book of Holy Communion and from the *Prayer of Humble Access*:

> *We do not presume to come to this your table, O merciful Lord,*
> *trusting in our own righteousness,*
> *but in your abundant and great mercies.*
> *We are not worthy so much as to gather up*
> *the crumbs under your table;*
> *but you are the same Lord*
> *whose character is always to have mercy.*
> *Grant us, therefore, gracious Lord,*
> *so to eat the flesh of your dear Son Jesus Christ,*
> *and to drink his blood,*
> *that our sinful bodies may be made clean by his body,*
> *and our souls washed through his most precious blood,*
> *and that we may evermore dwell in him, and he in us. Amen.*

Certain phrases were used: *We do not presume, O merciful Lord, trusting in our own righteousness, we are not worthy*. The crucifix was plunged deeper, anchoring the seed of disgust, loathing, and hatred of all things alive, bright, creative, and vibrant. *You are not worthy to gather up the crumbs from under our table. But we are the very masters whose character is always to have mercy. Therefore, our gracious Lord grants us grace to eat your flesh and drink your blood.*

The imagery in this prayer disturbed me. Forgiveness was radical. I had to forgive myself. And not a moment before was I able to share what I had discovered and remembered of my childhood with my parents. The church teaches to forgive others. I did not find this to be the correct way to understand forgiveness. It is I who needs to be forgiven, for having lost my way and forgotten God's love for me, twisting the word to be unsavory and feel wrong. I had buried and forgotten the deep and beautiful roots which connected me to Mother Earth. I had grown strong feelings of hatred; I feared Nature and being alone, outside anywhere, which was not my natural and original state of presence. I startled easily, popping out of my body at random and inopportune times! This was caused by a state of extreme fear, a rooting of primal terror, which used imagery and lies to capture the hearts and minds of people, followers, and believers, by the millions, around the world.

I realized, when I was able to forgive myself, that my parents and my perpetrators were automatically released from the deeds that they acted out against me. The Souls of my perps will be dealt with through the karma they created. Worrying or taking any responsibility for my perpetrator's actions was not my job. I didn't need to give a second more of my power to the head priest and his cronies through fear— the black crows. I chose not to go after them in a court of law. We have a history of crazy women in my family, and the door to recovery had not yet opened for an empowered and safe passage, for survivors to shed light on this ancient practice in our patriarchal society.

SourceLove had another way for me.

Months passed, and finally I was ready. I invited a girlfriend to take a road trip with me and my portfolio to my parents' home in Bridgeport, Connecticut. We sat in my parents' colorful living room—them on the couch, my friend and I opposite in comfy rustic leather chairs that they had shipped back from Ecuador. I was nervous. My palms were sweaty, and my armpits stank from sweating fear out. My eyes roamed the walls, and I loved the wall hangings collected from Ecuador: the brightly painted pottery candlestick holder depicting the Tree of Life, complete with the snake, Adam covering his private parts with a fig leaf, and Eve, bare-breasted, hiding behind the snake as it wrapped around the trunk, climbing the branches. The leaves were shaped to hold the candles.

The colorful room calmed me, captivated my mind, and flooded me with comforting memories of Costa Rica. This brought my Soul back into my body. *I am safe.* I repeated this silently as a mantra: I am safe. I was also very nervous. My palms and armpits were wet with sweat. I reeked of fear. But I was safe.

SourceLove filled my body with unconditional love and compassion as sweet memories awakened in me. I felt the breeze on my face, which carried the ripe coffee bean smells as I inhaled deeply, held my breath, and exhaled fear out. I did this several times, inhaling the memory of sugar cane ripe and at its peak. I exhaled through my vagina as the memory of the scar tissue was triggered, activating the release of fear. I then breathed in unconditional love, joy, and called forth sweet memories to fill my heart with unconditional love and support of my highest good and the highest good for all involved. I sat and breathed for a bunch of minutes, scanning my parents' home, settling into my heart, and calling forth the courage to go through with this revelation!

Mom and Dad

I asked my parents to withhold comments until the end. I was clear of needing anything from them. I radiated unconditional love! My heart was joyous; finally, the moment had arrived.

I opened my large portfolio case that was laying on the coffee table. And one by one, I moved the paintings slowly, allowing my story to unfold. I didn't speak a word. Nor did they. No words were needed. In this moment, silence was golden. The silent space allowed for wild and primitive feelings to emerge as the story told itself, as one painting at a time was revealed.

Dad began crying at the end and thanked me for speaking up and speaking my truth. "Now we can begin talking with each other in a meaningful way," he stated emphatically.

Relief flooded me! I hadn't realized I'd been holding my breath. Inhaling and exhaling deeply, I gave thanks to SourceLove as I inhaled another breath and focused on sending love deep into my bruised and battered heart on the exhale.

This was written on January 29, 1990, shortly after my visit, by my mother, Gwynneth Kelley:

WOMAN

Ayla, a woman, our daughter
Came to show us—
herself.

Colors danced before my eyes—
Vibrant soul-dance colors
singing a jubilate of this woman's journey
in tempera, pastel, and watercolor.

Wandering alone, afraid to return home,
for denials pathetic vagary
points its condemning finger, chanting all the while
"It's you, it's you, you're the bad, bad one."
I feel the burning rage,
That's why I feared insanity.

Why?
Because I died a thousand deaths
As each child I raised.
Letting go, letting go, letting go
of my dreams, of my needs, of myself.

My precious daughter—this started out to be your accolade.
Forgive me for digressing—but we are both women.
And that black phantom spirit hovering over you—
the one you said was me—
that kept you down
was all that I abhorred and feared
repressed in me and absorbed by you.
No wonder your beautiful spirit had to vacate for awhile
haunting me with its energy,
wooing me, calling me to embrace my sexuality,
so, your tabernacle home could be safe for you again.

I was flooded in an ocean of gratitude almost sinking in the torrent of joyful tears. It felt like a Holy Baptism as I birthed joy!

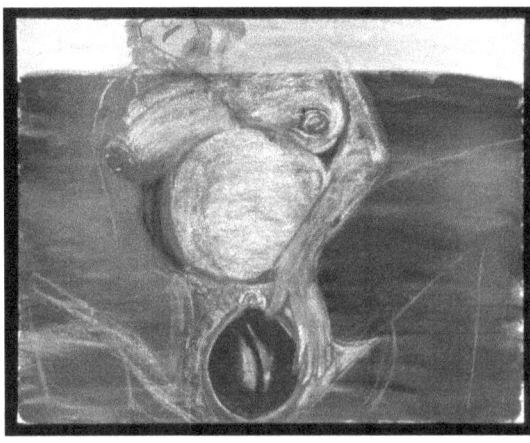

Holy Baptism

• • •

There are no words that express the gratitude I felt for my parents—especially you, my mama bear. I wondered how life could have been different if we had been friends, you know, living in a healthy mother-daughter relationship while I was growing up. I wondered how life would have been different for us both if you had been your beautiful artist self, sculpting, painting, writing, and thriving. Would you have hated me so passionately and been so jealous of me, or would you have embraced your own repressed sexual energy and expressed it through your art and writing? Giving me the space to sing and dance, write music, and live my dreams. Who knows? What I knew was: My journey so far had been amazing, magical, and mystical, beyond what I believed possible, a dream. I had discovered courage deep within where fear and love collided, scattering my energy. Breathing in SourceLove, I exhaled terror and kept choosing love. Repeatedly, I looked for the silver lining, believing that love will win. With this, I realized I was choosing to create from the ashes of devastation a beautiful life I love and the real mission: to fall in love with myself. My Holy Grail! Deeply, passionately, adoringly in love with my healthy body, my solid and flexible mind, my strong, courageous, and open heart, and my ability to speak and create my truth to offer the world, in service to love. I desire, through my service work, for people to realize how lovingly powerful we are, to create a unified world where peace reigns, creativity is expressed, love is the way, and the connection to SourceLove is realized... This is my passion, unleashed!

My healing continued as poems, songs, paintings, and movement all merged and exploded. I was an artist. I had many gifts and a powerful voice with which to share this enormous soul-inspired creative that I now know myself to be! This creativity was my superpower! Words came, some as little ditties, like children singing on the playground.

> *Just a little girl when I was first abused.*
> *Just a little girl when I was first abused.*
> *I'm just a little girl*
> *when someone took me*

for their very own.

This was sung to the tune of a jump rope slapping the ground. Refrain times three:

Mama is gone,
Daddy is around
but he doesn't care for me at all.

I recorded these melodies with a simple recorder, with which I could lay down up to four tracks. I had no clue what I was doing! But it was a blast. More songs, more paintings, and poetry arrived through my heart, eyes, and onto the paper, in whatever media SourceLove asked me to use. I used acrylic, watercolor, creating a relief with oil stick pastels, allowing the watercolors to flow around the shapes drawn; glitter was added as my joy infused these images. Some of my paintings became quite detailed, surprising me always with the imagery I was seeing emerge.

Purging the hatred infecting me by painting; I vomited the evil in colors splashed across my paper.

Emotions are free

Sometimes the images came so quickly that one image emerged on top of another. I followed what I was seeing as best I could. As I painted, my body violently trembled as though my cells were shuddering and shaking to release the molecules that were not *authentic*. Painting was a thrill that freed me. I felt the cords that kept me bound, releasing; returning me back to love, with the ability to express it.

In 1991, serpents began entering my dreams at night, and then serpents were slithering, it seemed, out of me and onto the paper. There were a lot of serpents. The serpents felt like they were wrapped around my insides and lashing out in my mind's eye, with their flicking tongue. I felt the Christian belief that decreed it an evil creature, transforming snake to serpent, with evil, sexual connotations flaring up within, burning me.

Forbidden Fruit

The first serpent painting I did was an abstract of a huge flower divided in half. Half was light and half was dark, and through the center wound a serpent crawling through both flowers. Was the snake/serpent part of the destruction of my innocence? What does the painting mean, I wondered. And snakes kept coming. I finally did two life-sized paintings...

I painted *The Bride Doll* dressed in the garb of a hooker. She wore a thong, a garter belt, had bruised thighs, a roaring-twenties feather in her hair, and her breasts were exposed. Snakes were slithering out of her vagina and were crawling up and around her body. Tanya, I named her, the "bad" girl. Painting her released her essence from me and fear that was attached to her legacy—I expelled the one who believes she must play the victim, onto my canvas.

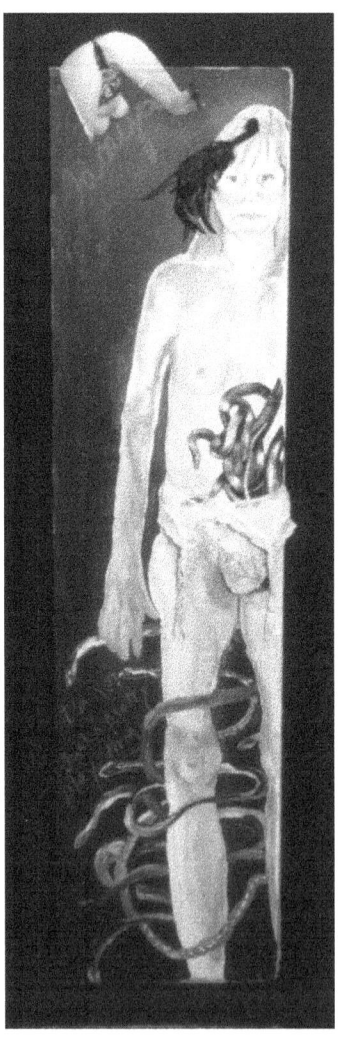

The Bride Doll

The next life-sized painting that followed was of me as a warrior woman. Ruby, who held a three-dimensional sickle, attached to a 3D plaster cast of my arm and hand, which was coming off the canvas.

The Warrior Woman

The Warrior Woman had flames coming up behind her, and she was wearing a fabric sarong around her waist. In this painting, the paper mache snake wrapped around her body and arms. The warrior woman is unified with snakes and is able to communicate with snake consciousness as she lives in harmony, as did the ancient priestesses from my indigenous European roots.

For weeks, snake paintings came.

Chapter 13

Mom Responded

I called my mother several weeks after they witnessed my story. I was checking in to see how my mama was doing. I was concerned. I hadn't heard boo from them, which seemed unusual, especially from my mother, until I received this written by my mother on February 25, 1990:

MY DESCENT

I am not sure what caused it,
My descent that is.
As the weekend progressed,
A provoking thought lingered in my brain.

Our daughter had called and we had talked,
And what was said hung furtively in half flight
in the recesses of my mind.

Friday passed and Saturday too.
It was the Sunday I was aiming for.

After the Sunday Eucharist when all was calm,

The afterglow of Christ's presence
Permeating our simple meal.

And so I said to my husband, her father;
"There is something I need to share with you.
Is now the time?"

And time stopped!

How does one share a daughter's plea
Fashioned out of honesty, courage, and agony,
from the dream world's fantasy and frozen reality?
Brought into light, through denial's veil of tears and
sobbing heart's admission.
Innocent mind, tormented heart, abandoned soul
hidden from scathing eyes for eight and twenty years.

How does one share the shame of life's tragic garb
worn unbeknownst by victim, while Mom and Dad, and
others look on and wonder why bother?

After I read the poem, I realized that, like me, after I have a huge aha moment which reveals truth to me, I, my ego/fearful self, freaks out. I tend to retreat and isolate until I feel safe. Truth revealing takes time and is best when it is gentle. When too much opens too wide, my human self can't handle the high vibration all at once. This was because past wounds, fear, jealousies. whatever we hold from the past that is unresolved, gets stuck. Mom was just temporarily stuck and observing herself. Here's another zinger when the evidence I sought to affirm this creative unfolding was being revealed to me. I was blown open as my memories were validated.

Gwynneth D. Kelley
February 20, 1992

I THREW IT AWAY

Yes, I did—it's hard to believe,
but I can't deny it.
I threw it away—trashed it—
what was written by my daughter
when she was only nine.

Ugly words and bleak thoughts—
I did not want to hear, so closed my ears
And veiled my eyes.
She wrote, I know not what—
but it's offensive nature
bounced off my brittle self, and I in arrogant authority
tore to shreds her blackest plight,
leaving her bound and gagged for thirty years.
Caught up in man's lust this daughter so fair,
to be used in the vilest ways.
As I stood by, her mom, not seeing,
not hearing, behind my window pane.
Anxiety gripped—screaming, screaming—
Engulfed in anger's hell,
As church bells rang and the organ played.

I was falling in love with me—this gorgeous self I was discovering myself to be. I spent time peering into my eyes in my bathroom mirror: *I love you. I love you. I love you, too. I see you. I hear you*, I'd speak to the eyes peering back at me, my heart wide open. At times it seemed there were different eyes looking back, the eyes of the different ones I'd been. Looking into my eyes was excruciatingly painful for the first several months. I couldn't stand the feeling of warm love flowing. What I heard in my mind, racing like a gerbil around its wheel, was a venomous loop of self-hatred spewing. I exhaled as I remembered,

THE GIFT

I don't remember her,
but I am told she was a gift.
When I was only eight
I must have played with her,
acting out the bride, as children always do.
But I have no memory of this gift
my mother gave to me.

I'm not surprised
by this gift.
No wonder it was easy
To fill those shoes my mother left behind.

She gave me the gift
to be my father's bride doll when I was only eight.
Frozen in time.
It was so easy to fill those shoes left behind.

To be my father's bride doll,
standing by his side
I was the gift,
when only I was eight.

This was written by me after I received Mom's poem and the self-portrait had begun. I saw that I was the gift! As I looked for the silver lining and realized that right where my feet were planted was the beautiful, creative, rich life I was desiring. This was the silver lining. It wasn't something outside of myself I had to find. Day by day, life unfolded before me. "You are living the life as a creative," I told myself as I looked into my eyes. "Your creativity is unlimited. It is mind blowing." The eyes looked back at me, soft and open.

To paint a life-sized portrait of myself, I had to put a full-length mirror in my bathroom. Stripped-down, buck-naked, standing in front of the mirror, I spent a lot of time studying myself. It was extremely uncomfortable. I felt so stupid and humiliated standing there gawking. As I allowed myself to sink more deeply into the experience, I saw a terrible and frightening sadness, like a gaping, unattended, festering wound. Each day, early in the morning, I began this ritual of studying my body. I'd study the shape of my breasts, how soft the curve at the bottom was, or I'd notice the softness of my "Kelley Belly" and kneed it like clay, accepting its softness and remembering the babies it carried, stretching my skin so tightly as my baby grew.

You stupid bitch, this is pathetic. Look at those flabby boobs and those stretchmarks. What an ugly, flabby body; you think this is going to make you clean and wipe away your past? Stupid bitch.

No. Beating. Up. On. Myself. Those old voices were losing ground. The hating was done! I could feel their powerful grip loosening. Gazing lovingly at the body standing before me, vulnerable, my heart exploded with a giddy, playful acceptance. I'm ok. And it's okay for me to have these crazy ideas that woo me into standing buck-naked in front of the mirror, looking intently at my body. It's my body. It's okay to see what I look like and to drop the judgments, because I realized in that moment, I don't care what others' think. I didn't give a flying fuck. I care about what I think and feel. I have a burning desire to know myself. And with this request, SourceLove invited me to take my work out into the world and share.

I knew I had to do this, because once again, I had hit a wall trying to dig the root of self-loathing out! I no longer hated myself so thoroughly as the superficial layers have been cleared. I was happy this had changed for me, but I still struggled with my self-esteem and feeling worthy of SourceLove.

This journey was the quintessential journey that mystics have called for centuries: *Dark Night of the Soul*, triggered by a deep soul searching or *kundalini*

Heart Wide Open

awakening! I became a stranger to myself, and my body was a mystery with the hidden information it carried from DNA stored from ancestor's business left unfinished.

I was enthralled with my life work and felt the beginning of joy bubbling deep in my Soul. I was dancing on the edge of my mind's excavation, staring into a great abyss in an altered state, feeling very relaxed, when the next thing I knew, I was slithering on my belly to the edge of Irazú, peering into a living volcano—the guardian of our home, protector of my Soul through fire. The great one I met in Costa Rica.

I blinked my eyes and my body shuddered as though I was cold. I was not. I had just changed realities, consciously aware of being in two places at once!

To be present in my body, Source guided me to take my work out into my community, and I pondered this, deeply. Holy shit, really? That terrified me to the core of my being. *Bingo!* The ball on the pinball machine just hit pay day! A rush of energy downloaded, and I was trying to process a ton of new information about confronting terror.

Emerging Selves

First things first and remembering how I had originally spelled my name, Sin-the-a, I prayed about the name I was to wear, as Cynthia no longer seemed to fit. I remembered reading the series *Clan of the Cave Bear* and loving the main character, Ayla, as she was strong, a survivor, who didn't fit in anywhere, and was a wise woman. I discovered, when I got home and did a bit of research, that Ayla was a Celtic and an Iranian name which means "light bearer." ***Ayla, a woman who brings her light to the Earth*** was born as I identified with that character in this new turn in my journey.

My paintings, about forty of them, went together in a slideshow. The music and poems I had been writing and singing were combined into the story, but it seemed recording everything was the next step. However, without any money, the show just needed to go on. I was dubious. SourceLove told me to trust. The support needed would follow!

In the first show, a shadow screen was made by using a white bed sheet stretched onto an extendible camping tent pole, which my husband and I shaped into a half moon. The feet were anchored with 2x4 pole braces, drilled at the base for the tent poles to sit in. By using the shadow screen and lights, the stage was set up with a friend sitting in a chair behind the screen and me standing beside her, telling my story. The way I placed the screen made my friend look like a mom and I was like a small child, telling my story to my mother. It was a powerful, knock-your-socks-off presentation, which in the beginning I called "Open Heart Surgery." It was simple, but the images with the words and story being told opened people's hearts, giving those who have not experienced sexual or physical abuse a toe dip into what it feels like to be a survivor of dehumanization. The truth is everyone has experienced dehumanization at some time, on some level, in some form. The fabric of our culture is based on annihilation of a people; how can we not have experienced dehumanization at some point? Those who seem to glide and slide through their lives choose to be happy for no reason, in spite of negative feelings. They don't appear to get stuck. Appearances can fool us, though! My audience's compassion was awakened.

Crayons and paper lay on every seat for the ending of my story, during which I asked for quiet as my sacred story-sharing time drew to a close. In the quiet before we spoke, I asked people to express what they were feeling.

WOW, WOW, WOW! What a gift. I was onto something. Ending this way was so powerful for all the people who were present. It proved to be a beautiful way to have closure and a very safe and loving experience for all of us. The terror and nausea that rose in my body I realized was able to be transmuted by super-soaking it with love. Energy is energy. It cannot be created or destroyed. It expands and contracts and it wears no labels. It morphs and changes. My human self was the one with language, who has named all things. When I name feelings, I assign these names a positive or a negative meaning. My feelings are judged acceptable or unacceptable—good, bad, values become right and wrong.

If I took the label off "terror" for me, it became a powerful, exciting, all-consuming vibration in my body, which triggered huge fear. As waves of love flowed towards me during my story sharing, the terror which had risen in me was crushed with ripple after ripple of love, from the willingness to be vulnerable... This mixing of opposing forces caused love to prevail. As the audience responded, the quiver of loving energy undulating through the room grew stronger. Acknowledging the presence of love, staying present to experience it, and absorbing it into my parched heart and dried up cells allowed me to transmute the terror as my heart filled with joy, overriding the twisted message implanted in my brain, years and years ago. When my energy system flooded with love, fear dissolved. And this dissolving of fear continues today. Every day, it is a choice.

It's amazing to me how we can hold such powerful emotions at the same time and be grateful for it all. I was beyond amazed and grateful that this was the next step for me. This was a dream come true for the girl I remember who dreamt of being on stage and then lost that dream!

What a tremendous gift and privilege I have been given for the colorful and amazing journey I have embarked upon and embraced to be happy, creating a soulful life in service to SourceLove. The jewel I found lies within. It has always been there, hidden from view, submerged for its protection until it was time!

Chapter 14

It's My Time

Dreaming in the creation of my multimedia soundtrack for the performance piece came as a gift from a musician extraordinaire, after his wife had witnessed my first ever make-shift performance! His generosity and support was overwhelming. Another dear friend sat at the piano while I shyly sang her the melodies I was hearing in my head. One by one, she sensitively picked notes, asking me if it sounded like this...or was it this... I experienced days of ecstasy, bursting with joy like the buds opening on a glorious spring day, an outstanding moment in my life! Family time was also filled with moments of ecstatic playful laughter and joy. I created six or seven songs with my friend, which were the ones I took into the studio. Creating a soundtrack for my performance was remarkable. It was a heady moment of generosity in action, grace, and tremendous faith at the work. I was rolling down the river of grace and ease! I also worked with a vocal coach, giving me instruction right in the moments prior to recording and as we were recording, urging my voice to grow stronger. I was painfully shy, but with such vibrant love and excitement for my project coming from these incredibly generous and talented people, my voice grew bigger and bigger still and has remained so today.

My creativity was a love story unfolding. And the story was a modern-day family love story. I loved every minute of it, as I fell optimistically in love with myself.

Painting, singing, dancing, and turning this all into a multimedia performance was touching upon the dream that my little girl had had: to be a singer-songwriter and dancer, shooting for Broadway.

A memory from Mathews, Virginia, 1966 surfaces: I'll never forget the first school dance I went to. I was in the 6th grade, living in Mathews, Virginia, and my school was not integrated. I was dressed up in a white lace dress, with a white corsage pinned to my still-flat chest. My hair was spray-starched into a flip. All the boys lined one side of the gym and the girls lined the other. When the music started, no one moved. I, being who I am, went and asked a boy I liked to dance. He reluctantly took my hand and followed me to the dance floor. Slow dancing required a teacher to come over and separate us if our bodies were touching with a ruler. We always had done this at Maria's house during birthday parties. Cuddling in close. My poor chosen victim must not have known what hit him. Next the music changed, to a favorite of mine, Diana Ross and the Supremes. The rhythm has my kinda beat. I start rockin' and shakin' my booty. Relaxed, grooving, and having a blast, I blast into my zone! Next thing I remember, the music ended. I was standing in the middle of the dance floor by myself. Everyone was standing around the edge of the gym, staring at me. Kids were giggling, embarrassed. Teachers and chaperones had their hands covering their mouths shaped in an "O," as they stared at me in horror. I was shakin' my booty, just as I had always done when I was little. I had forgotten my mom's original reaction of horror—same thing here. My white-skinned Anglo people, I figured, had forgotten how to dance. I was uncomfortable being the center of their gawking and disapproving attention. Out of my body I popped, splatted, and then into a body of shame. My face was crimson and my ears burned from the heat of embarrassment.

With this memory, it's like the key finally fits the lock because all the components lined up perfectly! A shift had happened within me. I realized I was not in need of healing any longer. I wasn't broken and in need of fixing. I never was!

I was strong, joyful, curious about life, and had grown comfortable with change. I was happy for no reason.

The *Dear Child* series was born. These paintings were totally different from the other paintings that had the outpouring of feelings unexpressed. In these paintings, I was imagining and daydreaming what a different life could have looked like if I had had a happy mom. This daydream was easy! All I had to do was look at my daughter and watch her engage with the small things around her, right under her feet. I loved learning and watching and heeding the invitations that were pouring forth from this mischievous daughter of mine. Out splashed a painting of Mom and me at the beach, holding hands. This joyful image sparkled with aliveness, vibrancy, and joy! Glitter became my new favorite medium. The next painting was of a little girl swinging high in a tree with a wild, gleeful look in her eyes, her toes reaching for the sky!

Dear Child, Happy Face

Dear Child, Mom and Child

It was March 1992, in Brattleboro, Vermont.

What a profound event to walk in from the street and bear witness to an art event like no others. We brought 3,000 people through our doors in three weeks, which was extraordinary and incendiary. This event, which I had spearheaded in the office of my therapist after having just participated in an art show in Portsmouth, New Hampshire, called *The Art of Healing*, in 1990, took two years of careful and sensitive planning. This was no ordinary show of art. This show was gathering survivors of violence and dehumanization who were courageous Souls and ready to share their stories. Those attracted to this show were willing to break eons of silencing and speak our profound truth. We had a hundred participants. We were artists, performers, storytellers, puppeteers, and educational speakers, and we had a support network set up for those in need, at any time during any of our events, including a trained sexual abuse therapist. We had a safe room with stuffed animals, paper, crayons, and big, soft, cozy pillows, and it was a peaceful sitting space should someone be triggered, have a panic attack, and need assistance, fast! All around town, in every available venue, we hosted an event. We had events for children, teens, and we even opened the gallery up to the prison, inviting perpetrators of sexual assault to walk through our Soul's injuries. Our gallery housed one hundred pieces of art in all media covering the walls. People's hearts were hanging on the walls, our voices emerging strong as one, through the myriad of painful, transformative, and beautiful expressions. On the program for this night's events was my performance piece, "Dear Child." Tonight was my night to shine! A whammy got thrown at me, making my armpits stink with fear. *Oh, shit. My parents are here. What am I going to do? Do I change the performance to protect them, or leave it as it is?*

After my performance was over, I noticed Dad waving his hands in the air, laughing, which meant he was most likely telling someone a story, oblivious to the stark feelings of vulnerability that were swirling around the room. My performance was the last event for the night, in the month-long multimedia event, *Heartwork: Art Emerging from Silence*, which took place in March, 1992, in Brattleboro, Vermont. Mom, on the other hand, stormed up to me. The veins in her neck popped out, her eyes had changed, and she stood a hand away from my face, up close and personal, and spit out, "If I had had a knife for every time I wanted you dead, I'd have stabbed you a thousand times." I was pushed back by the force of her words spoken so clearly and unadulterated. The hatred I felt was thick enough to cut with her imaginary knife. I stepped in closer. I reached my arms around her and embraced her, whispering, "Thank you," in her ear. "This is an amazing gift you have just given me, Mom. Because I felt that knife a thousand times, yet you never laid a finger on my body in punishment. It was emotionally that you beat the shit out of me. So, yes this is a gift. I know now I did not imagine your hatred of me."

Mom stood stunned, silent as my words sunk in.

"I am a work in progress as I forgive myself, every day, and every moment in every day, for believing the lies I was told by Dad, and his cronies, and your silent compliance, and hatred. As a result, I shut my true self away, safe from ever loving myself, which twisted my natural self-love into self-hatred. A hatred so deep that I believed that if my love for my baby touched her, she would die. I believed I could kill the most precious gift in the world, my child, born of my body, of my flesh and blood, just by loving her."

Mom came back into herself and was amazed at my work and the voice she saw painted across canvas, telling such a painful story, and with images that were stunning. "I am flabbergasted by your work. I had no idea...you are so talented!"

Her comment told the story of where my mom and I are in our relationship. After that comment came racing through, busting up my joy after a successful evening, I told Mom that we needed to take a break from one another for a year, so she can work on owning her role and speaking her truth. I felt her jealousy oozing, like a vampire: she wanted my life force.

"If we are to have a relationship with one another, you must own your evil one. The one that has hated me just for breathing. Otherwise," I tell her, "you will not see me or enjoy a relationship with your grandchildren, ever." I let that sink in while standing at arm's length distance from her.

Our year of silence was about to be broken. In four days' time, Mom and Dad were driving up to Vermont to be a part of the Unitarian congregation, which was hosting my sacred performance work. They would be staying in New Hampshire at my sister's home. My mother wrote beforehand in a letter, "I hear you. I am thankful that you are inviting me to join the congregation and witness your story and its impact on the receivers. I will do my work. It's what I've always wanted and what my poetry screams out about. So, Ayla, thank-you for this gift. For your strength and courage to break this cycle of violence in our family. Thank you."

My mother writes: *Journaling about a time in New York. Looking back.* The date is January 8, 1998:

In four days' time we will be driving to the Unitarian church in Vermont to be a part of the congregation involved in Ayla's celebration. John and I leave Saturday and will stay with Katherine. She asked me if she could bring her little girl—Oh my. I wonder if Katherine really understands just what Ayla is performing. My antennas are reacting! I have been working very hard to prepare myself—allow my feelings to come out—how do I really feel, how will I feel as she reads the Bride Doll poem and sings her jump rope song? Just mentioning it now makes my stomach swirl. Why? Because I want to shout at Ayla "NO, no. It's a lie. I never set you up. How dare you say such a thing about your mother—about ME. Don't say it, don't say it. Please don't say it. Even if it's true, don't say it. Sweep it under the rug, away, bury it away—don't expose it, me, in the glaring light."

And yet if I forbid her—what happens to our relationship?

As I sink down into my inner self, there is the tiniest little, frail voice who says in a nearly inaudible voice, "But I did do it. I bought the bride doll for her." She was so beautiful, her blond hair, curls cascading over her lovely, white satin gown. I had to have it and bought her for my daughter's 7th birthday, instead of the baby doll I had intended to buy her, that she wanted. A week later when I chose to enter a mental institution, I remember sitting on the sofa with my four children around me, crying my heart out to them—feeling totally inadequate, incapable of caring for them, of loving them, totally fragile, feeling less able to be their mother than they themselves.

Our three-year-old Katherine sulked all day in the Victorian rocker, thumb in her mouth nearly mute with fear and unhappiness. She was to go and stay with my mother and father, along with our six-month-old Kevin, who was maybe too young to realize that anything was wrong. Greg, nine years old, was able to board at the choir school, so it was Cynthia who was left to fend for herself—a little girl of seven, was to remain with her daddy. Why? To keep him company. He asked that she stay with him, and so she did, taking it upon herself to take my place.

It was at this time that my most fragile, inadequate inner child, who did not feel safe, bonded with my little seven-year old's determination to "care for her daddy" while her younger siblings went to stay with loving grandparents. She was somehow helping me. The small child in me melded with her. This part of me needed Cynthia's grounding and her energy, thus making it possible for me to leave. She was there for her daddy, easing her daddy's loneliness, his anger, even furry, his worry, his anxiety over his wife's departure. Our daughter must have wondered why she couldn't have gone with her brother and sister. Why didn't she need to be cared for? If she didn't need a mother figure to care for her, then she must be specially chosen and able to fill the role of her mother.

Working with my therapist:

I want to deny that this happened, that I left my children, my husband. That Cynthia was dreadfully hurt by my actions. How dreadfully sad I am that I had hurt her; that I was not able to mother her, had missed those beautiful, important years, had caused her to miss them, too.

I want to deny—but I feel a split; a part of me doesn't believe I did it, but another part does. My therapist asks me to rub my heart clockwise, as I repeat three times, "I love myself even though I left my daughter", three times, "I love myself even though I hurt her by leaving her", three times, "I love myself even though a part of me thinks she is angry with Ayla for accusing me", three times I say while rubbing my heart clockwise, "I love myself even though a part of me feels like lying". I realize if I deny that it happened, I will lose her energy. This frightens me.

My therapist asks me if I want to reclaim my energy. I say "Yes." She asks me to allow the energy to enter and command Ayla's energy also any others that don't belong, to leave. My feet become cold, then my legs as the energy from the Universe moves into the vacated space. I feel I am beginning to make sense of all of this.

Gwynn Kelley

I began visiting my parents again. Mom had evolved and grown open to seeing her own role in the silencing of me. She was involved in many different paths of healing, working with different modalities as she felt drawn to them. Her poetry changed in its courageous voice, embracing the horror of being one of my perpetrators, which supported the silencing of me. She has been a seeker her whole life, seeking to understand her emotional self, which we all knew, was out of whack. She hadn't yet directed her seeking to embrace her own inner demons which allowed her to project rage on her firstborn daughter, as it had been done to her, by her mother. She was an obedient girl/woman/wife. She railed against these roles, as she was an artist and an empath, a fantastic listener, and loved being engaged at the Soul level, in the rich, deep, vibrant life of a mystic. The year had passed, and our visits were better. Honest, more open; I was not on high alert, feeling the tightening in my chest and the frightening expectation of chaos to ensue, in their presence, when together.

Finally, a much more challenging shift occurred as SourceLove guided me to bring my mother's story into the performance.

Hell no, I argued with Great Spirit. *No way in hell am I bringing Mom into this. How would I do that? That's crazy.*

SourceLove gently but relentlessly guided me to invite my mom. I kept hearing, *Reach out your hand to your mother. Reach out your hand. She will take it.*

Gentle and persistent, God whispered, *She is ready and will take it. Offer your hand to your mother. You will change the world with your story of a mother and daughter healing in this fashion, as you both have done. It is a beautiful gift to the world.*

Mom was intense, no getting around that. She, a highly sensitive empath without the self-acknowledgement of this truth, was an introvert, a wonderful artist, and poet, but she was stuck believing she was without an outlet for her voice to be heard. This drove her crazy. I got it! I watched my dad emotionally torture her, throwing nasty, rude words at her—"It's a joke," he'd say, when I challenged him to lay off.

And then my invitation and this new burgeoning talent came. Dad didn't know what to make of this! It was puzzling me how she went from acceptance and support of my sharing the truth I had uncovered into the resistance that arose. It made sense to me, though, after a while. As I saw it, we have to shrink back into the fears after we've had such a bursting of the bubble experience; the ego, the human self gets frightened and wonders what they have just done. And clamps down. But it's never the same. The trapdoor hinges have been oiled and access was now open. It's the ebb and flow, the yin/yang; the Universe is full of expansion and contracting...all the time! So, too, are we human experiencers of this in our own emotional bodies!

Chapter 15

We Shall Overcome

As I walked together with my inner child, through my memories, I had to remember to breathe. Sounds silly, but I had learned how to disassociate from my body by not breathing. I still spent many minutes looking into my eyes in the mirror. It was frightening in the beginning. I burst into tears, unable to make contact and see who was looking back at me. I had to tell myself, while looking in my eyes, how much I am loved, and how much I love the child looking back at me. The child within needed to be super-soaked with love from my adult self. She needed to see me, reaching out to her, in her cave. I had to breathe her into feeling safe. Freeing my authentic voice allowed me to live joyously upon our beautiful Earth. I envisioned a New Earth where living from my heart and speaking truth, allowing the differences, celebrating our shadows in rituals with dance, song, our creativity in ceremony, was the norm. And peace prevails.

Now when I look in the mirror, who I see looking back at me is a compassionate, empathetic, and kind woman. Cross me and I am fierce, a warrior woman. Courage was something I began growing as a seed when I was little. I remembered the first time I felt courageous was when Mom was away at the hospital. I traveled down to Virginia to visit my dad's mother Joyce Lee, my most favorite grandmother, for a summer. It was going to be just her and I. And I loved having my mamma all to myself.

It was the summer of 1963 when I visited my grandmother Mamma in Gloucester, VA, for the summer. I loved my Mamma, my dad's mom. She was British, with a lilting accent, a twinkle in her eyes, and long white hair, braided and wrapped around the top of her head, like her crown. She let me brush her hair at night and in the morning, while sitting at her delicate Victorian dressing table, which had a silver and bone brush, comb, and mirror set; her beautiful jewelry sat in a silver box, and the sweet powder scent was heavenly. She lived in a cozy little house at the end of a cul-de-sac and had beautiful English gardens surrounding the perimeter. Lush, wild color abounded in her backyard, along with the homes of fairies and gnomes. Her stories were rich, lively, and real for me as we made a bed out of a matchbox for Hoppity, the fairy that lived on the land. The tiny droplets of pancake batter in the morning, which dropped and sizzled on the hot, cast-iron skillet, were for Hoppity. And there were countless other aspects to Hoppity which my grandmother, Joyce Lee, laid out to me throughout our days together.

I remember one time we walked to the "old witches" house up in the center square of town. The neighborhood kids told me it was haunted, and it sure looked that way as we approached. Heavy ivy was taking over the front of the huge Victorian house, growing up over the windows, covering the stone pathway in, which was flanked by what once were beautiful English gardens, now overgrown and unruly. A bright blue dreaming ball looking out of place, stood alone in the center of one of the gardens with sinister looking vines almost covering it, reflecting the sky on its surface. I decided it was a good idea to grab hold of my grandmother's hand as we walked up the front steps. Mamma lifted the large knocker on the tall, dark, mahogany door, and let it drop with a loud clang. A small, bird-like Black woman answered the door. She was dressed in a black dress with a white apron, and had a beautiful, serene smile on her face, with dreamy, soft brown/golden eyes. She was not much bigger than me in stature but was warm and strong in her embrace of me.

Birdie was her name. Miss Daisy was her friend whose house we were visiting. Miss Daisy's pink jowls hung soft and hid her chin. When she talked, they puffed out. It was funny to me, I suppose, because I was nervous. Miss Daisy and Birdie had lived together their whole life. Birdie was her constant companion, playing with her, brushing Miss Daisy's hair, helping her with her petticoats and dresses, etc., when younger. This allowed them to fall naturally into silent but understood roles of mistress and servant. But they soon grew beyond their roles, becoming fast friends, and they loved one another deeply, maybe they even became lovers over the years. Who knows! Miss Daisy was called a "spinster," which is partly how she became known as a "witch" by the neighborhood kids. When I met them, my Mamma said they were in their 90s, much older than she, my grandmother Joyce Lee, who was in her 50s or 60s maybe.

We were seated on an old Victorian couch covered in dark red velvet with mahogany wooden arms. Heavy dark burgundy drapes covered the windows, and beautiful Tiffany lamps were lit on several tables. It was a stately, regal, old house filled with Victorian artifacts and tchotchkes in glass cases and sitting on delicate tables covered in lace doilies. Birdie served us tea with an array of homemade baked cookies.

After we finish our tea and Birdie has cleared the tray away, she sat down on a footrest, leaning forward on the edge, with her face close to mine, and asked me, "Chile, will you make my heart happy and sing me a song I'm gon' to teach you?"

Shyly I replied, "Sure, I'll try," as I feel my ears turning beet red and cheeks aflame.

Birdie moved in closer to me and looked deep into my eyes. "You know this song, chile. You know this. Here, let me sing it." She began singing in a beautiful, passionate, sweet voice. It grew in strength and was full of emotion as her body swayed, she sang,

"We shall overcome,
We shall overcome,
We shall overcome,
some day.
Oh, oh, deep in my heart,
I do believe,
 we shall overcome someday!"

Tears were flowing down my cheeks as I opened my mouth and struggled to sing. As I began to sing, my voice was weak and scared. Birdie stood up and began to sway on her feet from side to side, humming, holding her hands over her heart, saying, "Yes, lawd, sing it, chile. Sing it from your heart. Yes, lawd. Hear your daughter sing so sweetly and strongly."

By the end of the song, I was belting out the words in a big, rich voice. I remember thinking that this feeling was a feeling I desired more of. I felt courageous singing so strongly. I would remember that feeling the rest of my life!

Birdie took my shoulders, looked me deep in the eyes and said, "God, gave you HIS power, chile. Use it."

Birdie was right! I've been learning about my superpowers for years now. I have offered my unconditional love and belief in love as the ONLY way to my family, friends, clients, and colleagues, and the world at large for years now. Now it's my time to throw this whole amazing story out into the sea of possibilities and unlimited opportunity to catch the big wave!

For the last year of my father's life, I was guided to call him weekly. So, I did. I had gotten in the habit of confronting Dad in the beginning of our journey, at the beginning of his Sunday morning ritual as he prepared himself for his service. This was the time in his life when his heart was most open and he was able to hear me. Quite often, he would tell me his sermon had changed after he had gotten off the phone and spoken with me. Good. My intention had been received and impacted my ego-driven dad. Dad was an amazing man and had enormous gifts, some of which he failed to really step up and grow into. He was afraid of a lot and didn't seem to be able to handle change. He was terrified of death and only had to perform two funerals in his thirty-year career as an Episcopal minister. I find that incredible and it makes me feel sad. In the end, I had the huge honor of assisting my father on his final journey. The phone calls I made weekly to him brought him and I closer together as each week the one question I asked him always was this: "How is your dying progressing?" You see, I knew he was dying, and he knew he was dying, slowly. I wanted him to know he was not alone and that I would keep his secret safe until it was his time. Right then, it was our time.

Dad was surrounded by people of courage, and he recognized, through his relationship with me, that he was not a courageous person. He liked to boast and brag but lacked substance to back it up. He was outspoken in his political views, supporting justice for the Hispanic people he loved and served, by writing many Letters to the Editor, in the local Clearwater, Florida, newspaper and the local Connecticut paper when he lived up north. I was proud of him for that.

Three weeks before he passed, during one of my Sunday morning calls, my dad was weeping on the other end of the phone. This was totally out of character for my father. He was not one to cry over the phone.

"Dad, what's going on?" I asked tenderly.

Sobbing heavily, he gasped as he said, "I am so ashamed of myself. I was a coward and never protected you. I didn't protect you when you were a little girl in my care, and I failed you when I allowed you to date Rusty, when you were going out with him. I never stood up to your mother when she forbade me to cuddle you in my bed, when you were frightened or sad." Silenced ensued for a few moments to let this sink in.

"Dad, thank you for this. I have waited a long time to hear you own your part and speak the truth. I never could understand where your love went. It seemed to just evaporate."

"I am a coward. I was always afraid of your mother's rage. I should have and could have stopped her many, many times when she was raging at you. The truth is, it kept her away from me. I am so, so sorry. Can you ever forgive me?"

"Dad, it is not my job to forgive you. I have forgiven myself, long ago, for how I belittled my authentic nature, believing who you all thought I was. The forgiveness you seek is for yourself. Forgive yourself! God bless you, Dad. And I love you."

It was never too late. Three weeks after his confession, I flew to Florida and visited with my dad in the hospital. He had an aneurysm which had exploded and was filling his entire stomach cavity with blood. He asked me to pray. I got his well-worn *Book of Common Prayers* from his side table and opened it to the *Prayers for the Dying*. I began reading it, gently and softly. I noticed Dad becoming super agitated the more I read the prayers he was so comfortable with. He clutched my hand in his big and bony hand. "Please pray your way, Ayla."

I put the prayer book down and picked up my rattle and began to swirl my rattle clockwise, opening sacred space as I knew how to. My voice grew strong and resonant as I prayed, singing over my father. I watched his body relax, as the prayers I knew in Quechua were soothing to his tired and tied up Soul. I sang for hours to him in Spanish and in Quechua, singing all the sacred songs I knew and watched my dad, my Father/God struggle with his fear of dying. My dad took to his grave the wound which tied him up in knots. The story recounted to me was that his mother, my grandmother, Joyce Lee, was an opera singer from England. She used to sing in a nightclub that Al Capone was said to have frequented. It was a club in Coral Gables, Florida, when he escaped the heat he created in Chicago, back in the late 1920s and early 30s. Joyce Lee (Mamma) was a gorgeous, boisterous, and a bodacious woman. She was quite a looker, too. Her husband, Beverley, my grandfather, worked on the railroad and traveled for his job. He did not like this connection she had made and had forbidden his wife to sing at the club while he was away. Dad accompanied my grandmother to her gigs and sat surrounded by women who loved him and gave him hugs, kisses, and all manner of attention. He was a youngster and forbidden to share their secret with his father when he returned home from traveling the country by railroad. I'm not sure if this story shared to me by my mother was the wound which created such fear in my dad, but something did. And I never found out in his own words what had happened. This made me sad as I know that Dad struggled in the end, afraid to let go, allowing his body to die, setting his Soul free to be home. Energy can neither be created or destroyed. It can expand and contract, morphing... I know you are resting in peace, now. You are forgiven. You are loved Dad, and all is well.

He bid farewell to me as I held sacred space for his transition. During the ceremony, I had called in his best friend, the bishop, Alfonso, to be his trusted guide accompanying dad on his Soul's journey home.

I made it safely home after a long drive up from Florida. As soon as I was home, I headed to the beach; the sun was rising on January 5th, 2015. Flying just ahead of my car, a few feet in front of me and several feet above, was a beautiful, pink orb that was illuminated and shimmering. I arrived and parked my car at the beach and acknowledged the orb as Dad's Spirit. As I did this, breathing slowly, simultaneously it broke apart into a million tiny, sparkling particles of light…joyful, "Dad, you're ok. All is well. You are loved and all is forgiven." I released a loud whoop in joy!

For days, I holed up in my home and painting studio, painting my grief, allowing it to morph and flow.

My Time *Book Cover*

My relationship with my dad was so complex. All I had ever wanted to do was to love him and be accepted by him, for me. At the end of his life, Dad grew in his respect for me and gifted me his miniature Holy Communion set that had traveled with him to visit his sick parishioners. When he gave it to me, he told me he recognized me as a Priestess in my own right and wanted me to be ordained as a minister. I took this as my ordination and registered myself as a minister with the Universal Church of Life, which recognizes that some Souls are called and need not attend a seminary for their calling to be fulfilled. He saw me as one of those people, as I do!

Chapter 16

Returning One More Time

I returned to the South Bronx years later, in 1993, after I had been offering my story sharing for a while. I was compelled to see if there was anything I could give back to the community in which I was most seriously imprinted by the light and dark. What I found in this community stunned me with delight!

The minister was a retired military captain, who had become a minister. She was a tiny, diminutive woman, but oh was she a powerhouse. The church community had been transformed into a loving, supportive environment for the children of the barrio. The minister created a "soup kitchen" and ran it for breakfast and dinner. The grandmothers ran this kitchen for the children before school and after school, so their mothers could work. On Sunday, after church, the entire community of women and children travel to the prison on the edge of the barrio for visiting hours. The women and children visited their fathers, husbands' brothers, cousins, and uncles, mostly. But there were mothers, wives, sisters, and aunts incarcerated, too. I have a vivid imagination and can see, in my mind's eye, the women dressed in their finest, bright, colorful dresses, pants, skirts, maybe some hats. The women, I imagine, are in a festive mood and have their make-up on just so. They are a mix of all colors in skin and clothing, shapes and sizes, and I imagine they sound like a gaggle of geese. The children, too, are excited with anticipation and are on their best behavior as they all wait to catch the bus that will take them to the prison, known as Rikers Island.

When I meet them again, I am deeply moved and humbled by the joy which exudes from the faces of these beautiful, forgotten people in our society, but not forgotten to each other. I was so happy for these people to see this huge change, working, on their terms, using their own resources, the children's grandmothers.

I discovered that my dear friend, Maria Carmona, the mother of my girlfriends, had been killed while sitting in her home by a stray bullet. This was devastatingly painful and shocking for me. For the community, sadly, this was not an unusual event. I will always remember Maria, dressed in her skintight, purple satin jumpsuit, with red nails and lipstick, on a regular day in June, my first time returning when I was in high school. And I remember Maria grabbing my hips as a seven-year-old little white girl and teaching me to shake my booty! Maria, you were an angel in my life, watching over me. I am forever grateful to you for showing me what a beautiful, proud, bodacious woman looked like! I'll always be grateful to you for awakening my passion to dance and to love others different from myself!

Chapter 17

Did I Do the Right Thing?

My life changed drastically after eight years of caregiving my mother and witnessing her demise with dementia. My mom was a soulful seeker. Creativity was how she expressed her journey and wrestled with her own demons. The dementia wiped that all away!

All of the plans that she and I had to get our love story out into the world were blown away with the winds of change! Gratefully, I have a beautiful portfolio of her poems, and someday they will become a book honoring the extraordinary courage she lived. My mother and I grew to become the best of friends.

MOTHER TO DAUGHTER, FRIEND TO FRIEND

I heard them from my room exclaim:
"Oh isn't she the most beautiful baby!
Come see!"
Copper-colored, silken hair so gently
framing her exquisite face-
fair and perfect all wrapped in pink,
this baby of mine.

Is she really? Did I in my tummy grow
a baby as lovely as she is to me?
Her ten little fingers, her ten little toes
and an upturned nose.
Did I really grow this baby mine?
So perfect, petite this elfin gift
was laid by my side
as she suckled my breast.

Yet, heart ache,
now, as I look back,
I wish I had another chance to love my baby daughter,
to protect her as she grew,
from violation that was to rape her.

Oh, heart ache,
I wish I had another chance to be mother to my daughter,
To nourish her, to watch her grow,
in a safe protected place,
where she can laugh in sheer delight
and I in awe struck wonder—watch.
Where mother/daughter spirit selves
Sing on moon lit nights, sending gleeful melodies
across a star strewn sky.

Oh, to move in rapture as our naked bodies sway
To feel the breath of heaven blowing gently on our skin.
Oh, to be alive together and pleased to be related,
as mother to daughter, friend to friend.

Gwynn Kelley, March 1, 1992

And in 2001, my response to my mother was:

SWEET WOMAN, MOTHER, MY FRIEND.

Who ever dared dream that one day I'd call you,
you, whom I taunted and despised,
my best friend?

The re-weaving of our lives
has had gifts rich and colorful,
textured to match my wildest dreams!

You are not a fragment of unfinished thought,
to me, sweet woman,
you possess the tenderest of heart.

Holy and strong, wise and wrong.
So many times, wrong, for so many years,
blinded by all your fears.

I knew at three, seven, and eleven,
I had to birth myself—
no matter that you shunned my pain.

It seemed natural to me to offer you my hand
and give you my heart—
so why not invite you to journey with me?

There was never a question, that into roles you never fit.
And I never doubted the aching in my heart
as a longing,
threaded years ago.

My love will set you free.
It's all I have to offer

for the sacrifice you made for me!

Let's be honest, I have been relentless,
to break the box, release the chain,
cut the cord,
and dodge the daggers that broke my heart.

But nothing has been strong enough to break the bond of love,
that crisscrossed over time,
passing down for generations—
denying us as mother daughter,
now, becoming friend to friend.

From Ayla to Gwynneth
Ayla Joyce Matheson
April 2001

I recently had to move again, but before we moved, I had a bazillion papers to go through that belonged to my parents. This was not the first time I'd done this. The first time I was responsible for their things it was about forty boxes of memorabilia from many generations: on my paternal side, the Lees and the Kelleys; on the maternal side, the Davies and the Borglums. Much of the stuff was tossed away, given away, or donated. Sadly, family members were not interested in our family's his(her)stories. I was in agony over this because I love family lineage stuff. I kept what I felt was important and released the rest!

This go around, I had my eldest sibling with me, Greg. Thank goodness he was present. It still was profoundly difficult, mostly with my father's things as I really didn't know Dad. Or maybe my perspective of who I thought he was was so strong that I missed seeing his shining soul. He had a sparkle in his eyes and deep dimples when he smiled his glorious smile. And I'll cut myself a break and say, Dad, I guess I did know you more than I realized! You stood up for what you believed. You did what you thought was right when it came time to bring change into your churches;

most of your parishioners loved you. Can't please everyone, so that's a great track record. And you gave me my love for dance, music, and the Latin culture, too. I'm fluent in Spanish, thanks to your influence and your musical ear which picked up tone easily, therefore the Spanish language was easy for me to speak because I inherited this too from you and learned Spanish as I was perfecting my English at age three, speaking with a beautiful accent just as the indigenous children in Costa Rica spoke. So thank you, dad. I realize you gave me way more than I have ever allowed myself to acknowledge! I am living a life of joyful abundance in flow with the Unified Field—God's creative envisioning!

I picked through boxes of papers, reading bits and pieces of my dad's writing. He was a prolific journaler with handwriting hard to read! I was very surprised to find one writing dated back to the late 1960s. In the writing, he expressed a concern: Shortly after arriving in Virginia, from New York City, at his new parish, our family had invited Greg's four best friends down to Virginia: Peachie, Frankie, Angel, and Eugene. All dark-skinned Puerto Rican kids who had never been outside of their South Bronx barrio with the exception of Peachie, who had attended St. John the Divine Cathedral choir school as a choir boy until his voice changed! The kids had a wonder-filled time. All of us explored the North River and the briny water of the Mobjack Bay. The blue claw crabs we were catching were prolific and gave us a scare or two as they pinched onto our fingers. We were not blue claw savvy yet and didn't know to pick them up from behind, grabbing their butt end. The "buck and riders," as we discovered they were called, were fascinating to us kids, never having seen anything like that before. We met the stinging nettles as their tentacles wrapped around our arms and legs, burning us in raised red welts that hurt like hell. The welts looked like a whip had lashed us. This made us terrified to go swimming again. But we did anyway, being curious and adventuresome kids. But the most poignant of writing that I found was his awareness that our friends were also coming face to face with racism for the first time. In the community where these kids lived, they weren't seeing the effects of racism. They were the embodiment of it, as it stayed hidden bubbling below the surface of everything. It was not in their faces unless they traveled outside of their barrio, which just wasn't the case very often. What they hit face on in Virginia was not the same. Same root, yes, their lives an outcome of it, but racism head on was frightening and very confusing! So our friends had an ignorance until their visit to the segregated south, Virginia. It smacked all of us in the face when we went to the movie theater, Donks, to watch a new film just released. Signs above the water fountain read "Whites Only." The stairs ascending up into the hot, stuffy balcony had a sign with an arrow pointing up: "Coloreds." Confused by all of this and not knowing what we were to do with our Puerto Rican friends, who were not "colored" to us, we all walked into the main theater and sat down. This created a disturbance as people moved away, changing their seats so as not to be in close proximity to us. Did people think the brown color of our friend's skin was going to rub off onto them? We, as kids, did not understand the depth of the disturbance. My brother and I paid dearly for this choice and ugly names took root and stuck like a fly trapped on a fly strip.

Dad's journal entry wondered if he had done the right thing to bring these kids down to the South where they were confronted face on with the cruelty and meanness of racism. He wondered if it had negatively impacted our friends to see the larger world outside the confines of their barrio. Did the trip south give them anything at all that they were able to hold onto as a sort of a "by pass jail" card, triggering an unstoppable momentum towards their own hopes and dreams? My curiosity remains unfulfilled as we lost track of our friends and Donk's theater was now closed.

As I bring my book to an end, I am proud of myself for digging deep to find the courage to write and share my story. Before this book, I had written hundreds and hundreds of pages, winnowing out the chafe, capturing the seeds that one day would take root and became my book. The root began to grow deep in the soil before I even knew I was ready to write my story, for real publishing! When I was twelve and we had just landed in the strange land of the South, where the dark, evil fruit from the root of racism was exposed and very present—in your face present—I heard a voice tell me I was to write my autobiography one day. I never forgot this. Back then, I wondered what kind of a life I would live that would give me something important to write about. I never imagined I'd be exposing my own experience with the culture of dehumanization. Let's define it in simple terms from the Merriam Webster Dictionary:

What is a simple word for "dehumanize?"

verb: humiliate, brutalize, poison, subvert, demean, animalize, bestialize, degrade.

Think about this as we envision a new Earth for our children's children. This is currently the norm in our country! What do you desire? This? We can, we are, and we must do better!

Epilogue

I celebrate and honor my mother, Gwynneth Davies Kelley, for having the courage to bring me into the world and to discover her truth. To my dad, John B. L. Kelley, I honor you for the courage you finally found to own your cowardice. Not an easy thing to do. Thank you!

I witnessed you both holding space for me, as painful as it was at times, and the joy in the growth and deepening of our relationships has been worth every step I have taken to discover my truth.

I know you did the very best you could with the limited tools you were given.

Mom and Dad

I became my mother's caregiver a year after my father died and her dementia was triggered. Let me tell you, in a million years I never thought I'd be the one to become my mother's caregiver. My thought was anything but THAT! The role shifting from daughter to my mother's keeper, or really becoming her mother, prompted the writing. It was time. Trouble was I didn't have "a room of my own" to write in. Our home, a condo in Quechee, Vermont, was beautiful but crowded and with no extra space for an office.

What I had was a beautiful deck. It sat high up off the ground, had nice, early morning sun, and shade most of the rest of the day. Huge cedar trees provided a beautiful umbrella from the sun, all afternoon. This was much to my chagrin as I am a gardener and wanted glorious full sun to feed my marijuana plants, hibiscus, geraniums, and various other flowering plants. No luck there! The deck became my outdoor office. I want to thank the Holy Spirit. Your presence and guidance flows like the rivers to the ocean and the tides that roll into the shores and roll back out again. Your presence flowing through me gave me the courage and the wisdom to know how to get this book written!

Every day, I rose at 4:00 a.m. This has always been my time to rise, the time when God speaks to me. I embraced the quietness, allowing it to impregnate me. The quiet, clear voice within becomes all I hear, as the world around me reflects the soundlessness of this hour! Every day, rain or shine, freezing cold or humid, sticky hot, I sat on my deck as the season's changed and wrote my book. I was lucky enough to watch four generations of downy woodpeckers, ladder-backed, red-bellied woodpeckers live not three feet away from where I wrote, pounding in the message to broaden my horizons, embrace new opportunities, think creatively, protect the vulnerable, and pay attention to patterns and rhythms. A pileated woodpecker even flew in one day to give his message! The downy families reminded me to look beneath the surface of things, for the hidden or deeper meanings within the lessons and opportunities being received. Mind you, these beautiful birds didn't show up at 4:00 a.m. They are still sleeping until the first light of dawn cracks the sky open.

I wrote all through the winter, no matter what the temperature, stopping when my fingers were too stiff to fly over the keyboard or my computer was getting sluggish from the cold. This was exhilarating, very courageous of me, and showed me a stamina I have to go the distance; no matter what it takes, I'll get it done! I am proud of myself and excited to let this book fly out there and rip apart some of the old structures that have deadened us to the truth and are no longer serving we, the people!

Opportunities for change are right now! The ones we have been waiting for have arrived! Look in the mirror and you will see... It's me and you. I've taught myself to ask for my assignment every day, moment by moment! And God/Great Spirit/my Dear Love provides it to me, moment by moment!

What's your assignment? Have you asked of late? If you are curious and have the desire to dive deep into Inherited Generational Pain, then you might enjoy the GraceWay Chrysalis journey! Check out my website: www.gracewaychrysalis.com You can see the paintings, poems, and read about the sequel to this, *The Grace Way*, coming soon! And so it is that I end this story and I thank you, dear reader, for joining me and caring!

Book Club Discussion Questions

Here are 20 probing questions for a book club discussion of *My Time, My Truth* by C. Ayla Joyce Matheson, based on the provided documents:

- Ayla describes her childhood as "bizarre." What specific events or experiences stand out to you as particularly unusual, and how do they contribute to the overall narrative?

- The contrast between Ayla's life in Costa Rica and the South Bronx is stark. How did these vastly different environments shape her understanding of the world?

- Ayla's father is portrayed with both positive and negative qualities. How did his role as a minister influence his relationships within his family?

- Ayla's mother struggles with mental health. How did her mother's struggles impact Ayla's childhood and her sense of security?

- The Bride Doll represents a significant moment in Ayla's childhood. What do you think this doll symbolizes in the context of her relationship with her mother?

- Ayla mentions feeling like there were "two Mes." How does this reflect the internal conflict she experiences throughout her childhood?

- Spiritual seeking is a major theme in the book. How does Ayla's understanding of spirituality evolve as she grows up?

- Ayla has encounters that she interprets as spiritual or mystical, especially in Costa Rica. How do you interpret these experiences, and how did they affect her?

- The "black crows" are mentioned in the context of evil and fear. Who or what do you think these "black crows" represent?

- Ayla mentions a recurring dream about being on a precipice. What do you think this dream symbolizes in relation to her life and emotional state?

- The open-door policy of the church creates a unique living situation for Ayla's family. How does this policy impact their sense of privacy and safety?

- Ayla's relationship with her uncle Clay seems particularly important. Why do you think she felt such a strong connection to him?

- How does Ayla's perspective on her own identity change as she navigates different cultural and social environments?

- The book explores themes of trauma and healing. What are some of the specific traumas Ayla experiences, and how does she begin to heal?

- Ayla's body plays a significant role in her journey, especially in the context of trauma. How does her physical experience relate to her emotional and spiritual journey?

- The book mentions Ayla's "Near Death Experience." How do you think this experience contributes to her transformation and self-discovery?

- How does Ayla's relationship with the church evolve throughout the book, and what leads to her eventual break from it?

- The book mentions Ayla's artistic expression as a tool for healing. How does creativity help her process her past and find peace?

- What role does forgiveness play in Ayla's journey of self-discovery and healing?

- What is the overall message or takeaway you get from *My Time My Truth*, and how does it resonate with you personally?

Acknowledgements

These acknowledgements are dedicated to the individuals who have provided steadfast support throughout my transformative journey. Your unwavering belief in me, even when I struggled to perceive the path forward, has been invaluable.

I am not able to mention all of you because there are too many who have been serendipitous guides, teachers, and inspiritors for me. I appreciate you.

My deepest gratitude extends to:

My Family

Kevin: My younger brother, who was the first within our family to truly listen and encourage our mother to do the same.

Greg: My elder brother, for our consistent and cherished Wednesday morning coffee meetings in Richmond.

Katherine: My younger sister, whose lessons for me have been invaluable in redefining our family's money story! Thank you for breaking the 'glass ceiling.'

Gwynn and John (My Parents): For your profound courage and openness, even when confronted with truths that significantly impacted your lives.

My Children: For their continuous love, joy, and encouragement, which has illuminated every step of this journey. When you were first born Heather you gave me the reason to live! Justin you came in happy! You have inspired me to choose to be happy for no reason! Now I have five amazing granddaughters born of my son and daughter; you and your families mean the world to me. You inspire me to live in joyful abundance with more than enough for myself and to share, therefore I am creating a legacy for us to enjoy!

My Supporters and Collaborators

Celeste: You were the initial champion of my narrative, providing financial support for my artistic endeavors for many years. Thank you for your generosity.

Stacia: My editor and dear friend, your encouragement and insights from the very first reading of my manuscript were truly exceptional.

Sifu Charles and Sifu Leslie, and the Breathing Lotus School Community: I am eternally grateful for the safe space you provided, allowing me to express and release profound fears during my most vulnerable moments in martial arts. Your encouragement to delve deeper and the assistance of Jesus Christ in moments of challenge were profoundly impactful. The relationships forged within this community are eternal bonds of strength and love.

Nadine: My dear friend, thank you for sharing music with me when I first began to perceive melodies. Your generosity was remarkable.

Anna: My longest-standing childhood friend, thank you for your unwavering steadfastness and for always being present through every challenge and triumph. Your family saved my family's ass so many times, offering us refuge.

My Ancestors

Joyce Lee Kelley, Mamma (My Paternal Grandmother): You consistently offered love and acceptance during my periods of profound sadness and confusion, serving as my safe harbor. Your love for me was uncomplicated and I thank you for that!

Aunt Harriet: Thank you for allowing me the cherished privilege of brushing your beautiful hair during my visits. This remains a precious memory and has inspired me to grow my beautiful hair out!

The Borglum brothers, my great-grandfather Solon and my great-grand uncle, Gutzon, and their parents, Christina Mikelsen and Jens Borglum: The immense artistic talent within our family lineage is deeply appreciated. The inherited patterns of rivalry, jealousy, and dehumanization through invisibility have been disrupted. I extend forgiveness and freedom to you, inviting your assistance in cultivating a life of joyful abundance and fostering right relations with both our ancestors and our Earth. I am listening.

And lastly, to Jeffrey Jack: Thank you for being true to your self. Your unwavering focus, diligent work ethic, and profound commitment to achieving your objectives have served as an unprecedented example to me. This coupled with your remarkably generous spirit, is admirable. I have appreciated being the recipient of it.

www.ingramcontent.com/pod-product-compliance
Lightning Source LLC
Chambersburg PA
CBHW042315120626
46547CB00022B/2052